STAGE BY STAGE

Brenda Collins

Lots of Love
and
Happy Memories

Brenda
xxx

Stage by Stage

Spiderwize
Remus House
Coltsfoot Drive
Woodston
Peterborough
PE2 9BF

www.spiderwize.com

ISBN: 978-1-908128-93-5

Acknowledgements

In being who I am I would like to thank the following wonderful people:

Firstly I would like to thank my Mam and Dad, they were always proud of me.....even when I misbehaved.

Miss Crampton my Junior School teacher who found out I had a voice and encouraged me to sing.

Mr Whittaker, my music teacher and Mr Bolt the history teacher at Bowburn Modern School for developing my voice and casting me in my first solo part.

Miss Sheila Mitchinson, my Guide Captain for developing my character.

My son's wife, Lesley's dad, Colin for pointing me in the right direction when I put pen to paper. Jill Bowerbank for all her help, support, knowledge and advice during the editing process. Sarah Black for her patience and support.

Thank you to David Forster for not only editing my photographs but also proof reading and photographing me for the front cover of my book.

To Graeme Paterson for his help with fixing things when I keep breaking them and finding things on the computer when I keep losing them.

And last, but not least, thanks to our Eileen for the final proofread and her approval !!!!

I dedicate my book to Alfie, my grandson

STAGE BY STAGE

Brenda Collins

My Mam, Catherine Annie May Johnson (Cathy), was born on 10th May 1913 in Tow Law, County Durham to a single mother, Ellenor. Seven years later, my Mam's sister Jenny was born. Cathy was brought up by her grandparents until the age of five when Ellenor married Anthony Dodds and the family moved to Chopwell, County Durham. The family lived in Wilson Street and Anthony must have had quite a good wage. I know that because I have photographs of my Mam and her sister Jenny taken when my Mam would be possibly ten years of age and not many pit families could afford to have photographs taken then! My Mam and Auntie Jenny had a good education.

Anthony Dodds was a union man and a very active one at that. Chopwell had the nickname "Little Moscow." The union men were very militant and my Grandad, Anthony, was part of a group called "The Fighting Men of Chopwell". In the 1926 General Strike in Chopwell the Union flag was replaced by the Soviet flag. Streets were named Marx Terrace and Lenin Terrace. After the General Strike ended Anthony was never offered his job back. He then moved to Ferryhill, County Durham.

Cathy left school at the age of 14 and went to work on a farm. Upon leaving the farm until 1945 she worked in service at various locations throughout the UK. After the war she returned to live with her parents in Ferryhill, County Durham and she worked as a cook in the school kitchen. Me Mam said she had a very posh accent when she came back to the North East. In 1945 she met Alfie Swainston at a local dance hall in Ferryhill.

Alfie Swainston was born in Brandon on 12th January 1916 and suffered every childhood illness: diphtheria, scarlet fever and rickets. (Amazingly he lived till he was 94)!!! His childhood was not a happy one. He had 4 brothers and a sister who died at a very young age.

Alfie's Dad was also called Alfie and he worked down the pit. His Mam died and his Dad remarried a lady called Rosie, who my Dad said, had been in the workhouse. He often recalled that his shoes always had holes in them and he didn't bother much with school – survival was his and the family's main concern. He left school at 14 and worked down the coal mines in Browney, County Durham. Nearly every young boy followed their father's footsteps and went down the pit. He used to lead the pit ponies who pulled the tubs full of coal. He later progressed to working at the coal face.

Alfie worked at various pits; one was 3 miles away. He would cycle there and back. In the winter if it was deep snow he would walk there then do a 10 hour shift. Crawling or snaking along, hacking at the coal with a pick axe. He would most of the time be crawling along in a seam with a depth of 16 inches and most of that would be in water. Then after the shift was over he would walk back home, utterly worn out. Miners like Alfie came back from a shift black with coal dust. There were no bathrooms in the houses the pitmen and their families lived in. My Grandad, Dad and my Dad's brothers, after a shift working down the pit, all had to wash that coal dust off every night.

They lived in two up and two down houses and there was an outside toilet, which I suppose was a "torture chamber" in the winter. Newspaper torn into squares nailed to the wall was, what families used as toilet paper? The houses were called the colliery rows and each had a large grey tin bath hung up in the yard. My Dad's Mam would heat the water up on the fire range and fill the tin bath, which was

4

in front of the open fire.

My Dad's brother Nicolas was only 21 years of age when he was killed down the pit at Bowburn. He was decapitated when a truck full of coal crashed into him. My Dad said that he had been a talented footballer as well as musician. He had played most instruments, including the accordion.

Alfie married Jane Wilson at 21 but she passed away six months later – he never ever discussed this.

Cathy Johnson and Alfie Swainston were married on 6th August 1946 and their first child born was a daughter, Eileen, on 5th November 1948. Then two years later on 24th October 1950 I entered the world!!

Oooh well, I wonder what happened next???!!..........

1955 - 5 years old

In the winter-time my Dad pulled our Eileen, my sister, and I on the sledge in the snow up to school, Bowburn Infants. The school was about a mile away from our home. The sledge was home made by "Uncle" Harry. He wasn't really our Uncle. He ran a mail order catalogue and in November of each year he used to drop one off at our house. Eeeh our Eileen and I used to be buzzing with excitement. We had a great time sitting snuggled up on the settee flicking through the pages looking at the toys we'd like Santa Claus to send. Eileen picked the girlie things like dolls and prams. I picked cowboy outfits, guns and cars. Yes, I was a tomboy!!! More about that later!!

My first day at school was not a very nice experience at all. I was taken into school by me Mam. I screamed and screamed when I got in that massive hall with a hard wooden shiny floor. We were told to sit on it crossed legged and arms folded. I hated it and wanted to go back home with me Mam to see my Dad.

Everyone sitting on the floor was told to stand up by a teacher who then led us to our classroom. My teacher was called Mrs. Moody and she was old but nice. The Headmistress was called Miss Addison. We sat at wooden desks where the seat part flipped up when we stood up. The seats were very hard. There was a massive, tall desk where Mrs. Moody sat on a very big chair. We all saw a jar of dolly mixtures perched on the top and we all looked at them and wondered when we would get a sweetie. We found out later on in the week that they were a reward for when a pupil did anything good.

Every morning we would sit again on the hard wooden floor in the hall for assembly.

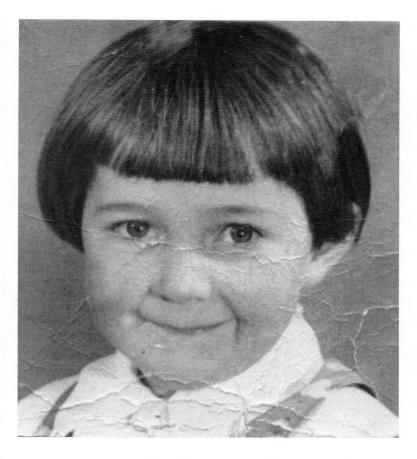

Me at five years old

"Good morning Miss Addison," we would chant, as soon as she made her entrance. I don't think anyone ever told us that we were to be going to school until we were sixteen. We were only 5 years old and none of us had ever been away from our parents. It was a very sad time for all of us children on our first day at school. We felt we had been abandoned by our parents and put in this enormous building.

I was glad when it was home time and me Mam would be there to pick me up and take me home. Trouble was I had to go back to that awful place the next day. I wasn't happy.

Our home was at 26 Prince Charles Avenue, Bowburn. It was on a brand new estate and building commenced in 1948. Of course, Prince Charles was born in 1948, hence the name. As each street got built they were named after members of the Royal Family. So we had, for example, Margaret Court and Philip Avenue. The house was a semi-detached council house built of breeze blocks. It was two-bedroomed with an inside toilet, bath and wash basin upstairs. There was a kitchen and a lounge downstairs.

Outside there was a wash-house and a coal house. Everyone had a coal-house. We got free coal because my Dad worked at Bowburn pit. A ton of coal got delivered outside our house in a big heap. Even at six years of age I helped load the coal into buckets and carry them to my Dad, and he would tip them into the coal-house. We all had to help get the coal in, even our Eileen!! Our Eileen would always be busy wearing me Mam's shoes, carrying me Mam's handbag and pretending to be a film star!!

The house was freezing in the winter and on the inside of the windows there were always patterns of frozen ferns. You could write your name in the ice on the inside of the windows. But we were always cosy. Eileen and I had twin beds with matching eiderdowns. If it was really cold, me Mam or Dad would come and put winter coats over us. We had hot water bottles too (still have)!!! No central heating in those days. To keep our home warm there was a paraffin heater in the bathroom, kitchen and bottom of the stairs. They were called Valour paraffin heaters.

Every morning Eileen and I would get up for school, run down stairs and get dressed in front of the roaring coal fire. Me Mam got up early to light it if my Dad was still at work. If me Dad was in from night shift, he would put the fire on. Me

Mam would have our school clothes warming up next to the fire: vests, liberty bodices and navy blue knickers and of course our tunics and blouses.

Winters were very bad in County Durham. There was snow, snow and more snow, from November to February. It was so deep we had to dig pathways from our homes to get to the local shop which was the only shop on "the new estate," as it was called. People from the colliery rows, these were the original houses for the pitmen and were back to back terraced houses; would ask where we lived.

"The new estate," we'd say, as if it was posher. In a way I suppose it was because we had an inside toilet and a bath. Our bathroom walls were so thin me Mam used to say, "Do you know these walls are so thin I'm sure next door can hear the toilet paper rattle. The toilet paper was the hard Izal type, which similar grease proof paper.

Sunday night was always bath night and we always got our hair washed on that night. We used to wash our hair with Vozene or Loxene medicated shampoo to keep our hair nice and shiny. Clean pyjamas, or nightie, a dose of syrup of figs and cod liver oil completed the day. When the next door neighbour's grandchildren were visiting and were having a bath at the same time we could talk to them through the walls. Eeeh it was great!!

"Hello you two." Our Eileen and I would shout.

"Hello Eileen and Brenda." We thought it was such fun. I don't think me Mam and Dad thought it was.

The only shop on the estate was a wooden shed owned by Mr. and Mrs. Johnson. Barry was their son and he was in my class at school. The shop sold everything you needed to survive the long winters. Mr. and Mrs. Johnson were looked upon as better than us. They were 'business people', so to speak. Mr. Johnson was tall and well made. He wore a brown overall coat. His hair was thinning, and he had a moustache. Maybe now when I think about it, he had a look of Mr. Arkwright, the character played by Ronnie Barker in the programme Open All Hours. Mr. Johnson didn't have a stutter though. Their shop also sold newspapers and of course sweets!! You couldn't walk into the shop. There was a hatch at the side which opened up and there stood Mr. and Mrs. Johnson ready to serve their customers.

"Yes, can I help you?" Mrs. Johnson would ask. She had a look of Norman's Mam from Fireman Sam. A lot posher, no Welsh accent, and definitely no headscarf turban on her head, or rollers.

Our entertainment in the winter months was sledging, making slides on the icy roads. Not a car in the street where we lived to hinder our playing because no-one had a car!! Simple!! We also had snowball fights usually with Ann and Christine Walton just because they lived opposite. Not because we didn't like them.

As girls, we never wore trousers; we wore long socks and wellies, skirts or dresses. We had red welly marks imprinted on our little legs and the snow always got down our wellies and made our feet freezing cold. Oooh not nice! Every now and again, we would go back into our house and get warmed up in front of the fire and change our socks and gloves for dry ones. Me Mam used to dry them out on a rotation system!!

I was known as the "little-un" by me Dad and our Eileen was known as the "big bugger." Our Eileen was much bigger than me you see. I was so tiny. I always wore our Eileen's clothes as she outgrew them. In fact I wore everyone's outgrown clothes. My friend's Mam, Mrs. Milburn, who lived at the top of our street, used to drop some of Joan's clothes off which Joan had outgrown. So I wore her tunic to school. She, Joan, announced in class that I was wearing her tunic. I was so embarrassed. You see I was so shy and quiet and anything like that was terrible for me. I hung my head, I suppose in shame. I wanted to go home.

In the school yard, after we'd had our milk, the girls used to play fairies and witches. The song would go – "Anyone want to play Fairies and Witches – one boy?" The one boy would be the witch. The boys on the other hand would play cowboys and indians and their song would be. "Anyone want to play cowboys and indians – one girl?" The girl would be the indian and would end up getting tied up with a skipping rope they'd robbed from the girls while galloping on their pretendy horses.

In Mrs. Moody's class we were taught how to count with shells and sometimes tiddlywinks. We had story time, which I used to enjoy and we were always told to bring into class the cardboard bit of a toilet roll in order to make models. I felt very important telling me Mam that I had to take something into school, albeit a toilet roll. This was eventually made into a Christmas cracker for the forthcoming Christmas party. Waiting for the toilet roll to be finished often felt like an age. In fact I do remember rolling all the paper that was left on the roll onto the floor so that I could take the cardboard bit to school the next day. Mind I got into big trouble for my actions.

"Brenda, you little bugger", me Mam shouted, "Why is all the toilet paper on the floor?"

You see everyone else had taken one in already days and days before and I hadn't. The rest of the class were busy making their Christmas cracker and I hadn't even started mine, so drastic actions had to be taken. Maybe we never used as much toilet paper as they did.

Me Dad always smoked a pipe and me Mam smoked Embassy cigarettes (not the tipped type). She never smoked when she was sitting down, like after a meal. She always smoked when she was working around the house. Even when she was washing up she had a cigarette in her mouth and she had an uncanny knack of balancing about two inches of fag-ash on the end of her cigarette before she blew it off into the sink at the side of the washing up bowl. She used to go phuuff and off it dropped!! When she was scrubbing the kitchen floor she would repeat the process but the fag ash would go in the bucket next to her.

Me Mam was a quiet lady. She suffered from psoriasis affecting the skin on her face. To cover it she used a heavy makeup she got from the hospital. She was very homely and motherly and always kept in the background, whereas me Dad took up position at the front. Me Mam was always there for us, making sure we were both cared for. She always wanted the best for her family. She devoted her life to her family. She was a good cook and baker. Every week she baked. She usually baked the same things, mostly for me Dad to take down the pit for his bait (his packed lunch). He liked cakes with currants in because they were moist for him to eat while in all the coal dust. When she made the cakes our Eileen and I we would fight for the privilege of scraping the bowl clean with our fingers. Ummm it was lovely! We would shout, "Bagsy the dish." Mam would make apple pies too. She was always immaculate. She protected her nice day clothes by wearing a nylon overall or a pinny. She kept our house immaculate too. Always dusting, hoovering and tidying every day as well as cooking dinners like leek puddings cooked in a cloth, corned beef pies and hot-pots. She was a good housekeeper. Her Sunday dinners were brilliant.

Every Sunday my Dad would go to the club, Crowtrees at the top of Bowburn. All the pitmen went there for a few pints. In the early days only men went to the club. They discussed the pit and their working conditions. Usually on a Sunday morning there would be a man walking through the streets ringing a bell shouting:

"Oh Yey, Oh Yey, Oh Yey There'll be a meeting in the Welfare Hall at 11 o clock." This was The Union's way of letting their members know there was a meeting. All the pitmen on our estate would make their way to the Welfare Hall for the meeting then make their way to the club to wind down. My Dad would get back home at 2.30 pm; have his dinner, which had been kept warm in the oven. He would then go to bed for the afternoon to sleep off the effects of the beer. I would lie with him because I had missed him. You see I was my Dad's favourite and our Eileen was me Mam's.

My Mam had her routine worked out for the week. Monday was washing day. We had a Hoover twin tub, a washing tub and spin dryer all in one well that's why it was called a twin tub. The tubs were joined together. We had a boiler, which was like a cauldron, in the wash-house. All the white clothes were boiled first. Then they were washed in the twin tub with a blue bag. This was a block of blue colour to make the whites look whiter. Me Mam used to bash me Dad's work clothes against the wall as they were full of coal dust, and then wash them last of all. During the summer there was never any problem getting the clothes dry but in the winter it was different story. On wet days the clothes were always hung around the fire on a clothes horse which our "Uncle" Harry had made. The clothes horse also miraculously transformed into a tent when it wasn't in use by me Mam for the washing. We used to turn it so it was in the shape of a tent then put a sheet over it. It was great. We played in "the tent" for hours.

During the winter if the weather was freezing and the clothes were on the line me Mam would bring them inside and the clothes would be as stiff as a board. They could stand up on their own. They would have to be dried in front of the fire. When the clothes horse was in front of the fire it made the sitting room cold. The heat couldn't get anywhere; the clothes horse stopped it. I used to push myself in front of the clothes horse and sit in front of the fire and my face used to glow as red as the fire. Me Mam used to go mad.

Tuesday was ironing day. Wednesday was housework downstairs, Thursday was housework upstairs, Friday was cleaning the bathroom and maybe swilling the yard and cleaning the step. I don't know why but housewives always liked a clean step at the front door. Then of course there was the stairs to brush down. The weekends were for us, her two girls, and maybe a bit of shopping in Durham.

At school there was always a regular visit from the "nitty" nurse. I never got nits but our Eileen did!!! The nurse was called "Nitty Norah the nit explorer". A few days after the visit from the nurse there used to be a recall for the pupils who had nits. They suffered the humiliation of being singled out as "a carrier". Usually it was the same children each time who were recalled. I think our Eileen would have been horrified getting them. Even if she had got them she would have said, "Oh they're not mine, I got them from someone else."

I never used to eat much that's why I was so little. Mam used to worry. But I used to love semolina with rose hip syrup and cake and custard; I'm sure that's why I had rotten teeth!!! I did! So I had to have all my front teeth extracted. My Dad took me to a dentist at the very top of North Road in Durham, just under the railway viaduct. I wasn't keen at all. In fact, I was frightened. We were sat in the waiting room. It was full of people. I was the only child. I hung onto my Dad's arm because I was so scared. A nurse came out of another room. She looked around the room then called my name:

"Brenda Swainston."

"Yes, this is Brenda," my Dad said pointing to me.

I wasn't happy by any means. My Dad came with me and lifted me up and sat me in a huge, leather chair, which was surrounded by items of torture all silver coloured, such as pliers and a hammer. A hammer, what was a hammer doing on that shelf, and tools with big long spikes and big long hooks on the end? I didn't like the look of any of it. I was scared stiff. The nurse told me not to be frightened. Haaaaarr!! Then the dentist made his entry. It couldn't have been any worse. He wore a white coat, a white mask over his mouth and wait for it he had a black patch over one eye. My head turned towards him and Aaaaaaggghhhh. I jumped out of the chair and ran away from the surgery, through the waiting room and down North Road towards the bus station. My Dad ran after me shouting at me.

"Come here you little bugger."

No way was I going back there. I kept on running. I was petrified. I imagined "him", the pirate dentist standing over me, looking at me with that one eye. He was holding the silver pliers in his gloved hand and smiling at me with his rotten teeth. Because all pirates have rotten teeth!!! I kept on running then my Dad caught me and carried me under his arm and returned me to the surgery. I was screaming and screaming when he put me back in the ginormous chair.

The dentist was nowhere to be seen. I kicked and kicked. The nurse got a mask. Yes a mask, and it was brown. It smelt awful.

"What are they going to do to me?"

"Breathe deeply Brenda," the nurse said. Aaaaaaaa! And I suppose then – I was asleep. At which point the dentist was able to enter the surgery again and he pulled all my bad teeth out without me even seeing him!! My Dad carried me home in his arms after my ordeal. I had one of his scarves with one of his hankies around my mouth. When we got home me Mam put me to bed where I fell asleep. I suppose when I awoke I had a wonderful story, a true story to tell our Eileen and my friends. I never went back to that dentist.

I suppose my first "stage" was going to tap dancing classes in Coxhoe. Coxhoe was two villages away. First there was Park Hill then Coxhoe. It had more shops than

Bowburn. In fact every village had more shops than Bowburn!! Coxhoe had a front street full of shops. One in particular was called Gatenby's owned by I think three brothers, all in their twenties and all very good looking. The shop sold everything from carpets to cookers, furniture and clothes. The brothers gave credit to customers who worked but couldn't quite afford to pay the full cash amount for say a new bedroom suite. Yes, buy now pay later. The brothers used to come around on a Friday night to collect their credit payments. All the older teenage girls and some of the young mothers used to swoon when they came on their "rounds" Some used to dress up for the occasion and have their hair done. Well, my Mam didn't, but I know some of my friends' Mams did.

Anyway there was a Community Centre in Coxhoe and it held dancing lessons. Our Eileen and I went on and on to Mam to let us go for tap dancing lessons. I think one of our Eileen's friends went and she said it was good. Well me Mam said we could go. Eeeh we were so excited. We were going to learn to tap dance. Eeeh.

The class was called The Vera Twitty School of Dance. Sounds brilliant, don't you think? Eileen and I went and started tap dancing lessons. We got our little black taffeta dresses, which we wore each week for our lessons. The dress had a badge on too!! And of course, we got our tap shoes. They were red and we copied the more experienced tap dancers and took the laces out and threaded our hair ribbons through. Eeeh, we thought we were great.

Once I got my tap shoes on I never had them off. I loved them. I loved the noise my wonderful red tap shoes made. I tap, tap, tap and tapped anywhere that would make a noise: in the yard, up the garden path, on the path outside our house on the tiles of the fire place, when the fire was out, even in the enamel bath. Me Mam heard the noise of my tap shoes.

Dancing on a carpet with my sister Eileen

"Where are you Brenda?"

"In the bath Mam."

"Get out of there. You just wait 'till your Dad gets home." At which point I jumped out of the bath. I even volunteered to go down the shop for me Mam so that I could hear my tap-tap-tap shoes. I drove me Mam mad.

"Will you take those bloomin' shoes off." she would shout.

Eileen and I were in a couple of concerts which were performed at Coxhoe Community Centre. In one I was a gypsy, our Eileen a Hawaiian girl in a grass skirt. Then, the next show I was a sailor and our Eileen was in a red robin costume. The costumes had to be made by the parents. Me Mam was good at mending and darning, but not so good at making costumes so we relied on good neighbours to help with the sewing. Anyway Eileen and I soon got sick of going to The Vera Twitty School of Dance so we packed in. I can still do the shuffle hop though!!!

At the same community centre I remember getting my polio injection. I was the first child to go in for the injection. Well I screamed, screamed and screamed again, which made all the other children waiting in line nervous and they all started to scream. The place was full of screaming 5 year olds. They thought I was being tortured and that was before I'd even had the injection!!

Our Eileen got a nurse's uniform for Christmas one year. Her friend Elizabeth had got one too. Eileen asked me to come along to Elizabeth's house, which I thought was strange. Eileen never asked me to play with her and her friends. She took her dolls with her. One of her dolls had rubbery skin and was stuffed with cotton wool. We got to Elizabeth's house and both of them were in their uniforms: white pinnies with a large red cross on the front and the nurse's hats around their brows. They were playing hospitals and guess what, I was one of their patients, along with all the dolls. I had medicine spooned into me. I was bandaged from head to foot. Our Eileen was injecting her dolls in the arm with a darning needle and she even tried to inject me with the needle. I wasn't having that, so I escaped from Elizabeth's house and ran home and told me Mam that our Eileen had been pushing needles into my arm. When Eileen got back me Mam said, "Have you been sticking needles into our Brenda's arm?"

"No." she said.

"Eeeh she did."

Myself, Arthur Bell and my sister Eileen

1957 Moving up to Junior School

My time at the infants' school was pleasant. I learned and sang nursery rhymes. I could read and could do a few sums. In the last year of the infants my class friends and I all felt very grown up when it came to time for us to go to the junior school.

Moving up to the "Big" school was an event. For one, it was bigger than the "baby" school. Yes it certainly was. Both the infants and juniors were on the same site built in the early 1900's. In fact all the schools in County Durham were of the same design. Built of red brick, they had very high ceilings and very long sash windows. They were heated by coke and I do believe the caretaker used to get to school at 5.00 am in order to get the boiler lit so that the whole of the school would be warm for 9.00 am.

It was a big event in your life because in the infants the teachers were nice and gentle. It was comfortable because as well as learning we played a lot. We even had dressy up afternoons and if you did something good you were rewarded by a dolly mixture, so I always strived to be good. There was discipline. If anyone was naughty they were put in a corner. If the whole class had been naughty we had to sit with our hands on our heads for quite a while.

In the infants we had a few gypsy children. Their camp site was in a field about a mile away. On their first day at school they sat underneath the desks. One of the children was called Penny and she was always wetting herself. Everyday a small stream of water would end up at the front of the class. Someone would always shout,"Miss, Penny's wet herself again." Poor Penny.

The big day arrived and I had our Eileen's tunic on which she'd outgrown - now it fit me - a white blouse and a tie. In the summer term we wore blue gingham dresses and short white socks.

It was a long walk to school, about a mile and a half. Usually Eileen and I would go up to school together with our Mam or Dad and on our way we'd pick other friends up as we passed their homes. Rain, snow or shine we always walked. Not like this day and age.

The big school had six classrooms and a very big hall, where tables would be set up for our dinner. The dinners were brought into school from a place that cooked all the school meals for infants and junior schools in the south Durham area.

This new school had a headmaster called Mr. Evans. Yes, a man. He was massively tall and had a very loud Welsh voice. When he shouted he terrorised us into behaving ourselves.

The site for the two schools was right next to the colliery houses. You see Bowburn used to only consist of the colliery houses. Then the new estate was built. The junior school had two play yards, one for the boys and one for the girls, so no playing fairies and witches.

On moving up to the big school we were graded: A class and B class. Surprisingly, I got put into the A class. My teacher was called Mrs. Smith. She was small with short black wavy hair in a side parting and she wore bright red lipstick which made her front teeth look bright and they stuck out a bit, not a lot though. I didn't have any so I was mesmerized by those teeth. She was pretty and wore fashionable clothes: nice colourful dresses or skirts with a big elastic belt. The fashion was of the 50s. Today when I watch "Call the Midwife", the midwives' clothes always remind me of Mrs. Smith. Mrs. Smith looked very different to the Mammies of my friends and of course my Mam. And she was young - maybe in her 20's. In the infants all our teachers were old. Well they looked it.

On our first day at school Mrs. Smith gave us homework. I remember bragging to our Eileen. "Oh we've got homework." I shouldn't have opened my big mouth because we got it every night for the whole time I was in her class.

Each night we had to learn 10 spellings and a set of tables. The next morning we had our spelling test and tables test and for every word we got wrong we got the board rubber across our hands. I was only little and the board rubber hurt. I wanted me Mam!!

My Mam helped me with my homework and I soon became a good speller and good at my tables. I didn't want to get the board rubber. I wasn't keen on this Mrs. Smith at first; in fact I would have liked to have gone back to the Infants. Our Eileen was in two classes or year groups above me. I always used to think she was clever.

I couldn't tell the time and one day Mr. Evans, the headmaster, told me to go into the hall and find out what time it was. It was a massive clock on the wall. I stood staring at the clock, hoping someone passing would tell me what time it was. Our Eileen even passed me on her way to the toilet. I asked her to tell me the time. She didn't, so there I stood until it was playtime. I was glad to hear that bell ring.

When me Dad was on night shift he used to come to the bottom of the school playing field to see me. I was always pleased to see him. Seeing him used to break up my school day - 9am – 4pm was a long time. My friends used to tell me he was there. "Your Dad's at the bottom of the field with your dog." All my friends would come and see my Dad and our Whiskey, because none of their Dads ever came to see them. I was always chuffed to bits.

We got our Whiskey, the dog, when he was just 8 weeks old. He was a wire-haired fox terrier. I remember going to get him in Durham. When we got off the bus at Bowburn my Dad carried him in his jacket to keep the puppy warm. I skipped alongside me Dad so happy that we had a puppy. Our Eileen walked behind carrying the bags of shopping.

When my Dad was on night shift he would get back

home at about 11 o clock at night. I used to lie in my bed at night and worry about my Dad being down the pit. I had heard stories of how dark and dangerous it was. I would trace his footsteps from the pit baths round all the streets and then up the path to the back door. If he wasn't there I would start all over again tracing his footsteps until eventually he was at the back door. Then I would go to sleep rested knowing that he was home safely.

Our Entertainment

Our entertainment during the summer months was playing 'two a baller' up against the wall, doing hand stands up against the wall with our dresses tucked into our knickers and skipping with me Mam's washing line, which we used to stretch right across the road. Or, if we dared, we cut a washing line down to make individual skipping ropes. Just like those we had at school.

The love of my life, apart from our Whiskey, was my bike. My Dad bought it from Durham Sale Rooms, an auction room. Apart from me Mam, we all had a bike. My bike was shiny and painted black. I used to polish it after it got dirty from a hard days riding. I used to pretend it was a motor bike. I even saved my pocket money up and bought a speedometer, a stand and even an aerial for it. No wireless but I wasn't bothered. It had a saddle bag on the back in which I used to keep my sandwiches and a bottle of water. Sometimes me Mam used to take our Whiskey for a walk and I'd be on my bike. Coming back from the fields I'd pedal like mad and Whiskey used to run like hell after me. Eeeh it was great. Other times me Dad, Eileen and I used to ride through the farms to a place called Croxdale. There was a weir here and so we took our bathing costumes and paddled in the river. Blooming cold but we didn't care.

Being a tomboy I used to love playing football with the lads of similar age to myself. For Christmas one year I even got a pair of football boots, in fact I still have my boots in the loft. After a game I used to go back home covered in muck and my knees were always covered in scabs. The lads and I used to compare our scabs to see who had the biggest one. Our Eileen used to just look at me and sigh. I didn't care. Our Eileen was a lady, I wasn't.

I must tell you about one piece of play apparatus we made. We'd ask our Mam's for two empty baked bean tins, wash them out and then get our Dads to drill holes right through so we could thread a long string through the holes. The string was tied to make a long loop. Then we stood on the tins, one foot on each tin and hold on to the string as support. They were makeshift stilts. We'd walk everywhere on them. Often calling for friends on them, who in turn would get their tin stilts out. Hey, I tell you they were a fashion accessory. We all walked a clonk, clonk, clonking. A bit like the way the young people do now on their massive high heels.

We'd also have water fights. We couldn't afford water pistols from a toy shop so we used Fairy Liquid bottles or Squeezie washing up bottles. Sometimes I used to go into the kitchen when me Mam wasn't in and empty the washing up liquid out and fill the bottle with water in order to go and play water fights. Me Mam used to go mad.

"Brenda!!!!" she'd shout. "Where are you, you little bugger? Have you emptied my washing up liquid bottles out?" She knew I had. She knew it wouldn't have been our Eileen; she'd be putting her make up on. I'd just put the washing up liquid in a bowl but it meant that when me Mam washed up she had to spoon it out into the washing bowl. I wasn't very popular.

I was ten years old when I found an old car which had

been dumped behind Ann Walton's house. I was over the moon. I loved cars, probably because we never had one. I spent hours and hours in that car. I used to pretend I was driving to places I'd been to on holiday with me Mam and Dad and our Eileen - to Butlins in Filey, Blackpool and Whitby. There was the gear stick and all the dials, oh and the pedals, but my feet couldn't reach them anyway, so it didn't matter. The car was an old Austin, a little black one. There was glass all over the seats and it rained in but I didn't care. I was in my element. Me Mam would probably ask our Eileen "Where's our Brenda?" I suppose she'd reply, "Probably Blackpool by now."

I just loved cars and wanted so much to drive. In the sitting room I'd move the furniture around in the shape of the inside of a bus. The settee was the backseat of the bus, and the chairs were the single seats. I was the bus driver sitting on one of the kitchen chairs. My Dad got me a steering wheel from the rag and bone man. Our Eileen was the bus conductress (clippie) and me Mam and Dad were passengers. Even our Whiskey had a seat in the bus.

Our Eileen got the conductress dressing-up set for Christmas. It had a ticket machine, and tickets and the strap to go around her neck. Our Eileen even had a bell to ring for me to start the engine and get going on our journey.

The door to my driver's cab was me Mam's baking board, which me Uncle Harry made. It had no hinges but I was still able to open it, climb in and then slam it shut. (You can picture it can't you?)

The front of the bus was my desk turned around so that when we broke down I could lift the lid which was the bonnet of the bus and hold it up with my ruler. Under the bonnet was my engine which was made up of items from my Dad's tool drawer. He didn't have a tool box! I also carried tools with me to mend the engine, such as my Dad's hammer and screw drivers.

On certain journeys we'd have breakdowns and I'd have to jump out of my cab, lift the bonnet and then mend the engine. The pedals, like the brake and accelerator for the bus were my Dad's slippers turned upside down, the soles facing up, the poker was the gearstick

Do you know, it was great and me Mam, Dad and our Eileen, enjoyed the journeys and "pretendy" trips into Durham. They had to get off and on the bus as our Eileen ordered though.

The children of the estate all had second hand bikes. These sometimes didn't have any brakes and we used our feet to stop. My Dad used to mend our shoes on a last.

We drank out of taps. A takeaway was from the fish and chip shop. We shared our bottle of water with all our friends. Mind you I'm pleased I wasn't the last one to drink from the bottle because of all the dregs at the bottom!

We stole turnips from the farmer's field to dig the insides out for Halloween. We'd put a candle inside and go around the doors. Halloween wasn't a big celebration like it is today. It was still fun carrying a turnip with a lighted candle inside!!

After playing all day we'd only go home when we were hungry or when it got dark.

Because we lived on a new estate and building was still going on, there were building sites for me and my friends to play in. We'd go there after school when all the workman had gone home. It was a brilliant play ground where we would climb the scaffolding, jump onto the pile of sand and after that slide down the pyramid of sand then makesand bombs and throw them at the newly built walls. The big planks of wood we'd make into a see–saw. I bet we were popular with the builders when they went back to work the next day.

There was always a night watchman but he was usually asleep. If he woke up he would shout, "Get away you little buggers."

Playing in the street with friends, making new friends and falling out with old friends was quite common. I had lots of friends and always went calling on them to come out and play depending on which one I fancied playing with.

Wendy Burn was a junior school friend. Wendy was very clever and was always reading books, whereas, our Eileen and I never did. Wendy always talked about a ghost called "The Blue Lady" who was on a hill just outside of Bowburn. We used to ride our bikes to the bottom of the hill and leave them there. While climbing up the hill up to where The Blue Lady was supposed to be, Wendy made up stories about The Blue Lady. By the time we got to the ruin, possibly the remains of a farmhouse, at the top we were all scared stiff. We used to scream then run like hell down the hill, get on our bikes and head for home where we would be safe.

In the early 50s skiffle groups were very popular. The lads and I used to put a group together. We made all the instruments. Shiny toilet paper wrapped around a comb made a brilliant sound (who needs Botox, when you can play the comb). A large round biscuit tin became a drum, using knitting needles as the sticks. A shoe box with elastic bands stretched across became a guitar. Hey what a brilliant sound we made.

Mod-cons

Wendy's family were the first in Bowburn to have a fridge. Her Dad wasn't a pitman, he was an engineer. I think that's why they always read books!! They lived in William Street. We used to cut through their massive garden to get home from school (only if Wendy was with us).

Wendy's Mam used to make ice lollies out of orange juice. It was great. I think our family were the second family in Bowburn to get a fridge. It was a Hotpoint Iced Diamond.

So we had our own ice lollies and I used to sell them to the lads and lasses in our street.

I also think we were one of the first families to get a television. Eeeh! It was 12 inches square and was in a nice cabinet. "A lovely piece of furniture." My Dad would say. He got a massive magnifier to hang in front of the screen to make it look bigger. My friends who didn't have a tele used to come in our house and watch the programmes like "Muffin the Mule", "The Wooden Tops", "Andy Pandy" and "Bill and Ben". We'd watch "Bill and Ben" with such concentration that it's a wonder we ever learned how to talk at all because of the way "Bill and Ben" spoke to each other. Bill would say, "Oh flobbalobbalobba." Then Ben would reply, "Ah flabbalabbalabba."

We used to be glued to the television. Monday was "Picture Book", Tuesday "Andy Pandy", Wednesday "Bill and Ben", Thursday "Rag, Tag and Bobtail" and Friday was "The WoodenTops". A lady called Cathie who was on one of my cruises reminded me of the order of the programmes. Then there were programmes like "The Lone Ranger" and Tonto and "Bonanza". These were all in black and white. The programmes only started at teatime and they weren't on for very long. After a while we got a second channel called Tyne Tees.

I daresay all the other areas in different parts of the country got their regional television station. Now of course there are about 199 stations to choose from!

Me Dad

My Dad used to cut workmates' hair. He had a barber's chair which he used to put in the kitchen. He had electric shears and used to give his mates short back and sides. That style would keep them cool while down the pit. I used to love me Dad to cut my hair. Our Eileen wouldn't let him near hers!

One Saturday afternoon I sat and watched my Dad cut one of his mate's hair. I was watching and staring, thinking I'd like to do that. Snip, snip, snip with scissors and a comb. So I went off looking for one of our Eileen's dolls which had hair. I couldn't find one. She must have hidden them from me. So I went in the bathroom and to my joy I found me Dad's shaving brush, the bristles standing tall. Well, I got the comb and combed the wonderful bristles then I got the scissors and clipped, clipped and clipped, combing at intervals. I clipped until there was about one quarter of an inch left of bristle. I thought it looked good and so off I went to play on my roller skates. I left all the bristles in the bathroom basin. Next thing I heard was, "BRENDA, where are you, you little bugger?"

Well I didn't know what was wrong but I thought a clout was definitely on the cards by the way me Dad was shouting! He still used that shaving brush right up into his 90's.

On a Saturday night my Dad would always go to the Working Men's Club at the top of Bowburn. In fact most of the pitmen went there with their wives but me Mam never went.

There used to be a "Go As You Please" on, which was like karaoke, but in those days the backing was an organist and drummer. Me Dad used to love getting up on the club stage and singing. His favourite song was The Story of My Life by Michael Holliday. The prize for getting up used to be three pint tokens, which meant three free pints.

Well this one night my Dad sang three songs. The committee gave him three tokens. My Dad thought he should have got nine tokens because he sang three songs. The committee said, "No Alfie you just get three tokens. "Well me Dad lost his head and threw the tokens into the audience and shouted to the committee: "Keep your bloody tokens."

He got summoned before the committee and was told he would have to behave himself or be banned from the club for a few weeks. I think he behaved himself after that. Well for a while at least.

When my Dad used to get back from a Saturday night at the club he always brought Eileen and I a Britvic pineapple juice. I later progressed to "Cherry B's" but that's another story!

The fruit and veg man, called Jackie Tarren, came around the streets with a horse and cart, selling his produce to the families on the estate. When the horse deposited its manure (or did a poo!) on the road, I was sent out with a shovel and bucket to pick it up. If the horse hadn't dropped one outside our house I had to follow the horse until it had done one, shovel it up and take it back to me Dad and he would put it on the potatoes in the garden.

Eeeh! That reminds me, I had a tortoise called Tommy and our dog Whiskey used to think the tortoise was a bone and we often used to find Tommy buried in the garden, along with the potatoes. We used to see one of its legs sticking up above the soil.

Our Whiskey's kennel was under the draining board next to the sink and whenever I knew I was in trouble and heading for a belting from me Dad I used to hide with Whiskey under the draining board behind a curtain. I could hear me Dad shouting.

"Where's that little bugger?" Our Eileen and I used to hide the belt from me Dad so that he couldn't find it when we were under the threat of getting the belt.

My Dad always used to make the chips on our open coal fire. It was too expensive to buy them from the fish and chip shop. He had a chip pan full of dripping and it went on a hot coal fire. The raw potatoes went in when the fat was hot hot

hot. The fat used to sizzle like mad. Oh yes my Dad was always in charge of the chips! Eeeh! Can you imagine health and safety standards now finding out about that!

My Dad making the chips gave me an idea – I started making chips in our backyard and I sold them to my friends in our street. This is how I did it. I got a large empty biscuit tin (the type we got for Christmas) then cut a hole in the centre of the bottom of the tin big enough for a large single Yorkshire pudding tin to fit in. I hope you're following. Turn the biscuit tin upside down and place the pudding tin in the hole. Under the tin I placed a saucer with a candle on it which I lit. Dripping or usually lard was put in the pudding tin and the heat from the candle heated the dripping. I put the chips in the dripping to cook. Well, they never did! I sold them you know. Yes I did.

Friends like Ann Walton from across the road and Marjorie Symons bought them and actually ate them!! They were raw waxy potatoes, covered in soot from the candle!! I remember one friend, who will remain anonymous, saying, "Eeeh Brenda these chips are lovely." Mind she was in the bottom class at school.

I also used to make suntan lotion too. You see my Dad loved to sun bathe and going brown. It was his recipe for the suntan lotion that I used. He used olive oil which you could only get from a chemists and he'd mix it with vinegar. He used to have a brilliant golden sun tan.

I got the bus into Durham and bought some olive oil. I was always a good saver and still am. When I got back home I found some empty bottles (any size and it didn't matter what had been in them). I filled them with the mixed lotion and sold that to my friends too. I'd convince them that they would end up with a glorious golden tan if they bought my potion. No one ever complained.

Durham Big Meeting Day (Gala Day)

Durham Big Meeting or 'The Gala' was brilliant. This is where all of Durham's mining villagers would gather. Every family would be there. There were brass bands from each village and they marched into Durham City playing their best tunes. The bands must have rehearsed for months getting the tunes right and of course marching at the same time.

Every village had its own banner which was carried leading the brass band into the city. We all "danced the banner in" which meant families and their children would dance in front of the banner while it made its way into Durham where each band took its turn to play their best tune in front of The County Hotel where the Labour Prime Minister of the day, such as Harold Wilson, would be standing on the balcony.

After that everyone walked to the fairground on a nearby field. There were hordes and hordes of people all crushed trying to make their way onto the field. I would be on my Dad's shoulders so that I wouldn't get stood on.

On the fairground there were amusements and rides such as the waltzer, the horse roundabout, ghost train and rides for the little ones and hook the duck. If you hooked a duck you won a gold fish. Eileen and I really, really wanted a gold fish and my Dad eventually won one but by the end of the day the fish hardly had any water left in his polythene bag he was swimming in and was gasping for breath. Just a quick mention: when we got the fish home and got proper fish bowl our Whiskey used to drink the water, so the poor fish was always gasping for breath. Anyway, there were hot dog stalls, candy floss, toffee apples, fish and chips and so on. You name it, it was there! All the banners by this time were all around the circumference of the field, with all the instruments in front of each village banner while the players of the instruments loosened their ties and opened their shirt top buttons and proceeded to get drunk. The band members were all dressed in a uniform to represent their village.

As soon as we got to the amusements our Eileen got a doll on a stick and I got a cowboy hat. My favourite ride was the donkey ride. Each donkey had its own name, usually of popular film stars. I begged my Dad for a ride on a donkey as this would be the nearest thing to a horse I'd ever get on. My donkey was called Frank Sinatra, while our Eileen's was Doris Day. It would be wouldn't it?

When I got on my donkey my legs were so short the gypsy man, who owned the donkeys, had to hitch the stirrups right up so that I could get my feet in. On that donkey I was "The Lone Ranger" on my horse, "Silver". I imagined Tonto was behind me. I thought he was until I turned round and shouted, "Come on Tonto." upon which I saw our Eileen toddling along on Doris. I leaned forward and stroked my horse. "Good boy Silver." I wanted him to go faster even gallop as my mind took me across the prairie. "Hi Ho Silver" - on a donkey!!

When the ride was over I was lifted off but I wanted another go.

"No," me Mam said, "There are other rides to go on, save your money for them." Aaawwww. I wanted another ride on Silver. Oh well, when I got home I'd have to make do with the arm on the settee and pretend "It" was Silver.

We always came away with a coconut my Dad had won. What a job we had getting the milk out of it and smashing it open with my Dad's hammer to get at the coconut, especially when my Dad was a bit drunk.

All the men from the Durham pits got drunk on that day. In fact, all the shops had their windows boarded up the night before because they knew there would be trouble, and there always was. The Police were always in full force, some on horseback.

Eeeh it was a great day and everyone enjoyed themselves. I bet there were some sore heads the next day. I know my Mam used to let my Dad stay in bed the next day. He wasn't very well.

Even today villages which were pit villages still keep up the tradition of the Miners Gala and it is still held on the second Saturday of July every year. The banners are still danced in and the bands still play. A political speaker still attends and stands on the balcony of the same Hotel they did in the 50's and 60's and the amusements and rides and even the donkeys are all there.

Unfortunately I'm always on a cruise when the Big Meeting is held. Maybe next year I'll get there and dance the banner in and maybe have a ride on a donkey.

Bowburn Community Centre houses the Pit Banner and the villagers are still very proud of their heritage. I regularly perform at the Community Centre at Bowburn to raise funds for The Durham Gala Day. The village need the funds to pay for the roads to be closed and to pay for the band and buses to transport the residents of the village into Durham. Bowburn doesn't have its own band and so the villagers have to hire one. I still feel part of Bowburn and often drive through the village on my way to Durham. Happy Memories!

My Dad lived in Bowburn until he was 94. When the local community banner group had a new banner made they told me that my Dad's photograph would be on the new banner. What a wonderful honour.

Here are the words to a song I recently heard. It was written by a man called Jez Lowe who was brought up in a Durham pit village. It describes The Durham Big Meeting Day through the eyes of a young Durham pitman.

When Big Meeting came round we knew
we'd have to beat the crowd

So we set off bright and early feeling
happy, pleased and proud

The day was ours to kill the golden sun
was shining downstairs

We found a parking place in Sherburn Hill
and strolled back into town

We walked along through Gilesgate
wondering where to venture first

And while we were a pondering that we
thought we'd quench our thirst

The pubs were full and so we bought a
crate from off a van

It was much too heavy to carry so we
drank it there and then

When we reached the market place it was
crowded fit to bust

We saw our colliery band go marching
past but only just

The woman next to me she said I'm really
over the moon

That's my husband on the trumpet; he's

the only one in tune.

*A man in uniform stood with a pint glass
in his hand*

*He looked alone and so I said, "I hope you
can find your band."*

*He seemed to take offence and put his
glass upon the bar.*

*He said, "I'm a traffic warden and I hope I
can find your car*

*Through the swirling crowd on Silver
Street I spied a friendly face*

*And though it seemed familiar it was one I
couldn't place*

*He made his way towards me as I tried so
hard to think*

*It clicked when he said to me, "Come on
now son, buy your Dad a drink.*

*A busload up from Murton they were out
to have a hoot*

*And to keep their driver sober they had
locked him in the boot*

*Before too long they'd all forgotten where
they'd left the bus*

"When the rest have gone," they said,
"The one that's left will be for us."

No-one in the company knew the way to
the race-course

Till someone spied across the crowd a
jockey on a horse

It was just a mounted policeman but we
still kept on his trail

My leeks would win some prizes if I'd only
brought a pail.

We slept all through the speeches and we
headed for the shows

But you shouldn't go on the Waltzer if you
brought no change of clothes

Then the crowds began to head for home
their banners rolled and furled

And the sun lit the Cathedral at the centre
of the world

You should've been in Durham such a
sight you never saw

Crowds and beer and chips and cheer
and banners by the score

Famous politicians perched upon the
balcony

As the whole of County Durham went a marching on a spree

I really like this song. It's funny and tells a brilliant story of Durham Big Meeting and its colourful visitors, including our family.

Shops

By this time Johnson's shop had had a face lift and was now a part of Mr. and Mrs. Johnson's home. They'd had a house built with the shop attached, so business must have been good.

Mr. Johnson's brother lived next door and they ran the fish and chip shop. That was the only type of takeaway food in those days. We used to take old newspapers to the fish and chips shop and get a free bag of chips. We took empty bottles of pop and got a refund on them maybe only tuppence in old money, but it didn't matter. Sometimes we'd get a bag of scrapings or fish batter.

A Co-operative Society store was next to appear on the estate. There was the grocery department, leading to the chemists, then the hardware department leading to the drapery department. The butcher's was round the corner. Everything under one roof. Who needed Tesco in those days?

One shop, which was in Durham City, was called Doggarts. It was a department store too and regularly visited by me Mam. When you purchased an item the money was placed into a small cylinder then that went into a very long tube and a handle was pulled and the missile would shoot off at a great speed to the cashier's office, who would deal the purchase. Then the cylinder would shoot back with the customer's change and receipt inside. Amazing technology.

Every Easter Mam used to get "a ticket" at the Co-op. This was a credit note. (Again buy now and pay later.) Our Eileen and I used to get new dresses and new coats and sometimes even a hat!

We'd wear our new clothes for Sunday School and then wear the dresses when we were invited to a birthday party or school Christmas party. This is what we looked forward to every year. We always had to take a cup, plate and a spoon and some cakes that our mams had made or even biscuits. We wore party hats which we had made a few weeks earlier. The games were fun, musical chairs, passy the parcel and pin the tail on the donkey, O'Grady says and blind man's bluff. Everyone got a present and had a great time. I think we even had red jelly!

The Club Trip

Every year all Social Clubs in the north east held a Children's Club Trip. Crowtrees Club in Bowburn used to send all its members and their children on such a trip. The thrill and excitement was obvious as we all travelled to a northeast seaside town by steam train. We all arrived at Shincliffe Railway Station and lined up to board the train. It was brilliant. Our Mams and Dads came with us.

We would go sometimes to Whitley Bay or South Shields. Somewhere where there was a fairground just in case it rained and we couldn't get on the beach. Me Mam would make sandwiches usually egg or maybe ham. She'd bake some cakes and a corned beef plate pie. We'd take our bathing costumes and the night before we'd all hope the weather would be fine for the trip the next day.

Most of my friends were on the trip as their Dads were

members of the club. Before we got on the train we were all given half a crown to spend when we got to the seaside. We were all giggly with excitement. Me Mam would take a bag packed with a travel blanket for the beach, towels, our costumes, two bats and a ball as well as an inflatable ball. Me Mam had the lot, making sure we had fun on the beach. Eeeh it was always a great day starting with a train ride where the carriages were full of loud children.

On the beach we played games like rounders and cricket. We splashed around in the sea. We ate our sandwiches, which were inevitably had a layer of sand. Didn't matter, it added to the taste.

Before we went home we went to the fairground. I went on the Penny on the Mat (Helter Skelter). The mat was a coconut mat. Very prickly when you're wearing a little dress. As I was older now I was allowed to go down on my own instead of sitting between my Dad's knees. We'd pick up our mats, which were nearly bigger than me and then clamber up the stairs to the top of the tower, sit on our mats then push off. Off we'd go weeeeeee! Round and round and round. It was brilliant, I loved it. Of course there were the older boys and girls who would go down the tower head first and crash at the bottom usually into the person who'd gone down the chute before them, unless they were quick enough to get out of the way.

I'd also loved going on the dodgems, where I would sit on me Dad's knee and I would be allowed to hold the steering wheel. It felt just like driving a car. Wow. We'd speed around the metal floor and sparks would rain down from the ceiling on me Dad and me. I'd scream with sheer pleasure. I didn't like it when some greasy haired lads with beetle crushers would hang onto the back of our bumpy car.

At the fairground our Eileen and I would eat the entire picnic prepared by me Mam then would go on to eat toffee apples, candy floss, ice cream and this was all washed down by fizzy pop. We arrived back home late in the evening totally exhausted. Eileen and I went to bed and slept a sound and contented sleep. What a great day.

The Pit Holidays

The pit holidays were usually the last week of July and the first in August and we always had a family holiday. We used to go to Blackpool and stay in a "lodge" or boarding house as they were sometimes called. We only stayed for one week, usually the first. Eileen and I loved staying at the lodge because we were sleeping in what we thought was like a hotel.

We would get up for breakfast when the gong was sounded. When this was rung it meant breakfast or dinner was ready. Woe betides anyone who was late for breakfast. We ate our breakfast and dinner in a dining room. Breakfast consisted of cornflakes and bacon, eggs and tomatoes. Oh we were so full.

Blackpool was a big place with a big beach, bigger than South Shields. Upon arriving in Blackpool in a coach there was a competition amongst the passengers as to who would see the Tower first.

"There's the Tower," We'd all scream. The Tower got bigger and bigger as we got nearer. It was massive. Our Eileen and I had never seen anything like it.The main street which was known as The Golden Mile was lit up on a night time, as was the tower. It looked beautiful.

Every day the beach, weather permitting, was packed with Mams and Dads sitting in deck chairs with hardly a gap between them. There were donkey rides and trams. Every child had their bucket and spade and made sandcastles. We always tried to bury me Dad in the sand but the full burial was never quite achieved.

We went to the Tower Ballroom on an evening, where Reginald Dixon played an organ which rose out of the stage in splendour whilst playing, "Oh I Do Like to be Beside the Seaside". We also went to the circus where there were clowns, acrobats and elephants and tigers. The ring would rise and fill with water and seals would swim and flip water into the children's faces. It was brilliant.

When we went to the fair ground in Blackpool just outside there was the laughing policeman. We would stand there for ages giggling and laughing before we went on the rides. Candy floss was always the order of the day.

Butlins at Filey was another holiday destination. It was great because we could go on as many rides as we wanted to for free. We stayed in a chalet and me and our Eileen had bunk beds. When we first saw the bunk beds we squealed with excitement. I always had to go on the top. We all ate in a massive dining hall. The entertainment was great. (I never thought I'd one day be working at Butlins, Filey). Me Dad used to go and watch the wrestling and me Mam went to watch the Bonny Baby competition.

Eeeh well one day I got lost and it came over the tannoy system as loud as anything.

"We have a little girl at the lost children's office, wearing a red dress and answering to the name Brenda. Will her parents please come and collect her." Me Mam and Dad were frantic, and so was I. Anyway I got a ride on a Red Coat's shoulders while I was crying my eyes out.

There were donkey derbies, four wheeled cycles, which held four people so all of our family could go on one of those. Me Dad doing most of the pedalling.

Another year we hired a 12 feet long caravan in Whitby. Eeeh it was tiny. The seagulls used to walk over the top of the roof when we were in it. It sounded like they were wearing me Dad's pit boots.

Me Dad and I used to walk across the cliff top first thing on a morning and scrounge some herring from the fishermen. I don't think me Mam was all that keen on gutting the fish.

All in all we had a brilliant time on our annual summer holidays. Most of the pit families from Bowburn would be at these resorts too so we never escaped them. Not that we ever wanted to.

Not a Happy Time

Apart from the lads I used to play with I had a friend called Mary Briggs who lived not far from me. We were both tiny and skinny. I had short brown hair and she had very long blonde plaits. She had very big blue eyes. Mary and I used to play together on our roller skates, skipping or anything we fancied doing.

I remember I was ten years old, still at junior school. I was playing on my skates. I hadn't called for Mary that day. I first heard, and then saw my Dad coming after me and shouting "Come here ye little bugger." Well the faster he ran the faster I skated. He was shouting:

"Your Mam wants to have a word with you." I knew she would at sometime. You see a big change had happened in my life. I wasn't expecting it and really I didn't understand what was happening to me and why.

I had started my periods. Yes at the age of 10 years old. I was still in junior school, still a child. My Dad didn't like getting involved in things like that. I hadn't told anyone I just washed everything out myself and dried everything on the tank. Anyway I skedaddled on my roller skates as fast as I could and I lost my Dad off and went to Mary's house where I was safe.

Well I knew I had to go back home sometime so off I went to face me Mam. She wasn't annoyed she just told me what I had to do.

I had no idea that this was to happen to me every month for the next 40 years. Me Mam never told me that! What she did tell me was that when this was happening to me I hadn't to wash my hair. How strange! Well I did once, I washed my hair and I actually thought that's how you got pregnant!!!

I worried and worried for weeks until one day we were all playing in the cornfield and one of the older lasses announced to everyone her knowledge of how babies were made! Well we were all shocked. No never. Anyway I was relieved that it wasn't if you washed your hair when on a period. What a relief and what a shock.

I couldn't wait to tell Ann Walton, who lived over the road, the knowledge I had acquired. She was younger than me and do you know what? She told her Mam what I had told her. Her Mam was furious and stormed across the road and had it out with my Mam. Saying I shouldn't have told their Ann, she was too young to know things like that. Oh dear I was in trouble again. I didn't get the belt though. Mrs. Walton was very, very angry with me.

"Touch your collar never follow, never get the fever. Touch your toes, touch your nose and never go in one of those".

This is what we sang when we saw an ambulance and we held onto our collar until we saw a four legged animal. Mary used to say, "I don't need to see a four legged animal because I have a "gg" (a geegee is a horse) in my surname."

Mary Briggs, my friend, was lovely and we spent lots of happy times playing together. We chatted about boys, walking up to school. We were in the same class and even did our homework together. She was my best friend.

One day her brother, David came to our house and said that Mary had been rushed to hospital in an ambulance but had died of a burst appendix before she got to the hospital.

I couldn't believe it. My bestfriend had gone and gone from my life. We were just playing together the day before.

This was a very very sad time for me. I was still in juniors, so young. Mary was eleven years old, too young to die. I went to her funeral, the first funeral I had been to. Her coffin was tiny. The church was full I couldn't believe that I was at Mary's funeral. I think I still expected her to be there the next day for me to walk up to school with.

At school we said a prayer for her in assembly. It took me a very long time to get over losing Mary Briggs. To this day I still think about her.

Finding My Voice

I didn't have any nickname while in the junior school, although my friends' Mams used to call me little Brenda Swainston. In fact Eileen and I were known as the Swainston girls; Ann Walton and her sister Christine were known as the Walton girls; Jean and Marjorie were the Symons girls and so on. There were a lot of sisters in the street. There were two boys Arthur Bell and David Attley, who lived round the corner.

My junior school years were alright. Teachers never noticed me. I was so quiet, never in trouble and not very clever. I was under their radar beam, so to speak, and I was tiny. I daresay a teacher who hadn't taught me thought I was visiting from the infants. I was so small.

The lesson I liked was music and dance in the hall. The girls stripped down to our navy blue knickers and vests and pranced around imitating animals, giants or trees swaying in the wind. You didn't have to be clever to run around in your vest.

I liked PE as well. I think you get the picture. I liked all the lessons where you didn't have to use your brain. Mind at the end of the school term I always got presented with a book as a prize. Not for anything academic, but for good attendance. Yes I was always there. "The hamster was in the cage but the wheel wasn't going round"!

In my last year at juniors I was still in the "A" stream, Mr. Bennett's. He was big, had short grey spiky hair and jam jar bottom glasses. The only lesson I liked in his class was gardening.

There was an end of term maths exam. I wasn't very clever and I knew it was the wrong class for me. Anyway Mr. Bennett caught me copying. I wasn't very discreet. I leaned behind me and asked one of the lads how to do the sums and what were the answers. Well they weren't going to tell me. I didn't get anything right in that exam apart from my name. When the results came in I was sent to the headmaster's office and he told me I was to be put in the "B" class. Mr. Bennett said that I would never amount to anything. Ha!

Do you know, it was the best thing that ever happened? The "A" stream was far too hard for me and because it was too hard I never listened. I would sit and day-dream all day. I was either looking out of the window, pretending to read a book or staring at the blackboard with a glazed look in my eyes.

I was put into Miss Crampton's class. When I went into the class I stood at the back of the room and Miss Crampton said, "Sit down here Swainston," pointing to a chair near her desk. Eeeh! I'd never been called by my surname before. The pupils in her class didn't make me very welcome either because they knew I'd been 'put down' and I suppose they were feeling very smug.

Both they and Miss Crampton after a while, when they got to know me, started to like me. Miss Crampton maybe felt sorry for me.

She played the piano and held singing lessons for our

class. I loved these lessons. Miss Crampton called me Brenda by this time. She helped me realise I had a singing voice. I suppose I owe everything, which was to be in my future, to Miss Crampton.

I certainly didn't think at this stage of my life that when I grew up I would be on a big stage cruising around the world singing.

This wonderful teacher also made maths easier for me to understand by sitting with me and going through the sums step by step. I really needed one to one. She made every subject easier for me. I was slow, but once I got the gist of the subject, I excelled. Well to a certain extent. I hadn't become Einstein over night. It was a 'B' class. I didn't care because at least I could do the work instead of copying

Do you know I enjoyed going to school and I looked forward to going to school every day. The pupils in Miss Crampton's class became my friends. She encouraged me to sing. She even had me in the school choir and, along with three other girls, I sang in front of the class.

I also became a member of the Bowburn Methodist Choir. My friend, Hilary, who was also in Miss Crampton's class, asked me to come to Chapel. She was in the choir and she thought it would be nice if we went together. The chapel was situated in the old part of Bowburn. The choir master was a very strict man called Mr. Strong. He was small with a bald head and big teeth. Mr. Strong was passionate about the choir.

The organ, and sometimes piano, was played by a lovely lady called Lilly Greener. She wore box pleated skirts; she was tall and with a big bosom. Considering this now, I think she had a bad chest because her breathing was always wheezy. Her glasses were thick and made her eyes look tiny. She was very nice to me.

Mam and Dad never pushed me into entering anything, for example competitions. I was in the Chapel Eisteddfod and me Mam helped me learn the words to the songs I had to sing. I'm still useless at word learning. In fact I was in a production show just a couple of years ago and I asked the audience, "Do you know the words?" to which they replied, "No." "Neither do I." I said.

Eeeh well getting back. I started to sing everywhere at home especially in the bathroom because in there my voice sounded great. Yes, the bathroom had a built in echo. Me Mam and Dad were shocked at this change in me. I was singing all the time. Up till then they had no idea I had a singing voice. I bet I got on their nerves.

Bonfire Night

November the 5th is our Eileen's birthday so she always had a party. Of course, it was always bonfire night too. A month or so before bonfire night my friends, who were mostly lads, would go around the doors asking for anything which would burn. We wanted chairs, old tables, and boxes. We'd pile them all up to make a bonfire just up from our house in Prince Charles Avenue on some waste land.

On this day our Whiskey never ventured out of the house. His place was under the table. I think he knew what was ahead. The bangs he did not like at all. He would shiver all day. Now and again our Eileen and I would go and check him out by rubbing his tummy. He always survived his ordeal of Bonfire Night.

We'd make a guy out of old clothes with a round piece of card board which had a face painted on. One of the lads would find an old pram to push the guy around in and we would go around the doors asking "Penny for the Guy." That pram was a precious piece of equipment as it later became a means of transport with, of course, some alterations. A makeover.

The guy would be put on the top of the bonfire, which would be as high as a house. Everyone from Prince Charles Avenue and neighbouring streets would be there. It was exciting when it came to the bonfire being lit.

We bought our fireworks from Johnson's shop or the store. On the box it said "Standard Fireworks" and inside there were Catherine wheels, jumping jacks, traffic lights, penny bangers, roman candles, silver rain and of course rockets. We were only allowed to hold the sparklers and spin them around and around to make a glowing circle. The lads would always get hold of the bangers and set them alight and frighten everyone out of their skin. Naughty!!

There was always a big crowd. A parent would take charge of lighting the fireworks. There was always great disappointment when a firework fizzled out. Everyone would sigh and say, "Aaawwww," while waiting in anticipation for the next one to light up the sky with great Ooohhhhs and Aaaaahhhs.

Because it was our Eileen's birthday she would invite her friends to our house to her birthday party. Me Dad would set some fireworks off outside our front door on the lawn.

Then we would all head off for the big bonfire. When the bonfire was blazing we'd throw potatoes into the fire and rake them out when we thought they'd be cooked. They tasted lovely. Our faces were as black as coal when we ate them. Nobody cared. A great day was had by all, especially our Eileen.

Christmas

At Christmas time we went around the doors carol singing. Just two or three of us and we'd share out the money we'd made. We were wrapped up well with coats, hats and gloves. And of course we had rosy cheeks.

Christmas time was great. Our Eileen and I were always excited about Santa Claus coming and bringing all our presents we'd asked for out of Uncle Harry's catalogue. We always wrote a letter to Santa asking for all the presents we'd seen, and posted it up the chimney when the fire was lit. We thought that the letters always got to Santa even though they got burnt on their way.

On Christmas Eve we put a pillow case at the bottom of our twin beds. We didn't have a stocking; anyway you can get more in a pillow case. We could hardly sleep. Just before we got into bed we'd look through the window up into the sky hoping we'd see 'Him'. We'd always leave a mince pie and a glass of sherry on the table for 'Him'.

When in bed Eileen and I would giggle and hide our faces under the eiderdown. We knew it was unlucky to peep. We heard a creak on the stairs.

"Eeeh is this Him?" I would say. No it was me Mam checking if we were asleep.

"Come on you two get to sleep or else Santa won't come if he thinks you're awake." The excitement was sometimes just too much and we couldn't sleep.

My Dad always went to the club on Christmas Eve. The organist and drummer would be playing and me Dad would get up to sing. Me Mam would stay at home with us and wrap some extra presents while waiting for me Dad to get back home. When he got back they both would sneak upstairs and put all the presents, they'd successfully hidden from us, into our pillow cases.

In later years it was a competition between Eileen and me as to who was the first to find the presents our Mam and Dad had hid. Our Eileen had sussed the non-existence of Santa long before me but she had been threatened by me Mam that if she said anything to me she'd get nowt. That was enough for our Eileen.

I had my suspicions at the club party when Santa Claus

appeared and his eyes, nose and voice didn't half sound like me Uncle Harry. What a shock it was to find out about Santa Claus and all the time it was me Uncle Harry. I always knew he was clever. I think I was 16 when I found out!!

Anyway back to where we were. Well the morning eventually came and we'd squeal as we ran into our Mam and Dad's bedroom.

"He's been, he's been."

We carried our pillow cases down stairs and sit in front of the fire, which was blazing and open our presents. We never got everything we'd ordered but who cared? We always got a selection box and a box of hankies, some nuts and a box of Quality Street.

One year the dog had eaten the chicken, which was for Christmas dinner, and then was subsequently sick all over the compendium box of games. We couldn't play snakes and ladders, draughts, ludo or blow football (that's where when you blew down the straw to chase the ball) as the boards all got covered in "slavver".That year the dog got put in his kennel and got no dinner. We got no chicken for dinner either! We always had chicken for Christmas dinner, couldn't afford a turkey.

After Christmas Day there was Boxing Day. We had a fry up of all the dinner left from Christmas Day and maybe for the next few days.

Moving up to Secondary School

Near the end of my year in Miss Crampton's class all the children in that year had to sit the Eleven Plus examination. If you passed you went to Grammar School if you failed you went to the local Secondary Modern School. All of my class knew they wouldn't pass but none of us were bothered. I didn't want to pass because I knew the lessons would be too hard.

It was the first examination any of us had ever sat. Our desks were set up in the hall and we were told to do our best, make sure we had our pens, pencils, rubber and ruler and to make sure our pencils were sharpened and to have spare pens on our desks. We were also informed that we weren't allowed to leave our seats until the examination time had finished not even to go to the toilet. I did my best.

When the results came by post to our house my Mam opened the brown envelope and said, "You haven't passed Brenda." I said that I knew I hadn't. So off I went out to play.

I went to Bowburn Secondary Modern School. I was placed in the 'A' stream, which delighted me. The class was called Tees 1 and my form teacher was Mr. Whittaker. He was the school music teacher, which was perfect. I loved my music lessons and my music teacher.

We had different teachers for different subjects. There was a Mr. Cherry, Mr. Bolt, Mr. Vest, Mr. Chesterton, Miss Smith, Miss Mitchinson, Miss Thomson and Mr. Roxby was the headmaster.

The school was a building built in the 60's, very modern with a flat roof and so much bigger than the junior school.

Our uniform was grey skirt, grey cardigan and white shirt with school tie. Some of the girls hated the uniform but I liked it. I felt very smart in my uniform. Of course the skirt was too big because it was one of our Eileen's she'd outgrown.

The pupils were not only from Bowburn but from neighbouring pit villages. So I made a lot of new friends. I enjoyed going to school and did well in all the lessons. Many of my friends from the junior school went to different Grammar Schools. Some went to Wingate, some Spennymoor and others Durham Girls Grammar School. This happened because of the lack of pupil spaces in the schools. Too many clever kids. There were always plenty of places in the Secondary Modern Schools though!!

At secondary school I was involved in everything; choir, netball, Scottish dancing, everything! My favourite lessons were music, PE, English, History, Geography, Biology and maybe a little bit of Maths.

Our headmaster was called Mr. Roxby. Everyone was frightened of him. He ruled by fear. When you heard clitty clatty shoes coming down the corridor you knew it was old "Rockbone," you lifted the lid of your desk and got a book out. I'm sure the books were all upside down but we pretended to read them. In our school the cane was used and the last thing anyone wanted to hear was "Go to the headmaster's room now."

All the girls in our class had to knit socks on four needles with white wool. Well mine ended up grey in fact nearly black because Mrs. McCallum, the Domestic Science teacher, used to say, "Take it out Brenda." She didn't think much of me. She thought our Eileen was great. Well she would because our Eileen could knit, sew, and cook; our Eileen even had a gondola basket to carry the ingredients for cookery.

I was always invited to parties held by our Eileen's friends. I used to make her friends laugh. I don' think our Eileen liked me being there because she used to say, "You have to go home Brenda me Mam wants you." I knew she didn't; you see I used to tell me Mam what she used to get up to and who she'd been snogging!!!

Well these bloody socks. I eventually asked me Mam if she would ask Mrs. Oliver round the corner if she could turn the heel on these socks. Mrs. Oliver was a good knitter. She did it for me and I took it into Mrs. McCallum. Well she knew I hadn't done it and told me to take it out again!!! Mrs. McCallum used to say, "You're nothing like your sister." Do you know she was right! I was pleased when the end of term came because the following term was cookery and so it was a different teacher!! I was useless at cookery too. I was hopeless at anything and everything domestic, whereas our Eileen was really good.

I used to go Youth Hostelling in The Lake District with the school. A few of the teachers used to take us and we'd climb some very high mountains. One of the teachers was called Miss Mitchinson. Two of the mountains we climbed were Great Gable and Helvellyn. Our Eileen would go on these trips too, along with all her friends. A couple of my friends would go. Most of my friends at school weren't into hiking and such.

The Girl Guides

Miss Mitchinson was our PE teacher and I was good at all sports. I got on well with her and she told me she ran a Girl Guide Company in Durham and asked if I would like to come along to a Guide meeting. I took no persuading. I joined The Girl Guides and took to it like a duck to water. The Company was the 6th Durham City Girl Guides.

As well as the uniform, I loved the adventures, the hiking, camping, singing and sitting test to get all the badges. We hiked in all types of weather sun, rain, wind and even snow,I loved it. I enjoyed learning different skills, skills which moulded me into who I am today. I learned how to build fires, build camp and survival skills too.

We camped in Jersey one year; in fact we camped anywhere as long as there was a field. My parents sometimes found it difficult to fund these outings but I always got there.

We were all in patrols. I was a very enthusiastic Girl Guide and so I became a Patrol Leader. Other Patrol Leaders became my friends. Some went to Grammar

School, others private school. I didn't care, I loved Guiding. It didn't matter at all what kind of education we had. We were all equals.

At camp we'd sing around the camp fire at night. It was great. Even if my patrol had to dig the latrines it didn't matter. We slept in ridge tents. There were no sewn in ground sheets and every morning our feet or our heads ended up outside the tent depending on which way we were lying. Fortunately all the cows had been herded out of the field.

We were taught all skills. We learned how to hoist our Union flag in the correct way. One morning, one of my girls in my patrol hoisted the flag the wrong way; it was upside down and at half mast. That meant there had been a death and we were in distress. She wasn't very popular with Captain, in fact, neither was I because I was the one who had taught her.

We had water duties. That meant keeping the water topped up for the kitchen and for the wash tent. There were wood duties too, ensuring the wood for the fire never got low.

We had to keep the camp tidy at all times as well as keeping our own tent tidy. We'd roll up the sides to air the tent every morning. We'd make shoe racks out of wood and string by square lashing. This was to keep our shoes off the ground. Really everything had to be off the ground so we made all sorts of racks to put our rucksacks and personal equipment on.

We'd make a tripod to rest a washing bowl on for our personal washing. We'd make hanging larders, this we did during the daytime, as well as our patrol duties. I loved every minute of it and at the end of all the duties there was games time. Then rest time or quiet time.

Accepting my Queen's Guide Award

Of course at the end of the day we'd all sit around the camp fire and sing songs. Every day was amazing. It didn't matter if the heavens opened or if it was scorching hot. I didn't care. Be Prepared was the motto and it is still mine today.

I was very sad at the end of each camp to have to go home. But when I got back home I looked forward to each Guide meeting which was on a Friday night.

In the winter or dark nights we were still kept busy at Guide meetings, learning new skills and teaching new members. We taught them skills such as knots, and identification of flags from different countries. At the end of each evening and we played games.

We also had to study for our badges. We were all proud of the badges we had. Thrift, music, in fact I just loved learning each skill in order to get the badge. I had an arm full of badges. Though I never did get my knitter's badge!! Thanks to Mrs. McCallum.

For part of one of my badges I had to darn 50 moth eaten blankets. Me Mam taught me how to darn. I'm not at all domesticated but I did it. The blankets were riddled with holes. Everywhere I looked there were holes. In fact I think the moths were still there and when I darned one hole another one appeared.

We were at one camp in Jersey. The weather was so bad the farmer allowed us to sleep in his barn. Well when I woke up I heard a noise and I thought it was me Mam's washing machine. I couldn't work out where I was. Of course it was the milking machine.

During my time at Guides I became a Queen's Guide, which I am very proud of. My Guiding friend Susan Holder also became a Queen's Guide. Today I have all my badges stitched onto a cushion with my Queen's Guide badge at the top and my "All Round Cord" stitched around the cushion. I have it on display to remind me of the good times I had.

My fellow Queen's Guide, I have heard became a scientist. Umm. Well done Susan!

Durham County Youth Choir

My music teacher, Mr. Whittaker got me an audition for the Durham County Youth Choir and I passed. My friends from the Grammar Schools were in it too, which was great. We sang with the choir all over the county and we even won the Llangollen Youth Eisteddfod. And we were all English.

Our choir Master was Mr. Hall. He was lovely. The songs he chose for us to sing I loved so much. One which I particularly loved was "Were You There When They Crucified My Lord. Eeeh I loved that song being sung in four part harmony. I also liked "How Great Thou Art." Do you know I still love these songs?

While in the County Youth Choir we were invited to go to Norway to stay with families in and around Bergen. Parents of the members of the choir waved bye-bye from Durham Bus Station. Me Mam was there as well. We boarded the coach for North Shields ship terminal. We got on the ship we went on the main deck and we sang in four part harmony as we sailed away from the port. It was very moving. It was very chilly but we were all wrapped up well. The passengers gathered around and applauded us.

Half way across The North Sea the biggest storm ever started. It was gale force 10 or 11! Crockery smashed, tables and chairs overturned, a port hole broke and sea water was pouring into the ship. No-one could walk. Passengers everywhere were being sick. People were shouting and screaming. The engines of the ship were stopped and we went along with the storm. Quite a lot of passengers stayed in their beds.

The ship was going up and down. Up and down. Then rolling from side to side. Side to side. Ugghhhhh

When one deck flooded passengers were moved up onto the next deck. None of our parents were aware of what was happening and just as well. No mobile phones in those days.

We were a day late arriving in Norway. A journey never to be forgotten. I wasn't frightened at all. I think I got my sea legs from this journey.

When we disembarked the ship we all noticed how beautiful Bergen was. All the wooden houses were painted different colours. There were high mountains in the distance and the lovely harbour.

Most of the families who we were to stay with were lined up on the quayside dressed in their National Costumes. They looked stunning. We'd never seen anything like this before. Even the men were in their bright red jackets, black breeches and white socks, and blonde hair, blue eyes and a suntan. They all looked amazing. Our Dads never looked like that. I think my Mam would be worried if me Dad came home one night from the club in a red jacket and black breeches. Me Mam would think my Dad was on something!

I wonder why we don't have a National Costume.

We were all so pleased to see these wonderful, friendly Norwegians. The family I was to stay with were the Eide family, a farming family from Os near Bergen.

The first our own parents heard of our ordeal on the North Sea was on the North East News at 6 when it was announced that members of The Durham County Youth Choir had been in a gale force storm on the North Sea and that emergency services had been on hand. They said that the choir were all safe and had arrived in Bergen. Oh my goodness, how our parents must have worried.

It was a very successful tour and one not to be forgotten. We sang in venues in and around Bergen. Jennifer Lynch, another member of the choir, stayed with the same family as me. We became very good friends. It was fun staying on Malfried's farm. Malfried was from a big family. Her brother and sisters could all speak English. Her parents couldn't, but it was no problem because their language is so much like the Geordie dialect. Can you believe that?

It all started when the Vikings raped and pillaged the North East coast, and we took on some of their vocabulary. For example, if we didn't fancy going to school. We'd say, "Aww I divn't fancy gannin to shcull." In Norwegian schull is their word for school. Cracket in Geordie is a small stool, as it is in Norway. A ganzie is a Geordie jumper as it is in Norway.

We had fun going through all the similar words. We learned the Norwegian phrase "takk for maten", thank you for the food. "Takk", thank you, "TusenTakk, a thousand thank you's. Of course "Hei" for Hello and "Ha det" pronounced Ha Da, for goodbye. And do you know? We have a Geordie saying Ha Da Way. This means, get yourself away. We were nearly fluent by the end of the tour.

We used to walk around fields and woodlands during the day. The weather was brilliant. Their food was similar to ours but had more variety of cheeses, which were all made locally. At home our cheese selection consisted of Cheshire, Cheddar and Edam.

Most of the farms had their own alcohol still in their barns because alcohol was forbidden to be sold in those days. On an evening we had concerts to go to. Malfried's choir sang during the first half of the evening, of course wearing their National Costume then our choir sang to conclude the evening in our choir uniform, which was a blue dress for the girls and blazer and grey trousers for the boys. It didn't quite have the same visual impact as our Norwegian host choir.

It was always very well supported by the Norwegian people, who were absolutely brilliant. I'm still in touch with Malfried and met up with her on one of my visits to Bergen while on a cruise. What a brilliant time. Never to be forgotten.

1960s

Sundays and Thursdays were special days for watching the television. Sunday was London Palladium night and Thursday night was Top of The Pops.

Eeeh! I never ever thought I would appear at the London Palladium, but I did many light years later! But that's another story.

I remember Juke Box Jury with David Jacobs and a

young lady who rated the record by saying, "I'll give it Foive" Janice Nichols from the Midlands. The record was a 'Hit' or a 'Miss'. I also remember Ready Steady Go with Cathy McGowan, 5 4 3 2 1 by Manfred Man was the signature tune. Well when these programmes were on the tele everyone stayed in to watch them.

The groups that appeared in the charts were: The Beatles with songs like Please Please Me, Gerry and The Pacemakers with How Do You Do It, Billy J. Kramer with Do You Want to Know a Secret. The music was amazing, all teenagers loved it.

Every week we'd get the bus into Durham to buy the latest hits from Woolworth's. It was brilliant. The Beatles had hit after hit with With Love from Me to You, and She Loves You, Yea YeaYea. It was fantastic. It's what we talked about at school, the groups. I had a crush on Paul from The Beatles. 1963 was the start of Beatlemania.

Around this time Bowburn Community Centre started putting groups on every Saturday night. They were all local groups, who were copying the groups in the charts. It didn't matter, they were brilliant.

Our Eileen and I used to go to the Community Centre every Saturday night. All the girls would dance the latest dance, which we'd seen on Ready Steady Go or Top of the Pops. Usually we stood in a circle and put our handbags in the middle and did the Hippy Hippy Shake. In our school some of the pupils came from nearby pit villages, Kelloe, Quarrington Hill and Cassop. Saturday nights at Bowburn Community Centre were very popular and the girls would all be dancing but the Kelloe lads always were in one corner, the Bowburn lads in another, Quarrington Hill lads in another and Cassop lads in the other. Well what do you think? Yes, every week there was a fight.

Fashion was changing. At first there was back-combed hair, sprayed with hair lacquer from a squeezy bottle bought from Woolies. It was called Bellair. The lacquer was in a sachet and squeezed into the bottle. If the hole was too big the lacquer would stick to your hair in globules. Some girls never washed or combed their hair from one week to another and if their head was itchy, which it used to be, they would scratch their head with a knitting needle. The hairstyle was called the 'beehive'. It was backcombed as high as possible, sometimes 6 inches high. There used to be horror stories of insects living in the 'Beehive' hairstyle. The girls also wore thick black eyeliner.

The lads were a bit slower with the fashion and at the dance they were still wearing the clothes which James Dean, Rebel without a Cause wore, white tee-shirts and denims and their hair style was combed back with Brylcreme. A quiff at the front was a must, copied of course from Elvis and Cliff.

Some of the girls used to be wearing flat shoes, short white socks, sticky out skirt and buzzy bee elastic belt. The lads wore Teddy boy suits with black velvet collars, fluorescent socks and shoes called 'Beetle Crushers' or winkle pickers. It was Rock and Roll.

But now it was changing, hemlines were getting higher. No more sticky out skirts. Mary Quant was a fashion designer for the stars and we copied the stars: PVC boots and PVC coats in black, white and red. Hair styles changed and the beehive gave way to bobs or pixie cuts made famous by Twiggy.

The lads copied the bands and their hair got longer. They wore black polo neck jumpers because the Beatles did. Shoes with Cuban heels came into fashion for the lads.

Someone else came on the music scene and it was a young lady by the name of Cilla Black. Her first song, which went to number 1 in the charts, was Anyone Who Had a Heart. Nearly all the groups and of course Cilla came from Liverpool.

Tom Jones came on the scene and an act called P J Proby, who wore such tight trousers that while performing on stage he split his trousers not once but on many occasions. This new decade was called the "Swinging Sixties."

At home we had a Dansette record player. We spent hours and hours dancing to the records in the sitting room or in the kitchen if me Mam and Dad were watching the tele. I remember buying "You were Made for me", by Freddie and the Dreamers. Eileen and I danced and danced all night, we even missed going to the dance at the Community Centre.

Our Eileen was made head girl at school. She was very well respected by teachers and class friends. When we lined up to go into class from break-time she used to pull me out and pull my skirt up (which had been hers anyway) she pulled it up because it was a box pleat and always hung well below my knees, which of course in those days was definitely not the fashion.

On a night time in bed we'd listen to radio Luxembourg on our 'with it' transistor radios under our pillow. Tony Blackburn, Dave Lee Travis, and David Hamilton were all DJs on a pirate radio station called Radio Caroline, which transmitted from a ship off the Essex coast. Eeeh! We loved it and often fell asleep to the music of the 60s. The batteries were always flat in the morning.

In about 1963 "Christ the King" Church was being built in Bowburn and Father Bill was the vicar. He was a very modern vicar who ran a Youth Club for teenagers. Oooh there was a lot of gossip about him, mostly by the older women of Bowburn. Our Eileen and I weren't allowed to join that youth club.

There was gossip that he held orgies in the vicarage. Someone had said that the young teenagers and the vicar were wandering around wearing very little in the vicarage. They said they'd seen them through the net curtain when they were passing on their way to the bus stop. It was all gossip, or was it? The people of Bowburn loved all the gossip, and even added bits to it!

I remember Father Bill came to our house and he asked me Mam if he could bless the home we lived in. She told him that everybody and everything mostly my Dad got blessed everyday! Even the dog. The vicar made a hasty departure.

Father Bill along with his young teenage parishioners built a very futuristic church, in Prince Charles Avenue. It was like a space station with a spire like a rocket. The spire was very high and it could be seen for miles around. Some people thought the roof resembled a pineapple. It became a land mark because drivers on the new motorway could see it. It was built on a budget. Father Bill begged and often had building materials donated for the Church. Eventually work was completed.

Father Bill had two buses, called Samson and Delilah to take his young teenage parishioners on holidays. They were a bit like Cliff Richard's on "Summer Holiday." I don't think the older parishioners were asked. I don't think they would have wanted to go either.

Father Bill eventually disappeared from Bowburn, never to be seen again. I don't think The Bishop of Durham agreed with the way Father Bill ran his Parish. The Church is all gone now and a new conventional Church has been built on the same site. It's just not the same!

Still Singing

I was in the Bowburn Methodist Chapel choir. I was told by Mr. Strong, the Choir Master, to learn "The Old Rugged Cross". I was to sing it at another chapel in Sunderland. I wasn't the only singer, Ann Fawcett, Christine Bowes and Carol Colman also sang. They had different hymns to sing.

I practiced with me Mam. We didn't have piano in the house so I sang without backing.

On the evening of the concert I was very nervous. Me Mam couldn't come because there were no tickets left and, of course, we didn't have a car. Well it was my turn to sing and I sang "with expression" as they say. It was my first ever solo and I thought all the other girls had better voices than me. Well do you know I loved every minute of it. Everyone clapped loudly and even cheered.

At the end of the concert I (little Brenda Swainston) was asked to sing again - an encore! I wished me Mam had been there to see me. I was floating on a cloud. I could have burst with happiness. I sang the hymn again for the chapel and when I finished singing everyone stood up and applauded. Oh my goodness! What a fantastic feeling, seeing everyone stand up and show their appreciation. I couldn't wait to get back home and tell me Mam. It was a great atmosphere on the bus home. We all sang at the top of our voices. "Bread of Heaven, Bread of Heaven." Fantastic.

Me Mam was over the moon. From then on I did more solos. I loved the fantastic feeling I got when everyone applauded and cheered. I wanted to sing, sing and sing more. I suppose today's expression is I loved "the buzz".

Next Stage – Changing Schools

I was 14 and had moved to Spennymoor West Secondary Modern School for a commercial course, shorthand, typing, commerce and accounts. I didn't want to move schools because I wanted to be a mechanic and I was very happy at Bowburn Modern School. All the teachers were brilliant and cared about each pupil, even if they were of average ability, which was what I was.

The Bowburn headmaster, Mr. Roxby, had a meeting

with me Mam and Dad and said he thought it best if I became a secretary!! Me a secretary. He had said that females couldn't become mechanics. So, it was decided that I would go on a secretarial course. I wasn't a happy bunny.

My Mam bought me my new uniform and I thought I'd better give it the best I could. A few of us from Bowburn were on the same course so I wouldn't be alone. We had to go to Spennymoor West Secondary Modern School.

Our first day at the new school was alright because there were pupils on the course from other schools. We met everyone and we all got on together straight away. The course was to last 2 years. The shorthand and typing teacher was Mr. Grieveson (Jacky). Mr. Stoddart taught us accounts, Mr. Abbly tried his best to teach us commerce and a lovely lady called Mrs. Coya taught us English. The music teacher was called Mrs. Newland.

We, the Bowburn gang, were nicknamed the part-timers because we used to get a bus from Bowburn to Coxhoe then from Coxhoe to the bottom of Spennymoor. If it was nice weather, we'd walk to school which was at the top of Spennymoor, but if it was not nice weather we'd wait for a bus. We dawdled up to school because we didn't like going into assembly. If we got into school early and assembly had started we used to hide in the cloakroom behind the coats. We'd find someone's big coat and get behind it with our heads up to the peg. We'd put our bags on our feet. Often we'd hear a teacher doing the rounds to see if anyone was skiving off assembly. I think the teacher knew we were somewhere, but hadn't a clue where we were. We used to hold our breath as the teacher passed the cloakroom. We were like Japanese Snipers. When assembly came out we used to come from behind the coats, mingle in with the rest of the pupils and make our way to our class.

We'd go to each lesson but come the last lesson we had

to set off early in the afternoon to get the buses back!! We were hardly there you know.

I had a nickname at this school. I was called The Duck because my arse was so near the ground. I didn't mind at all. In fact I quite liked it.

H.M.S. Pinafore

I got a letter from Mr. Whittaker, the music teacher, and Mr. Bolt the history teacher, from my previous school stating that they were producing the Gilbert and Sullivan opera "H.M.S. Pinafore". They asked me to perform the leading role of Josephine (without an audition). Oh heck! Well I was thrilled I jumped for joy. It was a Wow!! Me Mam was over the moon for me.

My headmaster, Mr. Prest, and music teacher, Mrs. Newland at my Spennymoor school were elated. But alas my old friends at Bowburn were not. They thought there were plenty of good singers at Bowburn Modern School and didn't want me back. Oh dear me.

When I went to rehearsals the atmosphere was not very nice. Anyway I told Mr. Bolt, the Director and Mr. Whittaker, the musical director and they must have had a word with the cast because at the next rehearsal everyone was friendlier towards me!!

Rehearsals after that went very well. I had a lot of songs to sing and a lot of dialogue to learn. I am not the best at learning words but I did it. I was so pleased I didn't have to make my own costumes.

Eventually the cast bonded and got on with rehearsals. Every week we worked so hard together. The leading characters had more rehearsals to do.

Not only was the Domestic Science department involved in the production of the opera, but also the Art department.

They made the backdrops and painted the props. The Woodwork department and the Metalwork department made the on stage sets. In fact, the whole of the school was involved in some way, including all of the pupils and teachers.

We rehearsed in school at Bowburn then we did a full dress rehearsal at Bowburn Community Centre. All the operas each year were performed at the Centre. We were getting nearer to the opening night. All departments were working flat out to get the stage set. Then the Big Night came, the opening night. We all got down to the Community Centre and into the dressing rooms early. Our costumes were already there hanging up. Oh we were all quite giddy with nerves. The whole cast were backstage and we each peeped through the curtains to see if our parents were there. You could hear the noise from the audience getting louder which meant it was filling up. The tension backstage was buzzing.

Would we remember our lines? Would the costume changes go well? Would we all sing well? But most of all, would the audience enjoy the opera? Then Mr. Bolt came backstage and said to everyone to enjoy the evening and told us that the hall was full to capacity. The hall held four hundred people. Oh my goodness. It was time for curtains up and the performance to begin. We all hugged each other. We were all in costume so quite unrecognisable. We knew who we were but would our parents?

The music started and curtains went up. The audience applauded. The chorus sang their opening song. By this time I was incredibly nervous. The worst moment was when I was standing alone in the wings. My heart was racing with expectation of what was ahead. The rest of the cast were on stage. I was waiting for my cue, for when I would have to step out there into the spotlight and perform in front of my biggest audience ever.

Myself in a production of HMS Pinafore

I went out. Mr. Whittaker was at the piano and smiled at me. All my nerves left me and I sang my heart out. I came off stage and waited for my next cue. Have I got the words right, will it go as well as my last song?

During one song my bonnet fell back onto my shoulders due to it being ill fitting. I undid it and put it to the side of the

69

stage, whilst still singing. Mrs. McCallum, who made or instructed pupils to make the costumes, suddenly took a liking to me and said that I was very professional in the way I dealt with the situation! Oooh!! The show ran brilliantly. Everyone in the audience cheered, clapped and stood up. It was a Wow! I came off stage and was on a big "high". The feeling was something special. It was exhilarating and it felt great being part of the production of H.M.S. Pinafore. We were a brilliant team, headed by Mr.Whittaker and Mr. Bolt. Both said that they were very proud of us all. Oh my goodness all that hard work of rehearsing learning words, costume fittings, makeup, stage direction, everything had paid off. It was brilliant!!

Back stage was buzzing even more after the performance. Everyone was hugging each other, congratulating each other; it was FAB!!! We had four more performances to do and we couldn't wait for the next one.

Up to this point in my life, I was extremely shy. After the performances of "H.M.S. Pinafore" I gained self-confidence in my ability to perform and I blossomed. I was not the little shy Brenda Swainston anymore. It was just brilliant.

The production party was great and everyone let their hair down. That was the last time I really had anything to do with the school and the pupils - it was the end of an era. I loved every minute of it and was sorry when everything came to an end. I enjoyed being on stage and performing and singing solos. I wanted to do it all over again it was so great.

Lads

I went out with lads at this stage and fancied quite a few but I always fancied a lad called Billy Jones. Everyone fancied Billy. He was so good looking, and he knew it. He was commonly referred to as Jack the Lad, a title he wore like a badge and he was a magnet to the opposite sex.

Well one day I got a message inviting me to his house that night. He lived in Cassop. I was skipping and jumping. Not outwardly to alarm me Mam! I knew she'd heard about this Billy and had warned me about him previously. Well he'd asked me, yes little Brenda Swainston!! I think I must have been next on his list. The evening came - Oh dear what could I tell me Mam? Oh dear.

I came up with a plan. Yes, I'd tell her I was going to Margaret Lister's house. She was on the same commercial course as me at Spennymoor. I got the bus to Cassop and knocked on Billy's door. His Mam let me in.

"Oh you must be Brenda. Come in and take a seat."

Do you know Billy came in the sitting room with another girl whom he said goodbye to. Then he said to me:

"Hello Brenda. Would you like to come and see me rabbits?" I'd never heard it being called that before. And I felt I was next in the queue.

Do you know it was sod's law because me Mam went looking for me on that night? She never usually went looking for me. She must have had a 'Mother's intuition' moment. She went to Margaret's home and of course I wasn't there, I was in Billy's rabbit hutch with Billy!!!! (Nowt happened, I was a good girl). I never did get to see his rabbits!!!!

When I got home did I get wrong? You bet I did. I think Billy in Cassop, which was ten miles away, heard me Mam and Dad shouting at me. You see when I got off the bus in Bowburn me Mam and Dad were at the bus stop waiting for me. In fact, I could see them as I stood up to get off the bus. Oh my goodness my heart sank because I knew I was in for it. Eeeh! Ooooooh! BIG TROUBLE. I never went out with Billy again.

Grandma, Granda and David

My Grandma and Granda on me Mam's side lived in a village called Fishburn. We didn't visit very often because we had to get two buses in order to get there from Bowburn. I didn't like visiting because I always used to get told off by my Grandma for maybe kicking me feet against the chair leg while we were sitting at the dinner table.

A young man lived with me Grandma and Granda and he was called David Johnson. I thought he was my cousin or an uncle.Sometimes he used to come to our house and he'd be on his motorbike. He used to say to me, "Do you fancy and ride on my motorbike Brenda?" "Is the Pope a Catholic?" He used to take me for rides all around Durham. It was fabulous.

I found out from our Eileen that David was my brother. I wasn't shocked at all; in fact I thought it was brilliant. Me Mam had David during the war years and my Grandma and Granda agreed to look after him while me Mam was in Service. It must have been very difficult for me Mam.

Our David met a young girl who worked as a secretary at The Northern Rock Building Society in Bishop Auckland. Her name was Jan. She was lovely and I got on so well with her. They got married at Sedgefield Church and our Eileen and I were bridesmaids. About six months after our David and Jan married, Jan became pregnant and had a son called Dwayne. They moved down to York because David was offered a better job as an electrician. I used to visit them there during my school holidays. They later moved to Middlesbrough and had another son Alexis. David got a job as school electrician and had the use of the school's swimming pool. I loved visiting them because our David, Jan and their two boys would invite me to go swimming. Bloody Great. Jan had her own hairdressing business and from then on she cut my hair instead of my Dad!

Next Stage

Leaving School

The careers department at Spennymoor school was well-advanced. You see even in 1965 our school organised work experience for the school leavers. I went to Smart and Browns (a local factory) and worked in the personnel department, where our Eileen was the Personnel Manager's secretary.

Every girl who worked in the factory went to work at say 7.00 am and went with rollers in their hair. When they got to work they styled it into the fashion of the day. They all wanted to look decent at work for anyone who they fancied.

I was 16 when I left school. I was very sad because I loved my school years. It had been a great time for me.

Mrs. Newland, my music teacher, encouraged me to do what I did best and that was to sing.

I thoroughly enjoyed my two years at Spennymoor West School. The typewriters we used were the heavy Remington type. We had to pound our fingers on the keys and practiced to the William Tell overture in order to get our speed up. My speeds were 100 wpm shorthand and about 65 wpm typing. I passed all of my CSE's and RSA's and I was a qualified shorthand and typist.

Philip Denton was Head Boy and Audrey Noble was Head Girl. I was a prefect. Again, as with Bowburn School, I was involved with everything, netball, hockey, drama and singing. They were all enjoyable and the teachers were just as nice; they were helpful, friendly and supportive.

In a typing lesson our teacher, Mr. Grieveson, (Jacky) came into the classroom and said, "Open all the windows please, Mr. Denton, Headboy, you have far too much perfume on."

There were two lads in our commercial course class: a

boy called Keith Long and Philip. I liked Philip a lot. We used to chat during our break-times about what we wanted to be when we grew up. On the day we left school all the girls cried and autographed each other's blouses. The lads never bothered. I think Philip did. The lads gave all the girls the bumps. We had to tuck our skirts in our knickers to save embarrassment. We said our goodbyes to our teachers and they all wished us every success.

As with Bowburn School the teachers at Spennymoor were enthusiastic to help the average pupil gain confidence in themselves and give them the best start in their adult life ahead of them.

My First Job

Time for me to enter the workforce! I applied for a few jobs as a shorthand typist while I was still at school. I had an interview with a firm of solicitors called L.J. Heron, in the Market Place, Durham City and I got the job as an office junior and shorthand and typist. I was "over the moon" and me Mam was too. I think what clinched the job was the fact that I was a Queen's Guide and that Mr. Heron's daughters were also Queen' Guides. Well me Mam was chuffed to bits for both Eileen and me. She was very proud of how well we had both done. We both had good jobs. Dad wasn't as chuffed; he wanted us to get work in a factory because that was where all the money was. In fact he always thought our Eileen would become a hairdresser and marry a 'good looking nowt'.

My first wage was £3 per week and I had my bus fares and board to pay out of that. Imagine the 16 year olds living off that now? How did we manage? I was very thrifty and tried to save money where I could. I used to walk to the next bus stop in order to pay less bus fare.

I started work at 9.30 am which was great because when I got the bus into Durham it was always quiet. Rush hour had been and gone.

First thing in the morning when I got to work I'd make tea and coffee for everyone, and then I'd go in for dictation. My next task was to deliver letters to other solicitors or maybe estate agents in the city, so as to save money on postage. I'd put the letters all in order of street locality, put me coat on, if it was winter, and then have a lovely walk around the city delivering letters. It was especially nice in the summer. By the time I got back it was time to make the tea and coffee for everyone again. Once I'd done that I had to get cracking and type out my letters for Mr. Burt, my boss. I can tell you it was all go in that office.

By this stage in my life I'd put a bit of weight on because at school I had a dinner then when I got back home me Mam had a dinner waiting for me. Two dinners in one day.

Our Eileen said that she thought I looked fat! Me fat? I've never been fat in my life. I went and looked in the mirror. Ummm maybe. So what did I do? I went on a diet.

I watered down all the milk I drank. I ate cream crackers. For my lunch I'd have two Ryvita with a bit cheese between. I never had dinners on a night. I ate so little that I my weight plummeted to 4 ½ stones. My legs were so thin that when I wore those Pretty Polly hold up stockings they would fall down to my ankles as I walked. How embarrassing was that?

One morning I was passing The Farm Shop on Framwellgate Bridge in the city on my way to work. There was a queue outside the shop and, just as I was passing, my Pretty Polly stockings ended up around my ankles. I quickly bent down and pulled them up as far up my legs as I dared, one at a time, because they were both down round me ankles. I did this trying not to make it too obvious as to what I was doing. I kept on walking quickly past the queue of customers. Only for them to fall down again before I got to the office.

My boss, Mr. Burt was very quiet and spoke quietly too. My fellow work mates were Christine Gibson, Pauline Fittzon, Margaret Lethbridge and little Joan, who did the accounts. Pauline and Margaret were older than me and lived in Bowburn. They were all great fun to work with.

Another lady, called Mrs. Durham, worked for Mr. Heron. She was lovely and was about sixty years of age, or maybe older. She walked as if she was walking on ice, very quick small steps, always in a hurry and always carrying files, even when she had her coat on and was leaving the office for her homeward journey. She obviously took work home to do. We didn't!

One morning it was break time. We got 10 minutes in which to have our coffee. Everyone always congregated in Pauline's office for their coffee and a natter. I made my entrance into Pauline's office bearing the tray of tea and coffee when my kitten heel of one of my shoes got stuck in between the floorboards and I lunged forward. Mrs. Durham was coming towards me. She couldn't do anything to help me. Away went the tray, the cups full of hot coffee, ahead of me.

Pauline's office was divided by a counter and all they saw was me walking past the counter announcing, "Anyone for coffee?" Then disappearing flat on my face. The laughter started and poor Mrs. Durham laughed so much her false teeth nearly dropped out. Pauline, Margaret, Christine and little Joan all lost control of their bladders that morning and even into the afternoon.

It was a very happy office but when Pauline and Margaret left L.J. Herons it wasn't the same, so I looked for another job, Christine did too. I got a job at another firm of Solicitors, Swinburne and Jackson which was also in the Market Place, Durham.

My boss was a female Articled Clerk, she was training to be a solicitor and I was assigned to be her secretary. The senior partners of the firm gave her the menial cases to deal with. So she didn't have much in the way of letters to reply to.

Eeeh when I went in her office for dictation we used to get gassing and she maybe only had a couple of letters to dictate but I would be in her office all morning, drinking coffee and eating biscuits.   We giggled about boys we'd been out with, and boys we were going out with at the time. She was also in the Durham County Choir, so we had a lot in common.

On leaving her office she'd say: "Take some extra files up to your office Brenda so that it looks as though we've been working hard." One secretary in the office didn't like it that I'd been taking dictation all morning.

"Have you got much work?" she'd ask.

"Yes loads." I'd say

She was in the same typing office as me and sometimes I'd type the same letter out three or four times in order for her to think I was rushed off my feet with letters. I'm sure she had an idea that I was bluffing. She'd Thump, Thump, Thump, Thump at those typewriter keys. It's a wonder the floor didn't give way.   Her poor fingers.

There was a lovely lady who worked in the office. Her name was Florence and she ran that firm. Her boss was a fabulous man called Jack Glendinning. The senior partner's secretary was called Sheila Chappell and she was brilliant. I really got on well with her. While writing about Sheila, I wondered how she was and if she was well. On that very night I was entertaining at Nidd Hall Hotel and a lady came up to me after my show and said, "I'm sorry to bother you Brenda but a lady who I live near sends her kindest regards. She said that she used to work with you and her name is Sheila Chappell." Well I couldn't believe it. What a coincidence. She must have got my vibes and I got hers.

Getting Tarted Up and More Lads

The fashion now was for higher hemlines. Everyone always went out on a Saturday night. We took ages getting dressed, or getting 'tarted up' as my Dad would say, putting our make-up on, and doing our hair.

With some of our wages we would try to afford a new outfit to wear like a new skinny jumper. I was still tiny and got most of my clothes from children's departments. In fact me Dad used to say, "Mother you can't let our Brenda go out like that, her belt is wider than her skirt." Eeeh and it was. This was the year the mini skirt took off, also bell-bottom trousers, bright colours or black and white checks; nearly everyone was a 'Hippy', 'Mod' or a 'Rocker'.

The Beatles released the album Sergeant Peppers Lonely Heart Club Band. Nearly all the lads had droopy tashes, those who could grow one. Twiggy was the model to copy. I had my hair the same as hers and my make-up. I thought I looked great! Again my Dad would say:

"She's not going out dressed like that."

"Tarrah Da," I'd say and off I'd go on a Saturday night usually to "The Boom Boom Beat Club" in Durham. That was the place. Oh yes. All the walls and floor were painted matt black and the lighting was very dim with the odd flashing disco light. I think it was all done on a budget. The floor was usually wet. Don't know how, but it was.

The music was deafening and we loved it. 'Psychedelic' was the new word. Although The Boom Boom didn't quite match that description but it was the only club we could get into because it was alcohol free. We were only seventeen. It was also 'The Summer of Love' with 'A Whiter Shade of Pale' by Procol Harum, Go Now by the Moody Blues and of course If You're Going to San Francisco by Scott McKenzie.

My favourite groups were of course The Beatles, The Who, The Tremeloes, The Kinks and Dave Dee, Dozy, Beaky, Mick and Tich. In fact I loved all the bands that were in the charts.

It was mainly the lasses who danced to the brilliant music, while the lads walked round and round the circumference of the club, looking to see which lass they fancied. I suppose it was a bit like a cattle mart. Once a lad fancied you he'd come up to you and dance. Not say anything, not a word, just dance. We used to think. "Oh he's nice or it would most of the time be:

"Oh bloody hell; look at the state of him and the price of chips." Then us lasses would make faces at each other and roll our eyes in as much saying, "I don't like the look of yours!" Upon which we'd pick our bags up from the minging floor, make an excuse and go to the loo and have a good giggle about the lads we'd just danced with and then dumped. The lads were only after one thing and that was anything with a skirt on. Anyway it was all good fun.

Sometimes a lad would say "Can I meet up with you again?" If I said, "Yes." Then we'd probably meet up in the pictures, (cinema) the following week. Usually the lad would say, "I'll meet you in the pictures." This meant I would have to pay for myself to get in. Inside we'd be shown to our seats by anusherette holding her torch towards two red sagging velour seats. When we sat down the springs stuck into our backsides.

The place was filled with smoke from Woodbines, Senior Service, or the new brand Embassy. We usually snogged our way through the film. If asked what the film was like I'd have not a clue. Sometimes, if he was a nice lad, he would ask at the end of the night "Can I take you home?" It was very nice being seen home by a canny lad. The evening would always be finished off by another snog! I'd always make sure that the lad would just walk me to the corner from our house because I'm sure my Dad would be watching out of the bedroom window waiting for me to get back. Me Mam would ask me the next morning:

"What was the film like Brenda?"

"Eeeh it was a dead boring cowboy film," I'd say.

One lad, who had a car, asked me to go out with him. He said his friend fancied Christine, my friend. So off we all went to a pub for our date. I didn't drink alcohol. I think Christine had a couple of "Cherry B's". My date had a canny few pints to drink.

On the way back with him in his car he dropped his mate off first then Christine. When he dropped me off at our house I went in the kitchen, filled a bucket with water and went out to his car and round to the driver's side, where he was sitting with his head moving like a nodding dog on the back of a parcel shelf. I poured the water over his head. He was drunk. If my Dad knew of that he would have lost the plot. I would have been grounded for weeks.

One lad I went out with was called George Paylor. He lived in the next village, Park Hill. He was ever so nice.

"I'll meet you on the TMS bus." The TMS bus was Trimdon Motor Service but it was nicknamed Trimdon Muck Shifter. He'd get on the bus first in Park Hill. Then I'd get on in Bowburn. He'd always pay my bus fare. He was a gentleman, a lovely lad. I hope he found a lovely lass and has had a happy and healthy life.

Another place I used to frequent and I loved going to was the ice rink in Durham every Friday night. The music again was brilliant and we skated round and round the rink.

The 'learner' skaters never owned their own skates and wore skates belonging to the rink. These skates were nicknamed 'Death Wellies'. They were blue and the laces were red. You had to be good or bloody clever to skate on those.

The lads were always there eyeing up the talent, even the ones who couldn't skate and were clinging onto the barrier, wearing the dreaded 'death wellies', their legs spreading like Bambi's. They would never be short of chat up lines. Shouting"Why hello pet," upon which the learners would fall on their arses.

One lad who I dated went to the ice rink and could skate and owned his own ice boots, had an Austin Mini with a number on the side. I only went out with him because of his car. Oh I loved sitting in the front of his Mini. I didn't think much of him. He soon clicked that it was his car I was after. That relationship didn't last long.

Joining a Group

On my way back home from work I used to sit at the back of the bus with the lads and lasses from neighbouring villages, who also worked in Durham, chatting about how our day had gone.

One day I was sitting with some lads from High Shincliffe and they said they were putting together a group. This would be about 1967. At that time every teenage boy was putting together a group. They'd got guitars or drums for Christmas, mainly because they'd seen "Top of the Pops", and the lads wanted to copy the groups that were on that programme.

The lads said that they were looking for a girl singer, and they'd heard that I could sing. I told them that the music they would be playing wasn't the type that I was used to singing, although I did love pop music, but I never sang it. Their music was "Jimi Hendrix" and "The Rolling Stones".

Anyway, after some thought I decided to see what they were like. One night after work, I went to a rehearsal which was held in the drummer's Dad's shed where he kept the pigs! There was electricity to supply heating in the shed to keep the baby pigs warm. The pigs were removed and re-housed in a neighbour's pig shed or as we call it in the North East a pig cree. The drummer's Dad had swept it out and it was quite reasonable. I didn't know that we were going to be rehearsing in a pig cree. If I had I would have put me wellies on.

The drums, amplifiers, guitars and a PA system, including speakers for the microphones were all set up. Hey it looked like a tiny club. All it needed was a bar!

I was excited. This would be the very first time I would sing into a microphone. Oh my goodness this was very nerve wracking. All the band members were in the pig cree. John Woods from High Shincliffe was the drummer. Alan Leyburn was lead guitarist and a lad called Ronny was on bass guitar.

They all lived in this lovely village called High Shincliffe and had grown up together.

I asked them what they wanted me to sing. They said that it was up to me; they weren't bothered. I'd taken some sheet music along with me of songs recorded by the Seekers, with Judith Durham singing the lead vocals. They all looked at the sheet music. I think they could only read the chords. Anyway they had a bash at playing through the song "Open up Them Pearly Gates for Me". I hummed along with the melody. Once they got the hang of it Alan suggested I sing it through the microphone and they would accompany me.

"Just say a few words into the microphone and I'll set the levels for your voice." Alan said. This was all new to me.

"Hello, one two three. Hello, one two three." I kept repeating this until Alan felt he'd got the right setting for my voice. I think all the Dads had clubbed together to buy the PA system. It sounded very good anyway.

The lads started to play the backing and I joined in and sang the song. My voice came out of the speakers and Eeeh it sounded good. Very different, but good. We got through the song.

"Let's play it a few more times." Ronny said. Do you know each time it got better. Alan, who was obviously the leader, said,

"Have you got another song we can try?"

"Yes, I've brought the music for "The Carnival is Over." They, as a band, ran through the chords, and then once again I hummed along with the melody and then sang it through the microphone.

Well, I really enjoyed it. I think the boys did too, although I knew it wasn't their taste in music but it sounded ok.

"Do you fancy joining the group?" said Alan.

"Yes", I said, "I'd like to join your group."

The drummer's Dad came along at the end of the practice and introduced himself as Bobby. He was really nice. John, his son said that I was joining the group.

Bobby said that our music sounded very good for a first attempt. He could hear the songs while he was in the house. I forgot it was only a shed that we were practicing in. That meant the whole of High Shincliffe could hear too.

I said my goodbyes to the lads and went to the bus stop to catch the bus home, which was just the next village. I was buzzing with excitement. I can only describe the feeling I was experiencing as "Electric" I'd loved every minute of the practice.

Alan had suggested that I look for more songs to sing and bring the music to the next rehearsal, which would be the same night the following week. I couldn't wait to tell me Mam and Dad about the practice and that I'd been singing through a microphone with guitars and drums. I was in a group! And I couldn't wait for the next practice.

I thought to myself I'm going to be doing something I love and eventually get paid for it. I found another couple of songs to rehearse: Bobby's Girl and Lipstick on Your Collar.

I told Jenny, Ann and Sheila my friends at work and they were all excited for me. In fact everyone who I told was excited for me.

At our next practice the lads ran through their songs and then it was my turn to sing my new songs. We needed to put 2x45 minutes together for a complete show. The lads thought of a name for the group and we were to be called "High Society." The drummer's Dad came to a rehearsal and said that he would go to a couple of clubs to try and get a few bookings. We all looked at each other. Well we'd have to practice and practice to get the songs to sound professional enough for the club audiences.

Working Men's Clubs and Social Clubs were becoming more and more popular. After a week of hard graft either down the pit or in another manual industry, a community of men formed their own club. There were Labour Clubs, Conservative Clubs, Catholic Clubs and British Legions. The group of men wanted to socialise with their own type and so in one district you'd have half a dozen clubs and maybe two or three in one village. Most of the clubs originally held 100-150 people, then as the clubs expanded, many had extensions built and then they could hold 500 – 1000 people.

The Northern Club circuit was a great place for an entertainer to serve their apprenticeship. It was fertile ground for many future big acts, who travelled to the North East clubs and who later became household names such as Bernard Manning, Marti Caine, Cannon and Ball, Little and Large, Les Dawson and even Bob Monkhouse.

Some acts only appeared in the North East clubs once and never returned because they found the audiences hard. But, the audiences for me were always 'easy going, generous and appreciative'.

At the beginning of the evening the members of the audience would buy their bingo books, raffle tickets, and get the drinks in. They'd place their cigarettes, lighters and lucky bingo pens all in a regimental order on their table. Some would bring their supper. This would include pickled onions, cheese, sausage rolls, sandwiches and pork pies and this 'picnic' would also be arranged on the table in front of them.

Week in and week out they'd sit in the same seats religiously. Mind woe betide anyone, regular or visiting stranger, if they should sit in 'Their Lucky Seats'.

There was usually entertainment on at the club every night of the week whether it was Country and Western, Go as You Please (where members of the audience got up and sang their favourite songs accompanied by the organist and drummer). Every club had its own organist and drummer. There were bingo nights, and nights where a group would be booked, such as a brilliant act called Brass Alley.

On the Saturday a comedian and singer would appear and on a Sunday possibly the same format. The audience turned up sometimes not knowing who the act was, but most of the time clubs advertised their evenings of entertainment in the local paper so as to attract an audience into their club. Quite often an act was booked because of their reputation of being good. The club would then be full to capacity and the audience would have a brilliant night enjoying themselves. If the act was rubbish the audience would become not so 'easy going and generous'.

Some local acts, such as Bobby Thomson, were in great demand because they were so good and popular. Every club wanted to book them. Some entertainers, got themselves bad reputations. They would accept a booking at one club for an agreed fee then a few weeks down the line they would be offered a booking at another club for the same night but for a much higher fee. They would turn up at the club offering the higher fee and would let the other club down.

In the 60s, 70s, 80s and into the 90s on a Friday, Saturday and Sunday night there would be queues to get into the club from 6pm and they would stretch way around the corner. Audiences made sure they got there early to get a good seat. In the early days of the 60s it was the club Concert Chairman who would book acts for the club. Agents arrived on the scene later.

During this era women were not allowed to be served at the bar. This went on for another 20 or so years until we were allowed to be served.

While we were just starting off performing around the clubs there were lots of acts who had been performing in club-land for years so this was all new to us.

About a month passed and John's Dad came to the rehearsal and said, "I've got you a booking."

"NO." We all shouted.

"Yes, it's at Blackhouse Club." He told us that it would be in a month's time. Well we were all so excited. A booking, our first booking as a group! He told us that our fee was £9 divided between the four of us. Not bad for 1967. Brilliant!!

"Right," Alan said, "we have to practice more." We all agreed.

It was an incredible feeling; we were all giddy with excitement. We jumped up and down squealing. I was going to do something that I loved doing, which was singing and get paid for it!

YES!!

The four weeks passed and the boys' Dads came to our last practice to listen to us to see if we were ready for the booking at Blackhouse. We gave it our best and they gave us the thumbs up. Oh my goodness!! Here we go.

I had learned more songs: Dusty Springfield's "I Only Wanna Be With You" and "There's a Kind of Hush" by Herman's Hermits as well as "Shout" by Lulu and of course "You're My World" by Cilla Black.

Two of the Dads had cars, so all the gear would be transported in those. We travelled in a convoy. They took the seats out apart from the driver's, of course. I'd found myself two nice long dresses to wear for each spot.

The day arrived and I was to travel with Bobby and John, the drummer. There was one speaker in the car, the drums, John and myself. Off we went to the club.

Me Mam had rang me Uncle Jack and Auntie Jenny (they had a phone and a car) to see if they could take them to my first booking. They said they would be only too pleased. Our Eileen and her boyfriend Alan were going to be there too, as well as our David and Jan.

We got to the club early to set the gear up. The lads set their own equipment up and Alan set up the PA. I couldn't help with anything other than carrying the gear I was capable of lifting into the club.

The Concert Chairman came into the dressing room and asked if we were ready to go on stage.

"Yes, we're ready," said Alan. Oh my goodness here we go. I didn't feel ready at all I was so nervous that my mouth was totally dry. My top lip was stuck to my teeth and my stomach was doing cartwheels.

We went on stage and the lads started playing. It was my song and I started singing. I looked out to the audience. The room was packed and heavy with cigarette smoke. I found myself moving towards my left hand side to stand behind a speaker. The speaker was about 5 feet high, so it was perfect. No-one could see me but I didn't care. I felt comfortable there. Every now and again I peeped around the speaker and had a look at the audience. Yes, they were still there. I didn't come out from behind the speaker at all during the first show. The audience seemed to enjoy it.

I was pleased to get back into the dressing room to hear what the lads had to say. They were over the moon with the first part of the show. I felt a bit better. Alan told me to take centre stage for the next spot. I did as he told me and I really enjoyed it. The dreadful nerves hadn't gone altogether but weren't as bad. The audience was brilliant.

At the end of the evening a fight broke out in the audience which, in those days, meant it had been a good night. Well that was good. When fights broke out in a club it wasn't just a fight between two people.   Oh no, the whole place went up!   When this happened, which wasn't very often, the first thing we would do was turn the speakers around and move all the instruments to protect them from damage. The members of the audience sometimes used to shout, "keep the music going" - we never did.

Again, not all the clubs were like this.

The next morning the perpetrators of the fights would be called to attend before the committee. Usually they were banned, maybe for six months.

The committee of some clubs were like the Gestapo!!! If you had to go before the committee you knew you were in trouble. The club committee men were a certain 'breed'. At work, they would work hard and be told what to do; but at the club they were the bosses, and they told the audience and the act what to do.

An act would turn up at the club and get the gear into the Concert Room. The Concert Chairman would then advise them of their times of appearance. Usually 2 x 45 minute spots with the bingo and raffle in between.

In one club our fellow act came off stage 5 minutes too soon they were told they'd have to go back on stage and fulfill the 5 minutes. We always fulfilled our times of appearance. Strict time keeping was a must. It never bothered me, I loved entertaining and would sometimes perform for longer than was required.

If a position on the committee became available, members of the club could apply to be nominated then seconded and possibly become a member of the committee. The successful candidate would have his badge pinned to his lapel, shoulders back, and what have we got? A Committee Man.

Krack of Dorn

Getting back to the show at Blackhouse, me Mam and Dad, in fact all of my family were thrilled to bits with the show even though a fight broke out. Actually I think what made me so nervous was that me Mam, Dad, our Eileen and Alan were in the audience. Even now I always get more nervous when members of my family come to see me perform.

John's Dad got us more bookings including one at Crowtrees Club in Bowburn, where my Dad was a member. Oh my goodness this would be another night where I would be wrecked with nerves because I would know everyone in the audience.

A few months after joining the group I started going out with John, the drummer. We got on really well and found we had a lot in common. Plus I thought he was lovely. He was clean shaven but I thought he would look lovely in a beard. So, to please me, he grew one.

We still had our jobs. John was a wood machinist and I still worked at the solicitors.

My first date with John was in the sand dunes in South Shields. Ummm. It was a nice night and fortunately the weather was nice too!! That sand got every bloody where!

We saw each other every day after work. Either he would come to mine or I would go to his house. Then, of course, there were the rehearsals and more bookings.

John's Dad worked on the roads laying tarmac. He did a brilliant job finding work for us in the local clubs during his spare time. John's Mam was very nice too. Like me Mam she wasn't keen on the clubs, but would always support her only child, John. As more work came in for the group I said to John that I would pack in entertaining around the clubs when I was 27 years old!! Do you know I'm 64 now and work is still pouring in, though not in the clubs any more, but on cruises and in Warner Hotels.

Club-land has been a big part of my life. I enjoyed working in the clubs and the audiences have been wonderful to me. As soon as I went into a club, either with the band, the double act or as Brenda Collins I was warmly greeted by committee men and members of the audience. My career in this wonderful industry has been what I can only describe as amazing. Can I also add that the club-land audiences for me have been like a pair of comfy slippers.

I was 17 years old and still in the choir and the Senior Guides, The Rangers, but life was becoming more hectic. I was still living at home in Bowburn with me Mam and Dad and our Eileen. Eileen got married to Alan Jowett and bought a nice bungalow just outside Durham City.

On my way to work I used to pass McIntyre's garage. It had a black Morris 1000 Traveller in the window for sale. It was beautiful. I used to look at it every day, wishing I could afford to buy it. The car's black paint work shone. It seemed as though the car was looking back at me and pleading with me to buy him. I told me Mam and Dad about the car.

"I'll come and have a look at it." my Dad said. My Dad knew everything about bikes, but sweet bugger all about cars. I said that I would take him and me Mam all over and for nice rides on a Sunday afternoon. Me Mam and Dad decided to help me buy it. £100!

I asked Fred who lived in the same street, if he'd take me out for some driving lessons. I had a few proper lessons too, but mostly my lessons were from Fred - he was cheaper!

Our Eileen didn't care for Fred. Do you know when the tread on the tyres of his little van were wearing down (getting a bit smooth) he used to cut the tread deeper with a sharp knife. He pop-riveted new panels to his little van. In fact, his little van was held together with pop rivets. I think Fred was as well. He was a scruffy character I don't think he ever combed his hair. But I didn't mind what Fred looked like, as long as I got my driving lessons. He was married and that's another thing our Eileen couldn't understand, what his wife saw in him. Anyway, his wife was very nice and they had a little girl who was born on my birthday. Fred and his family emigrated to New Zealand. Fred probably got a job cutting deeper treads on the tyres with his sharp knife for the Kiwi's.

I finally passed my driving test. It took bloody ages. I thought I'd pass first time but I didn't. "Failed, Failed." Then at last I passed. Me Mam said she was scrubbing the kitchen floor on her knees and whilst she was down there she said a little prayer for me. I passed and drove back home in my Morris Traveller. Me Mam was so pleased that I had passed but my Dad wasn't happy at all. I can understand how my Dad felt now that I am a mother! You see, he was worried about me being out on the open road on my own where other drivers might not be as careful as me.

The group was getting more popular. It would be about 1968. Alan and Ronny both had good jobs and were finding it hard doing their day job and being in the group. So they left. I knew there was a lad who worked at Burtons was keen to join a group. He was a bass player. We asked him if he would join our group and he was chuffed to bits. His name was Paul and his Dad, Jack Brandes, was a bespoke tailor in Durham City. John, Paul and I discussed the name of the group and decided we wanted a different name. We came up with the name Krack of Dorn. I think it was Paul who suggested that name. So that was the new name of our group.

We still didn't have a lead guitarist. Paul's Dad put an advert in the local paper and advertised for a lead guitarist as well as a rhythm guitarist. A man called Jack Newhouse applied for the lead guitarist's position and got the job. He was a lecturer at Durham University. He was about 50 years old, but it didn't matter because he was a brilliant guitarist. Absolutely brilliant! Jack was amazing and would teach us a lot. A lad called Ray Shields got the rhythm guitarist's job.

We rehearsed for a few weeks, after which we were ready to entertain the audiences of the North East. Paul's Dad, Jack, said he would become our manager and deal with all the bookings and dealings with the clubs. I think John's Dad felt a bit put out by this, but just let Jack get on with it. Bobby said Jack was a business man and that would be good for the group. Jack Brandes found us rehearsal rooms in Durham City instead of the pig cree.

We included music by the Shadows in our programme

and an instrumental called Albatross by Fleetwood Mac. Jack, our lead guitarist, said that it would be nice if I played the cymbal with a soft felt drum stick while they played their instruments. I was so pleased; all I had to do was keep in time with the beat. What talent.

Jack Newhouse was with the group for a short while and had to leave because of his commitments to the University. So once again we were without a lead guitarist. John's Dad said he knew a lad, Alan, who worked at the Council Depot who played lead guitar. He asked him to come along to a rehearsal. He was great and a very witty person as well as a good guitarist. Alan joined Krack of Dorn.

One night in a club, I tripped up on stage and fell over. Well the audience started laughing. At first I wondered if I should lie there and pretend I'd hurt myself, but when they laughed I turned my head and looked at them and they laughed even more. I got up and ran into the dressing room. They even laughed at that.

The boys in the group said during the interval, "Hey Brenda everyone was laughing at you when you fell over." I said that I knew they were.

"Well you'll have to fall over every night so that we can become a comedy show group and get more money" they said. So, yes, this is where the comedy started and after this we began to think of comedy sketches.

Each night I fell over. Then Alan would come over, pick me up and give me a piggy back off stage. I was strong and very fit. So we swapped over in the dressing room and I gave Alan a piggy-back out into the audience.

We were thinking of comedy ideas all the time. The Cadbury Smash advert was out at the time, the one where they wore strange round helmets and said in dalek voices:

'On your last visit to earth did you find out what the earth people eat?' So we bought four colanders to put on our heads to look like the Smash Martians. Then Wings had a song out called "Mary Had a Little Lamb". So I went out and bought a toy lamb and a water pistol. I squirted the audience with water. I bought a child's tricycle and rode around the audience to "Leader of the Pack". We all still had our day jobs; I think our fee for a booking now was £25 per night. This was divided between the five of us.

John and I had just got engaged. Bill Golightly, who was a Legal Executive at the solicitors and dealt in conveyancing, told me one of his clients had died who had a nice terraced house which was up for sale in Framwellgate Moor, which is a lovely village two miles outside of Durham. This was handy for me and forJohn. John worked in Framwellgate Moor. The price of the house was £1,800 and Bill thought it would be nice for John and me. Imagine what it's worth now.

So from then on, all the money we made with the group we saved up for the deposit on the house. We set a date for our wedding, the 27th February 1971. I asked Anne Shoulder, who I worked with at the solicitors, if she would be my bridesmaid.

We bought the house and decorated it from top to bottom so that it would be ready to move in as soon as we got married. John's auntie's mother had died so we got all of her furniture. We both worked hard getting the house ready. We went there every night after work stripping wallpaper off the walls, painting and scrubbing floors. We asked a lady, who me Mam knew, if she could come and wallpaper for us. She did a good job papering every room.

When she finished we emulsioned the walls and ceilings, scrubbed every floor for the carpets to be fitted and for the furniture to go in. We were shattered.

We had fun doing it though; often we'd be covered in paint because John would come over to me with a brush full of paint and slap a bit of paint on me and I would return the favour with my brush full of paint and slap paint on him. And so it would go on until we were in hysterics and both of us covered in paint, me screaming and John shouting, "Come here you little bugger." Happy Days!

Next Stage - Getting Married

Our Wedding Day came. 27th February, 1971.

On the morning I got my hair done at Jackie Brown's at Framwellgate Moor. I had a cut and blow. My dress was made by a friend's Mam. She said that if I supplied the material she'd make the dress as a present. I had my shoes and my head–dress, which was a beautiful fur hood. I'd seen it in a Brides magazine so I sent for it. A winter wedding.

John wanted a white suit but in those days you couldn't get them. So he settled for a grey suit with a blue shirt and white tie. Anne, my bridesmaid, wore pale blue. John's best man was Paul, the bass player; he wore a blue suit with a white shirt and blue tie, which matched my bridesmaid's dress.

Our wedding cars were booked and coincidentally they were from North Terrace the street where we'd bought our house in Framwellgate Moor. Ronny owned the taxi firm and when we moved into North Terrace he became a great friend of ours. He was a good mechanic too and often helped us to get the van or our car started years later.

I was at home and everyone had left to go to the church apart from my Dad and me. Our Eileen did my make up, so she went to the Church with me Mam and my bridesmaid Anne. The church was in a village called Quarrington Hill, which was right at the top of a hill. There was only my Dad and me in the house, oh and Tiger the dog (a whippet). He'd bitten next door neighbour's daughter so he wasn't popular. My Dad said, "Have a sherry Brenda, I'll have a whiskey. I hope you'll be happy" Then our car arrived. My Dad went out into the street and threw money and local children were there to pick it up. An old custom. Then we got in the car and made our way to the church.

It was a freezing cold day but it wasn't raining. My Dad and I got to the Church, got out of the car and we walked arm in arm to the door of the Church.

'Are you ready Brenda?' he said.

"Why yes Dad." I replied. He took me down the aisle to meet my future husband John. John looked at me and smiled. I smiled back at him. My organist was Malcolm from the County Youth Choir. He also played the organ at Durham Cathedral. If he was good enough for the Cathedral, he was good enough for my wedding. The service was brilliant. We had the wedding in February because it is always a quiet month for entertaining and we had more time on our hands.

Usually in February, it snowed, but it didn't on my wedding day. It was a lovely service and both John and I were nervous. I said to John the night before:

"Make sure the price is off the bottom of your shoes." I can't remember if I checked mine.

Our Mams and Dads were both very happy for us. Malcolm the organist played The Wedding by Julie Rogers as we walked up the aisle as man and wife. Mr. and Mrs. Woods.

We had our photos taken outside the church very quickly then everyone rushed off to the reception because it was bloody windy and cold.

John looked great in his suit. Paul looked nice too as did Anne. It was all very nice and everything on a budget! We never had much money and what we had we had spent on our new home in North Terrace, Framwellgate Moor.

Our reception was at Bowburn Hall, part of the Ramside group. My Dad was there with the waiter handing out sherry and whiskey for the guests arriving and making sure no-one took two. The photos were taken inside and outside the hotel. They were in black and white. Everything was in black and white in those days, even the tele programmes were still in black and white. All the members of the group Krack of Dorn were there. A great time was had by all. It was very memorable. I loved it.

After the reception guests went over to North Terrace to our new home. Me Mam and Dad went over to the house as well but took the key to their home in Bowburn where all my 'going away' clothes were. Fortunately, they'd left a little window open (not like my Dad)! So John my new husband pushed me through it. Tiger the dog didn't know what was happening.

Our honeymoon was in Penrith, Cumbria in a lovely posh hotel called The George. On our way the car broke down, not my Morris 1000. John had sold that and bought a grey mini van. It had started snowing as well!!

When we got to the hotel we found that our reservation had been cancelled!! Oh what more could happen?

Earlier on, I mentioned a girl called Joan Milburn who I went to school with and who's clothes I wore when she out grew them. Well do you know, she and her boyfriend, who had an E type Jaguar, had got to the hotel before us and as a joke cancelled the reservation. She popped her head around the corner when John and I were trying to work out what we were going to do next and shouted,

"Surprise!"

Well I was gobsmacked. We had a great evening together and her boyfriend paid for the meal. This was very nice as we had run out of money on the repair to the mini van!

For the rest of the honeymoon we went to visit John's Grandma in Ollerton, Nottingham. It was a brilliant honeymoon, and I loved every minute of it and loved being with my new husband.

We got back from our honeymoon and settled nicely into

North Terrace which was like any terraced street but all the outside walls of the houses were painted different colours. Ours was a light blue, next door's was dark green, there was a cream one and a yellow one and so on. In fact, driving up to it the street looked as though it was part of Tobermory, such wonderful colour and the resident's characters were colourful too.

The village of Framwellgate Moor was an old mining village. The houses on our street were built for the miners. The top three houses, one of which was ours, were bigger because that is where the deputies lived. There was a long street of shops ranging from newsagents, butchers, a small supermarket, DIY shop, chip shop, four pubs and a fruit and veg shop which also sold eggs. If John fancied an egg for his tea I used to go to the fruit and veg shop and buy one egg. Every time I went in they knew John was fancying an egg. The same went for when he fancied a tomato. I always bought plenty of potatoes for when he fancied chips. I still wasn't very good at cooking, but I got by. When I went into the shop the shop assistant used to say, "Is it egg or tomato?"

We had lovely neighbours, in fact, they were fantastic. At 2 North Terrace, were Jean and Austin. They shared a wicked sense of humour, so we got on really well with those two. Jean and I used to sunbathe together at the back of their house. Austin was an RSM at The Territorial Army and we often went to Army functions together. Then at number no.3 were Marjorie and Bill Allen. We called them Mr and Mrs Allen. Marjorie was a sister at the local hospital and Bill was a bus driver. Mr and Mrs Allen moved to Newton Hall, which was a much posher area. It had a reputation in those days of "fur coats and no knickers"! Although Mrs. Allen wasn't like that, she would have paid cash, I daresay, and she was a lady.

Jean and I used to visit her for a coffee but always

ended up on the sherry. We'd get back to North Terrace and Jean would hang out of her front door and shout,

"Tarra Brenda"

"Tarra Jean." I would shout back, both of us very merry.

Jean and Austin attended their youngest son's open night at school and when they read Philip's diary his entry for the previous day was:"My Mam came home drunk again." Eeeh she never drank sherry during the day again.

Sheila and Mac lived opposite. Kevin Tweddle lived about 5 doors away and he was in a band too. He had a girlfriend, Christine who he later married. We all were a great gang!!

They all regularly came to see us perform at any club where we were working locally. We would also go and see other comedy show groups who were at a club on a night when we weren't working. They were all very funny: The Don Juans, This That and the Other, Pendleton Tyler and many more. Each band entertained the North East audiences with their own unique special brand of humour, each writing their own material. They would also come to see us when they weren't working. We'd meet up with other acts at the motorway cafe near Birtley to have a chat after we'd all finished working, discussing how we'd performed and discussing the club we'd been to.

A lot of the clubs had their own reputations. One act would say that they'd been to a particular club. We'd all say in unison:" Oh no, not that one."

I still got nervous while waiting to go on stage and while on stage, but I always had the lads to turn to. I could also turn around and smile at John sitting behind his drums. John had a Premier drum kit. He always said he would love a particular sized tom-tom drum to add to his kit. His drum kit was in pearl grey and he could never get this particular size in that colour. Well, I went out of my way ringing music shops all over the North East. No Google then. In fact no computers, although I think there were some computers but they were the size of two rooms! Anyway I found a shop which could order one for me.

It was John's birthday in a few months time and I really wanted to surprise him with the tom-tom. It would have been lovely. The shop said they would have it in for well before his birthday. Well time passed, weeks passed, months passed and it was getting nearer John's birthday. The Friday before his birthday, which was on the Saturday, I got a phone call (at work). As I mentioned I was working in a solicitors' office in Durham and I had given them my works number. They said that the drum was in.

"Right," I said, "I'll be through to pick it up." The shop was in Darlington. Well I had to think of an excuse to tell my boss so I could get out of work to go to Darlington to collect the drum for John's birthday the next day.

"Well," I thought, "I have got to get through to Darlington before the shop closes." I had to think of an excuse to tell my boss so I could go and get the drum. Eeeh, I know it's awful, but I told my boss my Dad had fallen off a ladder at work on the building site. I didn't say which rung. (With hind-sight, I could have said that I had a dental appointment). The excuse was accepted. So off I went to Darlington to collect the famous drum.

Unknown to me (again no mobile phones in those days, in fact, only posh people had line phones in their houses, everyone used to use work phones or the phone box at the bottom of the street), my brother, our David, rang the solicitors to speak to me.

One of the staff told him that my Dad had fallen off a ladder, (they added a bit more on), and said he was in hospital in Durham. Well our David then rang our Eileen (he added a bit more on and said that he had hurt his spine). Our Eileen, who was at work in Spennymoor, about 15 miles away rang me Mam, who was also at work. She was a cleaner for a Doctor of Science at Durham University. Anyway she rang me Mam (but added a bit more on) and said that me Dad was in Intensive Care in hospital with spinal complications all because of a fall from a ladder on the building site. Mrs. Smith, me Mam's boss, rang her husband at the Labs at the University. She told him of the situation. He in turn came out of tutorials in order to take my Mam to the Hospital. Me Mam was frantic. Our David, our Eileen, me Mam, Mrs. Smith and Dr. Smith all got to the hospital, expecting to find me Dad in a critical condition. The receptionist said that no Mr. Swainston had been admitted.

"You must be wrong, try Intensive Care"

"No Alfred Swainston has been admitted to Intensive Care." After discussion they thought they had better make their way to the building site. He may have been taken to a different hospital because of the complications of his injuries.

They all got to the building site to find my Dad driving his dumper truck around the building site all in one piece!!! Oh dear. Was I in Trouble with a capital T?

I got back home and they were all there waiting for me. Did I get told off? Oh YES. Mind, they were all relieved that me Dad hadn't fallen off a ladder!!!

My motto is Never Tell Lies. Look what trouble it got me into. It kind of took the edge off getting the drum for John's birthday. Mind he was over the moon with his drum! A lesson learned. By the way my boss never found out the trouble I had caused.

Hair Colour

I still visited Jan, the hairdresser and David, my brother, in Middlesbrough.

"Do you fancy a colour on your hair?" she asked one day. Jean from the top of our street was with me.

"Yeah, I fancy green hair." I only said it as a joke. Eeeh well, she did, she coloured my hair green!!! When I got back home John went mad. He said in a quiet voice (he never raised his voice):

"You just do it, don't you?" He asked if I would go back and get rid of the green. I did but the only colour Jan could colour it was post office red.

"Dare you go back with that colour on your hair?" Jean said.

"I have no other option." I replied. When I got back John looked at me and shook his head. He knew what I was like!!!

Krack of Dorn

By this time, 1973, Paul had left the group. Paul had a good job. He was working at Burtons the tailors, but then got a job at Durham Prison training as a medic.

We were doing two shows every night. This meant working at a Working Men's Club first then, travelling to a night club and performing a show there. Jack, his Dad, had his tailoring business so they were both feeling the strain. So when Paul left his Dad did too.

John, myself and John's Dad were all sorry to see Paul and his Dad leave the group. Alan and Ray both felt the same. They too had good jobs and so they left the group.

We advertised in the Northern Echo for a bass guitarist and a lead guitarist. A lad called Stan, from Darlington got the bass guitarist's job. We nicknamed him "Wing Commander" because he was a pilot and flew small planes as a hobby.

Our new lead guitarist was John from Witton Gilbert. We called him Jonathan to save confusion with my husband John. Jonathan was a brilliant guitarist and a very quiet young man compared to Stan.

We used to rehearse at North Terrace with acoustic guitars so as not to upset the neighbours. Stan used to bring his girlfriend, Sue. He also had a MG Roadster car with a soft top. He used this to woo his girlfriend, Sue. Eeeh he was a lovely and funny lad.

We used to travel around the North East and Cumbrian clubs in a green Commer van. We loved it. In that van it was men behaving like boys, bad rude jokes, stopping the van while each of them had a wee on the grass verge. I was the only girl. But I was part of the group and they treated me as one of the lads. That's how it was.

One day we were travelling to a club and it was in the winter time. There was steam coming from the engine and we realised we'd ran out of water. There was snow on the ground so we started pushing snow into the radiator. The lads in turn all weed into the radiator as well. I'm pleased it was an impossibility for me because I would burn my arse on the radiator.

If you turned up late to a club the committee would not be the most understanding even if you'd broken down.

We later upgraded the van to a Bedford long wheel base. Stan and John converted it so that the gear was behind a partition at the back of the van. We got some aircraft seats for us to relax in while travelling to the bookings. We put windows in the sides. The aircraft seats were able to recline. We found a six inch black and white television and put it in the van so that we could watch it while travelling. I tell you, that van was good enough for the Beatles to travel in. There was a cassette stereo at the front too.

In the winter time, getting the gear into a club was always difficult. Sometimes we had to carry our heavy speakers and amplifiers up a back metal fire escape covered in snow. Other times we had to get the gear through emergency exit doors which were in the concert room.

"Shut those bloody doors. It's freezing in here. It's taken all day to get the room warm." The audience would shout.

We'd turn up at a club in the North East and, there would be children playing in the car park. As soon as the act turned up to get their gear into the club one of the kids would say:

"Can aa look after ye car mister?"

Audiences in clubs were very territorial. If an act came from Newcastle and was entertaining in a club in Sunderland the audience would give him a bit of a hard time and vice versa. This was all to do with their loyalty to their respective football clubs.

The doormen, who were usually in their 70's' would sit in a little cubicle taking the entrance fee. In most clubs in particular CIU clubs every visitor had to be signed in by a member of the club. This was all the responsibility of the doorman to make sure every visitor was signed in. The doorman took his job very seriously.

If an act was good then the audience showed them their appreciation by applause or even a standing ovation. If an act, usually a comedy act, upset someone in the club, by say criticising their wife, then the act would be in trouble.Which was understandable.

Working in the clubs on a night and working at our day jobs wasn't easy at all. In fact it was hard work.

In the early 70's there weren't many agents in the North East so I used to ring the clubs and speak to the Concert Chairman of each club and fill the diary that way. It worked well.

I think the secret of being successful in the North East clubs was always being polite and kind to the audience because it's best not to upset them. Most of the audiences were nice to me. I could test out an audience when making my way to the toilet. I'd smile at a few people who I passed on my way there; if they smiled back I'd think, yes this is possibly going to be a nice audience. If no-one smiled and they looked as though they were chewing wasps I knew it was going to be a hard night.

I was always courteous and polite to the Concert Chairman because he had our money in his pocket.

By this time I'd started drinking alcohol: Cherry B, Milly Sherry, Robbie Mac and Pony were my tipples. Eeeh I loved them.

One night at a club I was walking down the stairs after our first show and I had a Cherry B in my hand. You always got a couple of cherries with the drink. Anyway I tripped down the last few steps spilling my drink and dropping me cherries. A committee man thought I'd cut myself on the glass. I hadn't it was the stain from the Cherry B which had spilled down my dress. I think he was going to ring for an ambulance until I put him right by saying, "No man it's just me Cherry B I've spilt down me dress."

Eventually more agents surfaced. In fact most of the agents used to be acts themselves. They thought there would be more money being an agent and they were right.

We were never tied to one agent at this point and I still rang clubs direct to fill our diary. There was loads of work for everyone, singers, comedians, guitar vocalists, show groups and rock bands.

There were 450 Working Men's Clubs, and then of course there were Labour Clubs, Catholic Clubs, Conservative Clubs, British Legions and the list goes on. Every act could work most nights of the week. A lot of entertainers turned professional because of the amount of work around. They gave up their day jobs to work in the clubs full time.

We entered a talent competition and came second. It was held in Titos Night Club in Stockton-on-Tees, which was run by the Bailey Organisation from South Shields. An agent called Tom Smith was in the audience and at the end of the evening; he asked if he could manage us. He said that he really liked what he had heard and enjoyed the comedy.

We couldn't believe what we were hearing. Here's an agent from Manchester wanting to make us stars! He said that we would have to turn professional, which would mean giving up our day jobs. Were we to turn professional or not? Comedy was a big part of our show now.

We had a 'roadie' by then called Ian Bateman. John, myself and Ian wanted to turn professional. The others wanted to keep their jobs.

We all went to Manchester for a meeting with this agent. He said he could make sure we worked every week. Stan said, "Brenda you always make sure we work every night of the week and deal direct with the club so there's no agent's commission to be paid. There's plenty of work in the North East without travelling all over the country." Stan also made a point that this agent's acts who lived in Manchester, worked mostly in the North East so why should we want to be managed by him.

This Tom said he would charge 25% + VAT for managing us. That was over a quarter of everything we would earn. Then we had more petrol, and digs to pay for.

Stan had a good job and Jonathan worked in a bank in Newcastle. So he didn't want to give up his job. Despite the high commission and everything Stan had pointed out, which was all true. John and I were so keen to become professional artistes and Ian couldn't wait. Our minds were made up already.

For Jonathan it was a definite 'no' and he left the group. We were so sorry that he decided to leave. Stan said that he would give it a go but still felt strongly about the fact that we got plenty of work anyway.

A lad from Shildon, County Durham, called Keith

auditioned to join our group as lead guitarist. I recognised him because I used to go to school with him at Spennymoor West School. He was good. But again he didn't want to turn professional.

Then a lad called Dave joined our group as lead guitarist. He was a nice lad. Our manager auditioned him for us because he lived in the Manchester area. But he was able to drive in his car to where we were performing as we did.

It was a very exciting time for John and I and we put in our notices at our respective work places. They both wished us all the very best for our future.

Tom Smith, the agent, or our manager, arranged an audition for "New Faces". Yes the talent competition on television and do you know we passed. Wow!!! Stan was a funny man. That's funny "ha ha". He was good for the act. John and Stan used to dress up in women's clothes and impersonate the Supremes. Men in frocks always make me laugh! I rode around on a small child's tricycle as I was such a little dot it was just my size. I also sat in the audience dressed as a tramp at the opening of our show and heckled the band. John used to say, "That lady is wearing New Harmony hair spray, no she's not she's wearing Pledge!"

We travelled down to ATV Studios in Birmingham went into the reception and informed the lady who we were, and she issued us with passes. This was all very exciting. We took a seat in reception and while sitting there Ted Rogers and actors from the soap "Crossroads" passed through. We saw a couple of other famous people whose names escaped us.

A young man came into reception.

"Krack of Dorn?" He asked.

"Yes." We replied in unison.

"Come this way please. I'll show you to your dressing rooms." Ooooohhhhhh, our dressing rooms.

We got changed into our new clothes, which we'd had specially made for the show, and waited to be called.

"Krack of Dorn please make their way to Studio 1," came over the tannoy. This was our time to rehearse. The rehearsals went well. The Director told us which cameras to look at.

"Keep an eye open for the camera with the red light on." He told us who would be on the panel. Derek Hobson would arrive later to meet us. We went for something to eat in the ATV canteen with the other acts that were on the show with us. I can't remember who they were now.

All four of us went into make-up. We were quite giddy with excitement because we were here at a Television Studio and were going to be on television.

Whilst I was having my hair and make-up applied, the comedian called Ted Ray fell into the make-up department. He was drunk and, do you know, he was one of the panellists who were going to judge our show. We eventually met Derek Hobson and he wished us good luck. We were very nervous. It was our turn to make our way to the stage where our equipment was all set up.

We recorded the show in front of four stony faced panellists. One of them, Ted Ray, was in a drunken stupor.

The sketch we did, we thought, went well, but the panel had other ideas. One of the panellists, called Clifford Davis, slagged us off. There wasn't much response from the audience either. He said: "Dressing up in stupid clothes is not comedy." Clowns have been doing it for years! I think Ted Ray was the only one on the panel who didn't slag us off. But of course he was well pickled.

We drove back home disappointed but hoped it would come over a bit better on the television than it did in the studio.

John, Stan and myself.
I'm starting to look like Cilla Black.

John and I even bought a Betamax video recorder
because we were working on the night it was televised. We
worked at the Ouston Club in Chester le Street and all our
neighbours came with us and then came back to our house
to watch "New Faces."

At the club I rang me Mam and asked what she thought.

"Oh it was great Brenda and your Dad loved it."

We all got back after our show and sat glued to the
television.

"Here we are, here we are." The opening music started,
"You're A Star, You're A Star."

"Shhhhuushh everyone," Stan said, "It's our turn, here
we are. Shhhuusssh everyone."

It wasn't bad at all. All of our neighbours loved it. Lots
of people watched that programme - in fact millions of

people watched it. Within those millions was a club which had booked us and the Concert Chairman of that club cancelled us.

"Oh dear." I thought it wasn't that bad! You can't win them all and you can't please everyone.

Stan decided to leave the group. Not because of his appearance on New Faces. I don't think he enjoyed living out of a suitcase. It was sad because we got on so well together.

He was replaced by another lad from Lancashire also called Dave. So we called them the two Daves. They were two nice lads, although I think their sense of humour was different to ours. Being in our group was a job to them and we had plenty of work.

The two Dave's were from Lancashire and of course we lived in Durham so we always made our way independently to the clubs where we were working.

This meant we had to get rid of our wonderful Bedford van. We bought a Rover; it was a lovely car. It was £6000 and we bought it by getting a second mortgage on our house. John loved his beautiful Rover: leather seats; doors that shut with a clunk; and in an amazing condition.

It worked fine making our own way to the clubs in our car and it was nice travelling in the car with John instead of with the rest of the group.

We were working all over the UK. This agent or manager mustn't have had a map. One night we were in Cornwall and the next in the Borders of Scotland.

Me Mam used to plot on a map where we were working - Allinsons, Wooky Hollow, Coconut Grove in Liverpool, London, Birmingham, Manchester, Glasgow, and Edinburgh. In fact we used to work two venues a night. . We'd set the gear up in a club first, perform, usually 2x45 minute spots, then travel to a night club set the gear up again and perform a one hour spot there before travelling back to the digs. This was the pattern every night of the week plus a Sunday afternoon show, where there were often female strippers appearing in front of an all male audience. The lads used to go out and watch them. I stayed in the dressing room.

After fifteen shows a week we were TIRED yes, but I loved it. The theatrical digs were something different. Usually boarding houses, run by a middle aged homely lady. They had a sitting room for the acts to relax in. This was a big room with settees and easy chairs situated round the walls of the room with a coffee table in the middle and a big television in the corner.

All the way up the wall on the stairs there was usually a rogue's gallery of all the acts who had stayed at the digs. They were always clean, cheap and always the lady of the house, who was always known by her first name, fed us well.

Every act got up late so breakfast would be about 11.30 and it would be a big English with all the trimmings and a lovely mug of tea. We'd have a lovely evening meal and then every act would leave the digs for their journey to their respective clubs.

When we got back from the booking after midnight, all the acts would bring some alcohol back with them so that we could sit in the lounge of the digs and discuss the evening's good shows and not so good shows. There would be about five acts staying in the digs. We always had late nights, late mornings and lazy afternoons, unless we were making our way to another area of the country to "clock in" at another theatrical digs and meet up with other entertainers.

In Scotland we used to stay at a lovely hotel called The Lea Park Hotel in Grangemouth. The acts got to stay there for a cheap price as long as they did a show at the hotel free of charge. All the acts every night would empty the drinks machine and often went to bed when the business men who were staying at the hotel, got up for their breakfast.

One act which also used to stay at The Lea Park was Buzz Sound. Leo and Willy. They were a brilliant double act. Leo was big and bald and Willy was little and black with an afro hairstyle. One night whilst we were staying at The Lea Park there was a knock on our bedroom door. John opened the door and there was Willy standing at the door stark naked with a shoe tied to his willy. Eeeh! The little bugger! He was drunk of course.

In the winter of 1976 our manager rang us and told us he had secured us a summer season. We all thought, "Oh brilliant staying in the same town for a whole season." The season would probably run from end of March until the end of October.

Butlins 1976

It couldn't have been further away from what we were told we had to do. He told us we would entertain at Butlins, Filey on Mondays and Tuesdays. Wednesday and Thursday we would be in Butlins Skegness. Weekends were spent in the North East clubs. This was for a whole season. We couldn't believe he had arranged this for us. It was going to be a nightmare.

In those days there was no Humber Bridge to get from Yorkshire to Lincolnshire in order to get between Filey and Skegness.

Every Monday we'd drive from Durham to Filey over the North Yorkshire Moors. We'd entertain for two nights at the Butlins Holiday Camp in Filey. Then on the Wednesday morning we had to make our way to Skegness via the ferry in Hull and get ourselves to The Butlins Holiday Camp in Skegness.

We weren't given any accommodation on the Holiday Parks so had to find our own. It was very difficult finding digs during a season. In Filey we stayed in The Royal Oak at Hunmanby. It was a brilliant pub and we got on well with the owner.

A farmer used to get into the pub and during harvest time we used to help him bailing. It was the best part of the season.In Skegness we stayed at a bed and breakfast. The landlady was called Sheila and her husband, John, was a builder. They were two brilliant people and we had a good laugh with them too. Sheila encouraged me to experiment with our home in North Terrace by redesigning the lounge and knocking the wall down between the hall and the lounge and hanging Sanderson poppy wallpaper with matching curtains.

At the Skegness Camp, as they were called then, we used to judge the Glamorous Grandma competition. They were all very glamorous so it was a hard job.

1976 was the year our Eileen gave birth to a baby girl.

Eileen and Alan called her Catherine Anna. What a beautiful baby.

During our season, our Eileen, Alan, Catherine, me Mam and Dad came to Skegness to see us. It was a red hot summer and we had a lovely time on the beach together. There were swarms and swarms of ladybirds. As soon as me Mam put her navy blue handbag down on the sand it turned red by being covered in ladybirds. Catherine's little hat was covered. My Dad even put his pipe down and that turned red. My Dad wasn't very happy about that. It was really lovely to see my family, even though everything was red from the ladybirds.

After our last show each week at the camp we made our way back home. It took about four and a half hours but it saved on a night's digs money. After the two shows in Filey, the two shows in Skegness and then driving back home we were shattered. It wasn't very good money either. I think for the Butlins work we got £400 minus 25% commission plus of course VAT, petrol and digs. We were so tired but by the Friday night we were so pleased to get back home.

When we worked in the North East, our own stomping ground, we found that we were working for much less money than before we turned professional. I remembered what Stan had said.

We brought it up with Tom Smith and his comment was, "You asked me to get you work and that's what I'm doing."

We hated that season, although the audiances were good. We had thought that we might get the odd meal at Butlins, but we weren't allowed that. One day we sneaked into one of the dining rooms in the Filey camp and we were having a meal and a fellow artiste saw us and reported us to the camp manager. A secretary contacted our manager, who in turn rang us and said,

"What are you doing eating on camp?" Again we felt peeved especially because of the amount of food which was thrown away.

The two Daves always stayed with us when we worked in the North East in order to save them paying for digs. What made John and I a little unhappy was that when we worked in the Lancashire area we had to get our own digs!

You see they still lived with their parents and so there was no room for John and me. Which was fair enough I suppose.

Also when we did our first shows at Butlins the manager wasn't happy because we only did two spots. We were apparently booked for four different spots. Our manager had agreed to this too without discussing it with us. Again, a complaint was made against us and so we had to put our thinking caps on and put another two different spots together.

At the end of that summer season we were shattered. One thing positive happened while we were working at Butlins; the two Daves got themselves girlfriends who worked on the Filey Camp. One was a red coat and the other a chalet maid. I do believe both Daves married the girls.

Our manager rang and said that he had booked us to go and entertain the British troops in Germany. We had heard from other acts that there was good money to be earned on the bases. Yes other acts had told us that. Ha! Not for Krack of Dorn.

We drove down to Dover in a van we had hired. Our manager said that we couldn't take the two cars we were travelling around in.Anyway we boarded the ferry and met up with our fellow acts. There were three acts that would make up a show which would travel around British Military Bases in Germany.

This is where we met a fabulous act called Pip and Geoff George, a boy, girl singing duo. They were from Lydney, Gloucestershire. The next act we met on board was called Clive Webb, a mad magician. We got on wonderfully well with both acts. In fact we never stopped laughing all the way through the tour.

On arrival in Germany we had the address of our first hotel where we were going to stay. It was a very Bavarian type hotel with shutters on the windows. We thought the staff would serve breakfast wearing leather breeches with a bib and brace, nice white shirt and a hat with a feather in it.

Our first show was in Monchengladbach. There were about 500 squaddies and each act went very well. When we were on stage and I was singing Clive walked on stage completely starkers. I couldn't believe it. The squaddies thought it highly amusing. Afterwards Clive said, "It's what they want." Clive was crazy and still is.

When we got back to the hotel guess what? We were served by a gentleman who was behind the bar wearing a Bavarian costume.

Clive ended up being my drinking partner, although he drank more than me!!! That night in the hotel we got very merry on the schnapps and we ended up dancing with the barman, slapping our thighs in time to the Bavarian music.

While in Germany I did the van driving. When we got to RAF Larbrook, I was looking for a space to park our van after we unloaded the gear. Clive had already parked his van. He shouted to me that there was a big space just around the corner where I could park my van. I went around the corner and oh yes there was a big space. It was the runway!

The whole show went down really well with the forces, both RAF and Army.

During the day we sometimes had time to ourselves. We went go-kart riding one day. Then we'd have a look around the town where our hotel was.

Sometimes we would entertain squaddies while other times it was Officer's mess or Sergeant's. We would get to the venue and we'd all say, "Right we are not drinking tonight; we drank too much last night." Then the Sergeant in charge of the evening would welcome us to their club and say:

"By the way everyone there are ...... so many marks behind the bar so just help yourselves." We'd all look at each other as if thinking, "Oh well here we go again." Well, Clive and I thought that. I don't think the two Daves were very happy because if I had a drink the night before, I couldn't drive the van the next day. So if we had a long journey one of them had to do it while I slept in the back. Naughty me.

Mind again, I don't think the agent in Germany had a map, as one night we were in the north then the next night we were in the south of Germany. It was a brilliant tour because we got on so well with each other. We kept each other sane and we jelled completely.

We were all very sad when the tour ended. Again it was hard work in Germany for little reward. We had the hire of the van, the ferry to pay for, fuel while in Germany and of course the fuel to get to Dover and back

When we got back to the UK we kept in touch with Pip and Geoff and Clive Webb it was really nice to have met and worked with such nice people while on tour for such a long time. After the tour we promised to keep in touch and we all did.

Because of the amount of work and the amount of singing I had to do while in the group my voice suffered. While in Germany an Army doctor came up to me after a performance and suggested I see a throat specialist. He noticed I was having trouble singing.

We had a heavy workload in the UK sometimes performing at two clubs per night for seven days each week. During the day I hardly talked in order to save my voice for the night time when I had to sing. John and I had whistle signals to communicate so that I could rest my voice.

Shortly after we got back from Germany I booked an appointment to see my own Doctor and he made me an appointment to see a Mr. Dawes in Jesmond who was an ENT specialist.

I arrived at this massive house and was greeted by a receptionist. I was later welcomed by Mr. Dawes who showed me into his surgery. He examined my throat by wrapping a piece of bandage round my tongue and sticking what seemed like a dentist's mirror down my throat. I felt like I was choking but it gave him enough time to see the state of my throat. He told me I had damaged my larynx very badly and I was to stop singing for at least two years. I wasn't expecting to hear that. What a shock. Mr. Dawes said that if I didn't stop he would have to remove my voice box (larynx) altogether and then I would lose my voice forever. I sat in front of Mr. Dawes silent. He said he meant every word of what he had said to me and suggested I go home and talk it over with my husband.

I got home and told John that I had to stop singing or Mr. Dawes would be removing my voice box and it would mean I would have no voice whatsoever. It came as a big shock to John because he then thought he was going to have to get a real job!! But his main concern was of course me.

"Oh well." John said "I wonder what the two Daves have got to say about the news?"

When we told the two Daves the news that Krack of Dorn was disbanding and the reason why. They weren't very happy at all but that was the situation. I think they were more shocked than anything. They certainly weren't expecting the announcement. John did all the talking while I sat next to him nodding my head in agreement. One Dave said, "But we're out of a job." Upon which John said,

"Well we are too." He also said that it had come as much of a shock to us as it had to them. We also told our manager, Tom, the situation. Of course he was shocked and sorry. That was the last we heard from him.

We wondered what we were going to do. Were we going back to the real world of working 9 till 5? We both thought we couldn't go back to that way of life, so we agreed that it was up to us to put some sort of act together because this was what we loved doing and we didn't want it to end, although we were a bit limited because of the fact I couldn't use my voice.

After some thought, we came up with the idea of a mime act. Remembering I couldn't sing, we looked at what was popular at that time; what was in the charts, and on the news. There was Demis Roussos singing Forever and Ever. Sandi Shaw, singing Puppet on a String, Rod Stewart and I am Sailing, Lena Zavaroni with Mama He's Making Eyes at Me, the Muppet Show with Kermit the Frog and Miss Piggy, Don Estelle and Windsor Davis with Whispering Grass and of course once again our Cilla. Not forgetting Margaret Thatcher. We put together many more artistes' sketches including Sooty and Emu, The two Ronnie's, Morecambe and Wise and Max Wall. John and I worked everyday thinking of sketches to put together 2x45 minutes shows and make them funny without singing or talking. I think it's called brain storming or is it thought shower now? We wrote everything down with pen and paper. There was a list a mile long. We also jotted down names of artistes who were very popular years and years previous.

I went out and bought as many comedy records as I could lay my hands on and listened to everyone, getting ideas. I went rummaging around junk shops, jumble sales, and markets. Hylda Baker was a source of inspiration as well as Norman Wisdom and Benny Hill. I watched comedy videos over and over again. We thought of a name for the act and that was "Krack and Dorn".

We had to put all the props, wigs and costumes together.

Demis Roussos's outfit had to look good and big enough to get me underneath. Stagewear Unlimited made most of our costumes and they were good. They had to look glitzy and look the business. Some of the costumes John made. He also made most of the props too. He made a pit helmet by using a colander as a base then building it up with papier mache.

I thought of a sketch where my arms would get longer as I was miming to the song by Max Bygraves, "You Need Hands" and I found a shop in Newcastle which sold devices to help disabled people. It was made of aluminium strips and was criss cross riveted together. We bought two. John made the hands to go on the end of the concertina aluminium strips. He made the costume and the sleeves for the arms to fit in.

We bought an old Singer sewing machine from a second hand shop in Framwellgate Moor. We bought masks too, ET and Star Wars. We purchased an Akai reel to reel tape recorder, and bought all the records for all the sketches. We may only have needed one small piece from that record. It didn't matter. We had to make up links for the show to run smoothly from one sketch to another. We had records galore. I searched record shops for obscure records. There were no websites or Amazon in those days.

We got BBC recordings of laughter, someone giggling, footsteps and even birds singing.

These recorded effects only lasted seconds. In fact most of the sketches only lasted a couple of minutes each including the links and we had 2x45 minutes to put together. One hour and a half. Oh my goodness. John had to learn how to splice the tape and edit. We had a record player on which we'd play the song or piece then I'd say,

"Stop." Then John would record it and then splice it into the show. It took several times to get it exactly right and the way I wanted it, edited cleanly and clearly. One hour and a half. We worked our socks off but we did it!!

Then we had to rehearse to see if we had the timing right and enough time for costume changes. Every prop and costume had to be in the right place. It was hard graft and we had to learn all the words even though we weren't singing them out loud, as we had to mouth the words. Rehearsals were all done in our home at North Terrace. It never bothered the neighbours maybe because the walls of the house were solid stone.

Krack and Dorn poster

Then it was time to find the work. Again I rang clubs direct, saving by not paying commission to an agent. I also contacted agents in the north east and had to sell Krack and Dorn Comedy Mime act. The agents in the North East all gave us work. The diary was filling up nicely.

Our first show was nerve wracking but it went down well. All the hard work had paid off, thank goodness. We were freelance now so we could work wherever and whenever we wanted to. We had control over our diary, unlike when we were in the group, being managed by the agent in Manchester. He used to send us all over the country. We were rarely at home!

Work now came in thick and fast. We had work every night of the week. Our day time was free so we weren't exhausted. Of course we only had each other to worry about instead of thinking about other members of the group. John did really well, from sitting behind a drum kit while in the group to becoming a front man in a double act. I never gave it any thought I just thought John would be able to perform as a front straight man and he did. He was great. It was a big step and I was very proud of him.

The show which we had put together was going down very well in the clubs. We had worked it out that while I was on stage John was getting changed into another outfit and vice versa, except for sketches where we were both on stage together for example "Whispering Grass." It was all a new experience for us both.

We also had the publicity for Krack and Dorn to sort out. I wanted the photographs to look good and to depict accurately what sort of act we were, i.e. visual comedy. I booked a company in Sunderland and we took all the costumes to the studio. Again, the photographs would be in black and white.

One sketch I wanted on the photograph was John dressed as Demis Roussos and me as Benny Hill. Maybe

Puppet on a String was a possibility then of course John and I pictured together. Yes, that's what I wanted. The end product was very good.

We would normally do 2x45 minutes spots but sometimes we would do a one hour spot when we were on with another act. We got on very well with our fellow artistes and some of them became our friends and we invited them to stay with us at our home in North Terrace. The acts that stayed with us lived in different areas of the country. This saved them paying for digs, all they did was contribute to the food bill. I made all of their meals and it was a very happy time having them stay with us.

Pip and Geoff, who we met in Germany used to stay with us then a house became vacant and put up for sale in North Terrace so they bought it. Quite a few acts moved into the North East because of all the work in the clubs. The North East circuit was still a hard nut to crack but if an act was good the audiences used to show their appreciation. I just loved entertaining in the clubs, even though they had their reputation.

We were performing at a club Sunderland and we came to the part of our show where I was miming to "You Need Hands" where my arms got longer. A man, who I later found out to be a committee man, walked past the front of the stage and I swung one of my arms across his head, just missing him. Or I thought I had. One of his hairs on his head caught in between the two aluminium strips where the rivet was and it stuck.

Unfortunately he was wearing a wig and the wig was stuck in the rivet and dangling. He always denied to the members of the club that he was wearing a wig but the truth was dangling there. He was as mad as hell. The audience were in hysterics. I apologised to him at the end of our show. I was very popular with the audience but not at all with him.

Another sketch we put together was where I dressed in a Victorian bathing suit, flippers, snorkel, mask and a fish bowl filled with water and carrots cut up in the shape of goldfish. The music was the song by the Drifters, "Say You Meet Me Down On the Beach Tonight." I'd come out on the stage and take a carrot out of the bowl shake it between my thumb and fore finger as if it's a goldfish and eat it. Then I would proceed to make my way into the audience and threaten to throw the water over certain members of the audience and maybe put a few carrots down their necks.

In one club in Hartlepool, which was nicknamed 'over the wall' because every act had to get their gear over a high brick wall on arrival at the club then up a metal fire escape in order to get into the club.

John and I got our gear into the club and the Concert Chairman told me that it was a special night and that officials from the CIU, (Club Institute Union) were at the club. It was a very important night. We were to be on at 9.00pm which was fine.

We started the show and I noticed all the officials and the committee were right down the front, right in front of the stage. We came to the part where I came out with the goldfish in the bowl and wearing the flippers. All was going well until I got to the front of the stage and threatened to throw the water in the bowl over the officials. Only pretending.

Well I stepped on my left flipper with my right flipper and tried to move but couldn't and so fell forward and the water tipped accidentally over the people sitting in the front seats. The officials. Oh dear me, the officials were not happy at all. It was only cold water but the way they reacted you would think it was boiling water. They were not amused. The audience thought it so funny and laughed their socks off. Anything that upsets the committee always makes an audience's night.

We went down very well but not with the committee or the officials. We were banned from that club in fact I think we got 'life'.

We used to do a sketch with the music of Mull of Kintyre. We got the idea when we were working in Scotland. There was an organist and drummer playing in one club. We never used them as we were a mime act. Anyway they started playing " Mull of Kintyre" by Wings; John and I were sitting in the audience, and when we looked over to the organist there was smoke coming out of the back of the organ. It looked so funny especially when it came to the part of "oh mist rolling in from...." and out poured the smoke.

The organist wasn't aware that his organ was on fire, which made it all the more funny. I thought we could do a sketch around that. Again getting around the logistics took time but we got there.

In a tartan bag we put a co2 fire extinguisher. John was in a kilt and I wore a balaclava, glasses, kilt and jacket and carried the bagpipes. The extinguisher nozzle went up John's kilt and I pulled the trigger, which blew his kilt outwards and up.

We got an afternoon show in Scotland, Helensburgh. It was at the Polaris submarine base. We got there eventually at 1 pm. The officer in charge came to the gatehouse and got in our car to take us to the venue. We set up and the officer offered us a drink. I had a sherry and John had a pint. I don't normally drink alcohol before a show but on this occasion I had one as we'd had such a long drive from Durham.

We did our show and then the Officer, who was very happy with our act, came over with more drink. Oh heck. Then we sat in the lounge and had another drink. It was time for us to make our way to the digs where we were staying in East Kilbride. We set off from Helensburgh and started the drive. Of course John was driving and he'd been drinking.

We got to East Kilbride and came to a roundabout which looked like the previous one. Then we came to another roundabout which looked exactly the same as the last one. This went on. Every bloody roundabout looked the same. We were well and truly lost and couldn't find the digs. The Police started following us.

"Oh dear me". John said, "The Police are behind us and I think we're going to get pulled." Yes, the blue light came on and we pulled over.

The Policeman came to John's side of the car, John opened his window. The copper must have smelt the drink on John and the fumes from me. It wasn't a police car but a dog van. John was asked to get out of our Rover and blow into a bag. John was asked to get into the back of the dog van and I sat in the front with the two Policemen. I couldn't believe that this was happening. The police put John in the cells to sober up. I think it was the first time he'd been in a cell. I sat in the waiting room and read a book. I'm sure it was upside down.

John was released the next day and we made our way to the digs. No-one was worried that we hadn't arrived at the digs late that evening. The next day we had a story to tell everyone of our experience with the Scottish police. Our car had been put in a pound. The police released John's lovely Rover the next day. We got to the pound and John walked up to his car looked around it, and he had the cheek to say to the policeman in charge of the cars in the pound:

"I hope my car hasn't been damaged in any way." I don't think the copper was impressed. Eeeh mind John felt terrible that he'd been arrested for drink driving.

We got back home and John told me not to say anything to his Mam and Dad and of course nothing to my Mam and Dad. I said to John that his Dad was sure to suss something by me doing all the driving for a year. He received a summons to appear at The Sherriff's Office in Hamilton, Scotland. His Dad never suspected that he'd been banned.

We sometimes got work in Yorkshire and Nottinghamshire. The audiences were fine and seemed to accept us. In both these areas children were allowed in the club. This didn't bother us as our show was "family friendly".

By this time we had a sketch of Kermit and Miss Piggy in the show. At a club in Scotland we were appearing at an Orange Order Club. The convenor of the club came in the dressing room and said, "I hope yurrnott wearing grreeentoneet." I said that I was wearing an outfit of Kermit the frog. "Ach ye cannae wear grreeenn." I tried to explain that we couldn't miss it out because it was part of the miming. So I went on stage in green as Kermit. Not a good idea in an Orange Club! We didn't go down too well.

It just proved we still couldn't relax, we had work to do entertaining in which ever area we performed. It was still great and I loved entertaining in the clubs. They were all quite similar. Again there were still the fights, still the Committee and the Concert Chairman. Acts still got "paid off". Eeeh thank goodness we were never "paid off".

Sometimes clubs would arrange pie and peas suppers if it was a special night, engaging an act or "turn" which the audience liked and had enjoyed on a previous engagement. Then of course there were Leek Shows.

Most pitmen had allotments and grew leeks, onions, carrots, potatoes and flowers and the gardeners were members of the local Working Men's Club and each club held a competition every year for the best leek and all the other produce. There was fierce competition. Some men slept in their allotments next to their leeks weeks before the competition because of the fear that their produce would be slashed by rival gardeners who were in the same competition.

During the time of growing their produce the men would

spend more time sleeping with their leeks than sleeping with their wives.

Some men even had secret ingredients they put on their leeks to make them grow bigger. It was usually urine. Ugh!

In the past the winners of the Leek Show used to win items of furniture, kitchen appliances all sorts of items for the household. There was even a day where residents of the village were invited to view the items for prizes and view the leeks and flowers.

By the 70s and 80s the prizes consisted mostly of money, £1000 or more. That was big money for any working man.

John's Dad had an allotment but he only used it for growing vegetables for use in the kitchen. My Dad never bothered he only had the garden at the back of the house.

Life in the Street

We had some wonderful parties at North Terrace, especially when other acts stayed with us. They would bring crates of beer back. I'd bring my Cherry B's and John would bring some lager back with him.

Jean, Austin, Sheila and Mac would all join us in our house. We were noted for our parties.

One night little Willy, who was an act, stood on the window sill completely starkers with the curtains open and poor Lilly's mother, who lived further down the street, couldn't believe her eyes as she past our house when she saw a little black guy with an afro bearing all.

She'd complained bitterly to her daughter the next morning, saying how disgusting it was. Lilly had a word with me on the afternoon and asked if she could come to one of our parties!

Leo, the bald one who was Willy's friend, used to hoover

up on a morning in his underpants, drinking the dregs of the drink which was left from the night before.

Clive Webb and his wife Jacquie also stayed with us while working in the North East Clubs. He was appearing at a social club in the North East. John and I said we would come along to see his show. We got seated in this enormous concert room, which had recently had a new carpet fitted. Everyone in the audience was on about the new carpet and how much it had cost the club, and how beautiful it was. The committee were strutting around like peacocks taking all the compliments.

It was nearly time for Clive to start his show. I had a thought! I went to the bar and purchased a soda siphon. The big type like a hand held fire extinguisher. John said, "What are you up to?" I said, "I'm going to get Webby."

Clive came on stage and started his show. It was going very well and the audience were laughing like mad. At this point I took hold of the soda siphon and proceeded towards the stage. When I got up to the front of the stage I squirted Webby with the siphon, upon which he shouted, "This is War!" The audience were in hysterics.

Webby proceeded to get off the stage and came to the big hose fire extinguisher on the wall and started unrolling it. Everyone was wondering what he was up to. Oh no. I knew what he was up to.

He held the unrolled hose and got the water to flow through. How? I don't know. But the water at a great force started coming out of the hosepipe. Oh dear me. He then turned the hose, still flowing powerfully with water, on the audiance. The audience laughed at first then realised that it was not only soaking them but also their beloved carpet. The laughs turned to boos.

The committee, all of them, came marching like a battalion, down the aisle towards the stage. Oh my goodness. I said to John that I thought we should vacate the club as quickly as possible because I had started the situation.

A committee man asked, or rather shouted at Clive, "Get off that stage."

When outside the club John said that I was well out of order.

We all got back to North Terrace and when everyone else arrived Webby took centre stage in our lounge and proceeded to tell everyone about 'the new carpet'.

When I meet up with Clive when he's appearing at The Theatre Royal in Newcastle in pantomime, we recall that evening. Clive still laughs. He's a bugger! A very nice one. He is still as funny as ever. He is now part of a double act with his son, Danny Adams.

Sicily

An agent rang me up and asked if we would like to work in Sicily for a week. I couldn't believe my ears and I said, "Yes," without even asking John. We wouldn't get paid but would get our flights and meals all paid for. So it would be a working holiday. How brilliant.

We asked about carrying on the plane all the props and of course the Akai reel to reel tape recorder, which was quite heavy. We got a letter giving us a higher baggage allowance which suited us down to the ground! We had to fly from Manchester Airport and when we checked in we had three suitcases and an unusual bag which contained my little bike.

"How long are you going for?" the girl at the check-in asked.

"Oh just a week," was our reply."

I don't think she understood why we were taking a child's tricycle with us either. The time came and off we went flying to Palermo airport Sicily.

We got there and went through passport control and a Policeman with a gun pointed at us, said in Italian "Come this way," He couldn't speak English and we couldn't speak Italian. "Oh heck," we thought, "We're in trouble now."

We went into an office with three official looking men in uniform. It was the tape recorder they were interested in. They were going to take it off us and give it back to us when we left the country. I think they thought we had brought it over to sell. We couldn't get them to understand why we needed the tape recorder. I even took a costume out of one of our cases and a wig and put it on, demonstrating that we were a comedy act. They just looked at me as if I needed to be sectioned.

Anyway they let us go but kept the tape recorder. We got to the hotel, The Saracen Sands Hotel. Very, very posh and all the walls were white. We went straight to the Manager and explained that we couldn't do our show without the tape recorder. He sent someone immediately to the airport and got our machine back. The wonders of being able to speak a foreign language.

The hotel was brilliant it had a lovely pool and the weather was hot hot hot.

Another act was there and he was a comedy vocalist. We got on really well with him and spent our spare time with him.

The small village where the hotel was situated was like an American cowboy western town just like what you see on tele with tumbleweed rolling down the centre of the road, wooden single storey houses with a veranda. There were a few shops and I needed some shoes, or sandals.

A couple of local people were walking along the street on the other side of the road and we shouted, "Excusae, caaannyooootelll us where there is a shooooshawwwp?" They replied, "No weeecaaannn'thelllpppyoooosorrrrrry?" Oh well we'd just keep wandering around. We bumped into

132

the same couple and we nodded to them, acknowledging them with courtesy. Do you know they were in the bar at the hotel on the night time and were from bloody Newcastle? When we heard them talking we thought, "Ye daft buggers!" They were no more Italian than we were. They thought we were Italian and we thought they were Italian.

When it came to our evening to do our show it went so very well, the audience were fantastic and we spent the days round the pool sitting with them. The men were daft as brushes and when I walked past the pool I would always get thrown in, no matter what I was wearing, either swimwear or eveningwear. In I went! Just as well I could swim.

It was an amazing week and we were sad to leave. Of course we had to meet up with the Customs Officers at the airport, when we did they nodded and moved us on through check in. Phew!

We were working in South Wales, usually staying at theatrical digs in Neath, but this time we stayed at Gareth Williams' home in Swansea. He was wonderful. A teacher during the day and a colourful character by night. He came to all our bookings with us and helped us carry our gear and generally mucked in. We loved his company and he loved the company of ladies. He wasn't married, but was forever getting his heart broken. Poor Gareth. I think he eventually married.

May All Your Troubles Be Little Ones

Digs were still a part of our life while travelling on the road. Another act staying at the same digs had a baby with them and they handed me the baby to nurse while she went to the loo.

Oh heck! I'd never even touched a baby never mind

held one and, we'd been married 10 years. ,

"Well I like this," I said to John. That night the earth moved and, yes, three months later I had a pregnancy test and I was going to have a baby. I was chuffed to bits.

When we were at home at North Terrace I used to play or entertain the little ones next door and over the road. I made them laugh and made them mud pies. We baked the pies in the sun and they took them home to show their mammy. I loaned them costumes for fancy dress at school like the Honey Monster and Kermit the Frog.

When our Eileen visited I would play with Catherine. I enjoyed the children's company and maybe I was preparing for our little family.

Eileen, my sister and I were pregnant at the same time! Me Mam and Dad were chuffed to bits. My goodness must have been something in the water!

John's Mam and Dad were also elated as the baby was to be their first grandchild. Bobby was ecstatic. He'd been on to us for some years.

"When are you going to start a family?" He'd say. When we told them they were jubilant. Over the moon as the Geordies would say.

Really we never thought about having a family as we were so busy with first of all the group and then the double act. I had every intention to keep on working while pregnant and I did just that.

We altered our show so that I didn't jump around as much, or do as many quick changes. Although I still rode my little bike. Comments were made by members of the audience especially the women.

"Eeeh she shouldn't be riding that thing in her condition." I was perfectly fine. I'm sure when they were pregnant they got up to more strenuous activities for example scrubbing floors and getting the coal in. In fact running a house full of children and a husband is quite exhausting I'm sure. I had a wonderful pregnancy. I felt brilliant and I blossomed and bloomed. Everyone said how wonderful I looked and do you know I felt wonderful too. I loved feeling the baby move and saying to John,

"Oh feel my tummy the baby has just moved." Although I was frightened to give birth I knew whatever was inside, whether boy or girl, it didn't matter, it had to come out one way or another. I was truly scared stiff about the birth.

All the way through the pregnancy we were still working around the clubs in the North East doing a less energetic show.

One night we were working at Mile End Social Club in South Shields. I was still riding my little bike around the audience to Leader of the Pack. I was on my bike in the audience peddling like mad and a lady got up and pushed her chair back and I was right behind her. The chair she was on hit me in the mouth and knocked my two front teeth out. Ugh blood everywhere. I still carried on and everyone in the audience thought it was part of the act where my teeth fell out!!

Next day I had to go to the dentists and I had to have my front teeth crowned. Of course I was pregnant at the time and so I got them corrected for nowt!!

A few weeks before I was to give birth I thought I'd like to learn to play the piano. One had been left in the house at North Terrace from the previous owner. My cousin Dennis knew a fellow fireman who was a piano teacher in his spare time.

I went to his home and knocked on the door.

"Yes can I help you?" the man said.

"Yes I'd like to learn to play the piano please."

"Yes, that's good."

"How long will it take?" I asked.

"Oh it could take up to three years." Well I didn't even get over the door step.

"Oh," I said, "I've only got a fortnight." He told me to buy a chord book. I learned the chords so quickly I could play Let It Be" by the Beatles, "All Things Bright and Beautiful", "We plough the Fields and Scatter" and of course "The Old Rugged Cross" (my favourite). Oh and another one of my favourite hymns "For Those in Trouble on the Sea" I just loved playing the piano.

With the chord book it was instant. I could play the piano in my own way and I loved it. Mind John didn't love it he did say that every tune sounded the same. But did I care? No way.

I'm sure this is how Richard and my second son got their musical talent from. You see, womb music. It got through to my babies. It might not have been very good but, I enjoyed it and I hope the babies in my womb did!

When anyone called to see me I'd say,

"Do you want to hear me play the piano?" John always shook his head to them meaning, "No you don't want to hear Brenda play the piano." Upon which I'd clip him round the head and say to them not to take notice of him.

Austin our neighbour enjoyed a sing-along round the piano and our Eileen loved to have a sing-along too. When our David and Jan visited we'd always end up singing around the piano always the same tunes but nobody seemed to care. Mind I only played my favourite hymns because that's all I could play.

Our Eileen had already had her baby on the 18th April, which was John's birthday too. She had given birth to a boy and they named him Daniel. He was beautiful. It was my turn next.

Nearing the end of my pregnancy I didn't work as much. I was getting tired. We had a pair of ladders in the garage and I said to John,

"Why don't we start a window cleaning round? We've got the ladders."

I'm a strong believer in 'use what you've got'. John wasn't keen. But it would bring in some money. The next day I said to John, "Come on we're going round to Newton Hall." (the posh houses) I knocked on several doors and asked the occupants, "Do you want your windows cleaning?" I was heavily pregnant remember. Some said, "Oh no, anyway you'd better not go up those ladders in your condition."

On My Bike

After several attempts we gave up on the posh houses and made our way to the council houses. We hit lucky and every house I called on wanted their windows cleaning. I was chuffed to bits but I saw the look on John's face as I wrote the ladies' names and addresses in my little book. He definitely wasn't keen, but I would say to him to try to encourage him "Come on John get up the ladders."

I went collecting the money too and by the end of the week we had a canny round. At least it brought in some money, which paid the bills.

John decided he would try and get some drumming work in the clubs. They still employed organists and drummers. He was lucky and got two jobs in the Newcastle area. One on the Saturday and one on the Sunday, perfect. So with the window cleaning and the drumming we could manage just nice. This would see us through until well after the birth of the baby. Nee problem!

I would, I thought, even go collecting the window cleaning money with the pram with John and his ladders in tow!

One night while lying in bed, the time had come!!!!!! Oh dear me! Here we go this was something I wasn't looking forward to.

"John it's time."

"Oh right, what should I do?"

"Get my bag that I've prepared for going into hospital."

I went up to Jean's house and said,

"Have you got any magazines?"

"What do you want magazines for at this time of the night, it's half past eleven?"

"I'm going into to hospital to give birth and I'd like something to read!!!!" Yeah as if I'd have time to read a magazine while giving birth!!! Ha!!!

"Oh my goodness" Jean said, "Are you alright, is the pain bad?" She was panicking more than me.

I rang me Mam and told her I was going into hospital and John rang his Mam too. He came with me to the hospital and sat with me in my little side ward. He really didn't know exactly what to say to me. This was all new to him as well.

I asked the Doctor at the hospital while he examined me if I could have a 'section'.

"On your bike." he said. To which I replied:

"Oh you've heard about my bike?" As if? The doctor said that everything was fine and I was healthy and the baby was all ready to be born.

Nothing prepares you for such bloody horrible pain. I screamed, screamed and screamed more. John was there at the beginning but asked me if I didn't mind if he went. I said, "Noooooooit'ssssalriiiiiiiiightjuuuuusssstgoooooo. Upon which he did.

The midwives offered me gas and air, which made me feel sick. I had injections in my leg. Nothing eased the horrendous pain.

While in labour I took a wander and went into other mother's to be cubicles, who had their husband's with them, dealing with their own labour. I said to them:

"I can't do this, no I can't, no I can't do it. This is horrible." I bet the husbands thought, "Who the hell is she?" and possibly, "Where's her husband?" Well John just couldn't cope, they weren't to know that. But of course I had to!!!!!!

The midwife was saying:

"Come on Brenda get back onto the bed." I was in terrible pain. "Come on Brenda push, push, come on again push. Now don't push, no not yet Brenda. No Brenda try not to push. Right now Brenda one big push. That's a good girl."

"I can't," I was shouting.

"Come on Brenda one more big big push! .... Well

done Brenda, you've done it!!" And do you know I never did get to read one of Jean's magazines!!!!

Next Stage – Our lovely little baby son

It took 23 hours of hard labour and after all that RICHARD JOHN WOODS was born at 7.05 am on the 3rd July l979. He was 7lb 1oz and beautiful.

Mind when the midwife put him on my tummy I was so exhausted and at the time I couldn't have cared less whether the baby was a girl, boy or a bloody monkey!!! Every woman reading this will know what I mean!! Once I pulled myself around, which took only a couple of minutes after that excruciating pain, I said to baby Richard on my tummy,

"Eeeh well hello I'm your Mammy and you're my baby boy!!"

I was stitched by a man who looked like Cosmo Smallpiece from a Les Dawson sketch. He had little glasses perched on the end of his nose. There was no conversation as my legs were strapped up high in stirrups, not a pretty sight! All my dignity went out of the window. I couldn't have cared less what the man looked like or even what I looked like.

Cosmo was very intent in what he was doing and I'm sure he enjoyed his job. I asked him how many stitches he was putting in.

"I've lost count." he answered. That was the end of that conversation. I'm sure a Singer sewing machine would have been much quicker. But to be honest his sewing would be very neat, I think, although I never did find out.

After he had completed his handy work the nurse unhooked my legs and they were lowered onto the trolley on which I lay. I made myself presentable and the nurse told me I should have a salt bath.

"Put plenty of salt in your bath," She added. I thought a little shake here and there but next to the bath was a sack of salt with a measuring jug. The nurse put the salt in for me. I was shocked as to how much. Two scoops!

I lowered myself into the bath I was dreading reaching the water because I thought it would sting but no oh no it was fantastic it was soothing, it was fabulous, I wanted to stay in the bath all day it was bloody lovely. The nurse came into the bathroom to get me out.

"Come on Brenda you've got a baby who is hungry."

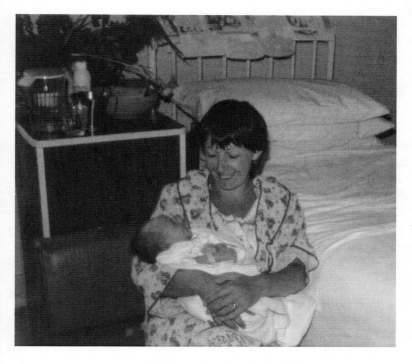

Richard - one day old

It took me ages to get out of that bath. I felt like a

geriatric and walked like one. My son had been looked after probably in a nursery with all the other babies. I was taken down onto the ward where all the mammies who had just given birth were. Probably the ones whose rooms I'd entered while I was in labour.

I said hello to everyone on the ward. The girls seemed very nice and very friendly. It was a nightmare getting onto the bed only to be told by a nurse to just sit in the chair next to my bed, it would be easier for me. So it took ages to get off the bed. She gave me an inflatable ring to sit on while I ate my breakfast with the other mothers. Charming, but it worked.

The sister of the ward made her round, checking that every new mammy was fine and comfortable. Our babies had arrived in their perspex cots and were next to our beds. Richard looked amazing and beautiful.

Oh my goodness, I couldn't believe it, I was a mammy. I did it. I gave birth. Me, yes. What a wonderful feeling cradling my son in my arms. A miracle. John and I had created a life.

He was perfect, ten little fingers and ten little toes. I couldn't stop looking at my little baby Richard.

John came into the ward and found the bed where I was and his new son. I looked at him and do you know he looked as though he had given birth.Yeah!! I was in my nice clean nightie and I think I looked a lot better than he did.

The Sister of the ward was Sister Quinn. She should have had a small black moustache! She only let the new fathers in when everywhere was tidy around all the beds, including cabinets and babies. Everything had to be shipshape. It was a military operation. All the new dads, who were as frightened of the sister as we were, came in together bearing gifts and flowers.

"How are you?" John asked.

"I'm fine." Then he held his son Richard for the first time.

It was a lovely moment. Richard never cried much at all. What a brilliant time!!!! What a wonderful stage of my life becoming a mother.

I learned how to breast feed. I changed my first nappy (not very well, may I add). We were surrounded by cards flowers and love!!!! It was amazing!!!! I asked John if he'd rang me Mam and Dad and his Mam and Dad. He said that he had and that he'd rang round everyone on the list I'd made before I went into labour. He'd done that, so that was good.

Unlike other girls I'd never babysat whilst growing up in my teens. Some of my friends had, so they were used to babies. The only baby I'd held was that one in the theatrical digs when I said to John, "Do you fancy one - a baby?"

Well here we were the three of us. All of us not knowing what to do next apart from Richard. He knew when he was hungry. I didn't even know how to put a bloody nappy on Richard. When anyone picked him up his nappy used to fall off.

The Doctor came around to check the babies and do you know he said to Richard?

"Your Mammy wants to learn how to put a nappy on." When he picked him up Richard's nappy fell off. Richard was lying on his back in his perspex cot and he weeeeeed in a vertical direction and hit the Doctor in his face. Yes well done Richard. A star already and right on cue!!!! Not a word from the Doctor. Well I was a new Mammy and it was all very new to me. Thank you Richard!

The girls on the ward were brilliant. We laughed and laughed all day long, whilst feeding our new babies, changing them and bathing them. The only time we were quiet was when we were nursing our babies to sleep! SSSHHHHH baby sleeping!!!

On the first ward the new mammies were all crying. On our ward and there was laughter. It was great. All the pain forgotten.

Ann Sables who was in the bed opposite to me was in her late 20's like me. I think we were the same age. I was 29. We were both in agony sitting down and walking. Ahggghh, ooohhhh, eeeehhh. Then there was a 16 year old in our ward and she hopped around her bed as if she hadn't had a baby. Well she would she was young. Anyway it was a great ward with happy new mammies.

It was day 9 and nearly release day. My bowel hadn't moved!!! You could go home if you'd "been." Well I hadn't and I'd eaten plenty of grapes too! I hid in the broom cupboard. I heard the nurse saying, "Where's Brenda?" One girl split on me and said, "She's in the broom cupboard." Richard was fast asleep, by the way. I knew I was going to get a suppository. I didn't want one of those. Anyway the nurse found me. When I heard her coming towards the cupboard to get me I suddenly had the urge to go!!!

I was allowed to go home. My case was packed; John brought the carry cot in. I had Richard dressed in a nice outfit. The nurse from the ward carried Richard to our car. I got in the car and she handed me our new son. Our little family was on its way home to North Terrace.

We'd bought a second hand cot. But of course Richard was too small to go in that just yet. John's Mam and Dad bought the pram which the bed part lifted off so Richard slept in that. It was lovely.

Richard became the star of the street. Me Mam and Dad bought the Harrington 'Gold Seal' terry towelling nappies, plus the sanitising bucket.

When we got back home all the visits started, everyone wanted to see Richard and hold him. Me Mam and Dad they both thought he was brilliant. John's Mam and Dad had their first grandchild.

John's Dad had tears in his eyes when he held Richard. He'd been waiting a long time for this moment. How lovely.

Richard had two sets of wonderful grandparents, who would love, cherish, and care for their new grandson. They were both over the moon.

Me Mam asked "Was the pain bad Brenda?"

"Yes, it really hurt but it's all over now." Our Eileen, Alan and their two children came to visit. In fact, there was a constant stream of visitors. John was forever making cups of tea.

Both John and I were up through the night. I breast fed and John ran about getting clean nappies and disposing of the dirty ones. No disposables nappies in those days.

For anyone who didn't know the news that I'd had my baby, putting the nappies on the line was the signal that we'd become parents.

"Oh look," passers-by would probably say, "She's had the baby."

For the next two weeks John was still drumming in the two clubs and cleaning windows. I think he couldn't wait for me to get back to entertaining. I felt really well and I rang an agent to start putting work into our diary but just a couple a week. I expressed milk into bottles so that it was possible for Jean and Austin and both sets of grandparents to share the baby sitting. It was hard work.

At weekends Richard would go to grandparents, which gave John and me a little rest. Yes, I went to work for a rest. Richard was a good baby, a real pleasure.

Our Eileen had Daniel just a few months before I had Richard so it was nice to share time with each other and our babies, although Eileen lived in Doncaster at the time. John and I found work in the Doncaster area so we stayed with our Eileen and she looked after Richard while we went to work. It was lovely that we had help with looking after Richard while John and I worked trying to make a living. We still just worked two nights a week which was enough to pay the bills and get food in.

In my handbag I carried a little photograph album full of pictures of Richard. When we entertained at a club the little album went right round the audience. I could hear all the oohhh's and aahhh's and I thought, "They think he's beautiful like we do."

While working in Yorkshire and staying at our Eileen's, John and I got a job at a club in a town not far from Eileen's house in Hatfield, Doncaster. Eeeh well, we died a death during our first spot. Eeeh it was horrible. I didn't want to go back on. During the bingo the curtains were closed and our speakers were behind the curtains so very very quietly we took the speakers down and loaded everything in the car and drove away. When they came to open the curtains after the bingo they'd find out that we had disappeared.

By that time we would be back at our Eileen's house and I would be holding my little boy in my mind thinking, "Oh what an awful night but so what I'm back with my beautiful son."

Whenever Richard was asleep I was forever checking that he was still breathing. If his breathing was quiet I'd put my head down to his face to listen and in some cases I would give him a little nudge, upon which he would wriggle. I was constantly worrying about him.

When feeding through the night I felt as though I was the only person up at that time, sitting quietly feeding and Richard enjoying every minute and finally going to sleep. Then time to put him back in his cot and I'd go back to bed contented. Mind there were nights when he just wouldn't go to sleep and I'd be nursing him and nursing him.

Bringing up babies is an exhausting task but so rewarding. I'm sure I looked permanently tired. Of course all the parties stopped, which of course didn't bother me. And the acts stopped staying with us too. We settled down to a nice family life.

I would take Richard for a walk along the front street.

People would stop and say how lovely Richard was and put £1 in his pram. It was summer time and Richard and I would go and sun bathe with Auntie Jean and Uncle Austin.

Our Eileen and I had talked about a double christening and agreed that it would be nice. We would have the christening at Christ the King Church in Bowburn.

The day of the christening came. Auntie Jean and Uncle Austin, our Eileen and Alan were Richard's godparents. Both Richard and Daniel behaved so well in church and it was a lovely day. Both grandparents looked on with pride.

Our Eileen eventually moved up to the North East because Alan, her husband got a job up here. Me Mam was chuffed to bits. John and I took me Mam and Dad down to our Eileen's in Doncaster a few times each year but this was better. It meant Eileen and I could meet up more and Richard and Daniel could play together.

Babies are not babies for long so I tried to treasure every part of Richard's early days. Enjoying his first smile, his first tooth, sticky fingers, sloppy kisses, and his first word, whether it be Dadda or Mamma. Soon he was crawling all over the house. Keeping an eye on him was a job and a half. Then of course after crawling he was up on his feet and walking.

Worms

Auntie Jean's son Gary came home from school to our house and said that his teacher had set his class a task. They had given each pupil £1 and, in some productive way, they had to double that £1. Auntie Jean came with him and we sat and thought and came up with the idea of buying a piece of fur for £1 and cutting it into the shape of a snake, finding some material, maybe some old curtains and cutting out the same shape. Sew them together, leaving a hole at the top and filling it with old tights. We made a draught excluder. Sell that draught excluder for £2. How's about that?

He sold it to me and he took the £2 to school. His teacher was well impressed. Jean and I came up with the idea that we could make these draught excluders and sell them round the clubs. So we both went to the market bought some fur, again got the curtain material. John cut the shapes out and Jean did the stitching, then I stuffed them with filling which we also bought from the market. We didn't call them snakes but worms because we didn't put any eyes in.

John and I took them to the club where we were working and at the end of our show I showed the audience one of our worms. I think we sold them for £3. I then proceeded to go round the audience up and down the aisles shouting, "Anyone want worms?" I used to sell the lot. That meant the next day I'd be off to the market to buy more fur and filling for the worms.

The profit we gave to charity. Local children's homes or whatever charity the club wanted us to give the money to. Every now and again we'd keep some of the money and treat ourselves. Now when it came nearer Christmas we thought about something different to make and we came up with the idea of Santa socks. I mean, now you can buy them anywhere but in 1980 they were nowhere to be found so we again went to the market, bought the red and white fur;red for the boot and white for the top. John cut them out and Jean did the sewing. I sold them in the clubs. They went like hot cakes. We couldn't make them quick enough.

Jean had a job too, she was a home help. I had our Richard and John well he had plenty of time, plus he was good at cutting out. I was useless at cutting out. John used to say:

"Come on Brenda try and cut the socks out." I did and it

looked nowt like a sock. Always do what you do best. I think John was trying to get out of the job.

He liked watching the television during the day. So whilst watching the tele he cut the socks out.

The Girl in the Afghan Coat

John and I got some work at The Flamingo night club in Darlington. The venue booked us for two nights. We thought it was brilliant because we were using the club's PA system so again only had our props to take with us.

We got to the Flamingo Club. Sylvia was the receptionist at the club. On our first night I was talking to her because we had to be in the club an hour before we went on stage so instead of sitting in the dressing room I'd go and chat to Sylvia.

While standing chatting at the reception, a girl with long hair came in wearing an Afghan coat and Jesus sandals. Well no one came in the 'Flammy' dressed like that. This audience were definitely not hippies. Sylvia and I looked at each other and quietly said. "Oooo, HummmmmEeeeeeh. What's a hippy doing in here?"

The girl was accompanied by a man who wore a denim shirt and had a perm or curly hair. He didn't look at all like a hippy and not the type of fella who she would go out with.

Permed hair for men was very popular, in fact, John had a perm. He wouldn't allow me to go to the hairdressers when he got it permed. I wonder why?

Anyway John and I went on stage and we went down very well. After the show I went looking for John. Someone said that he was playing pool with the manager of the club. I passed through the reception and saw that girl in the Afghan coat and Jesus sandals arguing with a man, the one she came in with. Or I should say he was arguing with her.

Ooooh, not good. Hummmm! Well I found John and off we went home. I told him about the girl, and then it was never mentioned again.

We were at the Club the next night and I saw Sylvia on reception.

"Do you remember that girl in the Afghan coat and Jesus sandals?"

"Eeehh yes, Sylvia I saw a man arguing with her at the end of last night. The man she came in with."

"You didn't."

"I did." I said. Then Sylvia said:

"You see that door opposite just go in there, there are some men in there, and tell them what you've just told me." I walked to the door, knocked and someone shouted,

"Come in."

It was the police - detectives. I just told them what I had seen. They told me that shortly after I'd seen the girl and man arguing she had been murdered!!!!! Oh my goodness. The detectives took my name, address and telephone and told me I was the last person to see her alive. They said they were making me their prime witness. Oh dear!! I felt terrible.

Poor girl. I went back stage and told John what had happened. That night we went on stage then went home quite subdued.

The police contacted me the next day and asked if I wouldn't mind going around pubs in Darlington to look for anyone who resembled the man arguing with the girl. I had difficulty trying to look for someone whose back I only saw. I only had a glimpse of his face. It was the girl's face which I saw. In fact most of the fellas in the pubs wore denim shirts and had curly hair.

A few days after the pub crawl, the policeman who was in charge of the murder asked me if I minded going under hypnosis to give more details of the man.

The police took me to a house in Ferryhill, County Durham and I was 'put under'. It was done by a doctor who held a pendulum in front of me and it swayed back and forth. I thought to myself, "I don't believe I'm doing this. This is what happens on the television."

The man I saw had black curly hair with a beard or a moustache. He had some sort of facial hair. I even went on an identification parade to see if I could pick him out of the line of men. I couldn't.

It was the time of the Yorkshire Ripper, but he'd already been charged and arrested so it wasn't him.

The police came nearly every day to take more statements. I couldn't tell them any more than what I had already stated. I went to court and the man in the dock accused of her murder was not the man I saw arguing with her. The man in the dock was sent to prison for her murder.

Sometime later while on holiday in Spain, we were walking around a town and I noticed in the English papers that the man in prison for Stephanie's murder had been given a Queen's pardon and released. It wasn't him who was arguing with her. I tried to tell the police but they wouldn't listen. I don't know whether they ever found her murderer.

Sacriston

Richard was one year old and we were looking for another house. We were very happy at North Terrace. We had brilliant neighbours, Jean and Austin and of course all our other neighbours down and across the street. We'd been there over 10 years and we'd had a brilliant time and I have wonderful memories. It's just I fancied a semi detached house, with a nice big garden.

We couldn't afford Newton Hall. So we looked around

houses in a village called Sacriston, which was about 2 miles away from Framwellgate Moor. We looked at a house in Valley View, a small housing estate. It had three bedrooms, lounge, through dining room and a big garden. We thought it was absolutely lovely and ideal for us so we bought it.

We had no problem in selling North Terrace. We thought maybe we should keep North Terrace and rent it out but after some thought we decided to sell. The house at Sacriston was £14,000 and we sold North Terrace for £9000.

When we told Jean and Austin that we were moving they were devastated. I felt terrible. I told them that I would still come and see them regularly and they could come through to Sacriston to visit us

We eventually moved into Valley View and it was lovely. It had a lovely big garden. The lounge and through dining room was nice too. The kitchen was a lot smaller than the one we had at North Terrace but I wasn't bothered. We even had a driveway for our car, albeit a shared one, but again we weren't bothered. We met the new neighbours; Ann and Malcolm and they seemed very nice.

The village of Sacriston had some good shops. Think of the song 12 days of Christmas and here are all the shops. One DIY, two butchers shops, three fruit and veg, four hairdressers, five social clubs. Not forgetting the pet shop, supermarket, Lloyds Bank, a betting shop and a small garden centre at the top of the street.

The DIY shop sold nails by the pound, putty and everything you can think of. It was better than B&Q because of the personal service and help Mr. Hattam offered. The little garden centre also cut keys, sold paint and also gave advice on gardening matters.

Do you know I could walk round to the front street with Richard in his buggy and do all my shopping for the week without even leaving the village? I found out that there was a mother and toddler group so I decided to join in order for Richard to mix with other children of his own age and for me to get to know some other mammies.

There were also schools within walking distance, and a good thriving community centre. There was another plus about Valley View where we lived. It was right next to a wood. It was fabulous and in the spring it was covered in bluebells. Brilliant! In fact that's what we called the wood 'bluebell wood' and we still do.

I couldn't get Richard into the local nursery but got him in one in the next village of Edmondsley, which was only a mile and a half away from us.

On Richard's first day at nursery when I left him at the nursery he cried and cried. I was distraught leaving him. Mrs. Kilner the teacher at the nursery said for me to ring when I got back home to see if he had settled down. He always had and enjoyed his days there.

Richard was an absolute pleasure. Not one ha'p'orth of bother. I loved his company and enjoyed teaching him new skills and playing.

We'd bought him a little pedal car for Christmas and when Daddy washed his car, Richard washed his little car, of course, with his dummy in his mouth. I missed him when he went to nursery but he was only there mornings so I'd spend the afternoon with him either down the wood if it was fine or playing in the house, playing shops, colouring in or, wait for it... I'd set the furniture in the shape of a bus with the settee as the back seat and the chairs as the single seats, Richard's desk as the bonnet and a steering wheel. I was reliving my own childhood. It was brilliant.

Another Christmas, we bought Richard a hamster. I went down to the pet shop in Sacriston the day before Christmas and bought a hamster and cage plus bedding and food. I hid the hamster in her little cage in the top cupboard in our bedroom. With hamsters being nocturnal I thought

Richard wouldn't suss where the hamster was. Anyway he didn't know he was getting one for Christmas.

On the night of Christmas Eve, Richard came into our bedroom and was asking about Santa Claus. All of a sudden there were squeaks coming from the cupboard. Richard asked:

"What's that noise Mammy?" I knew it was the hamster going like hell on her little wheel. I said,

"Oh it's just the water pipes making a noise; they do that now and again."

Christmas Day was amazing and Richard loved his hamster. She was called Molly. She was named after my Norwegian friend Molly, who was visiting Durham with some colleagues from her school in Norway.

She stopped and asked a taxi driver if they could take her to Brenda the comedian who lived in Sacriston and do you know the taxi driver brought her straight to our door. Amazing how many people know me.

We still didn't have much money and John loved the television. Well he said, "Why don't we get one of those televisions with a remote control?" We couldn't afford it so Richard and I went down the wood as we always did when it was nice and sunny. We used to pretend we were cowboys on our pretendy horses.

While we were playing I found a big long stick, it was nice and straight. I said to Richard,

"This is a present for your Daddy." We took it back home and I said to John that he could sit in his chair and from his chair he could hold the stick and change the channels by pressing the buttons with the stick. Who needs a remote control? Well it didn't go down well. Oh well so much for ingenuity!

John's Dad used to call in at the nursery to see Richard. He doted on Richard. If John's Dad was working on the roads anywhere local I used to take Richard to see his

Granda at work on the big machine he drove. He used to drive a machine that burnt off the old tarmac in preparation to lay new tarmac.

Granda Bobby was always chuffed to bits when he saw us drive up to where he was working. You could literally see his chest expand with love. He was proud to show Richard the big machine.

He had an allotment and used to take Richard to the allotment to collect the vegetables for Sunday's dinner, which Grandma Audrey would make. Like my Mam she made brilliant Sunday's dinners, especially her stuffing. She would never tell me the recipe. Not that it mattered I wouldn't have even had a go at making it.

My Dad used to put Richard on the seat at the back of his bike and take him for rides around the small roads and farm lanes of Bowburn to Croxdale. Just as he did with Eileen and I when we were little. We all had bikes and cycled to Croxdale and bathed in the River Brownie. WONDERFUL. I'm sure Richard has wonderful memories of being with both Grandparents. They were great.

Ann and Malcolm next door had a son Mark and twin girls called Helen and Jane. The twins loved coming in our house and playing with Richard. We nicknamed them 'the girlies'. I loved having them involved in our everyday life. Richard adored them both.

He loved dressing up in outfits I'd made for him and often using our stage masks. Richard would be dressed as Darth Vader and go in try to frighten Malcolm. Malcolm would play along and pretend to be really scared. Richard would come back and tell me that he had scared Malcolm to bits.

We had work at Primrose Valley and Reighton Sands so we asked the girlies to baby-sit for us. We had bought a little caravan so they came with us to Filey. It was great fun. During the day we hired bikes, went swimming and went to the beach. The girlies were great at looking after Richard. They looked after him in the caravan while John and I went on stage at the holiday venue.

Going back to when I was young, when it was raining, I used to go out in my wellies and raincoat and sweep the water down the gutters. I used to be the only child out in the rain with me Mam's brush trailing around the streets. I don't know what our neighbour's thought, but I didn't care. I was very happy. Well, I passed this onto our Richard. He carries on the tradition because I asked him what he remembers of his childhood and he said,

"Sweeping the gutters when it was raining."

My mam and dad

Castles Night Club

The neighbours in our cul-de-sac, Ann and Malcolm, were lovely and very friendly. We got on really well with them both. Malcolm was also an entertainer and was the compere at Castles Night Club in Annfield Plain. He invited us to spend an evening with him at the night club. I think it was The Bachelors who were appearing that night. It was a massive club. We really enjoyed the evening and Malcolm was a good compere.

The next day he came to our house and asked us to become the support act for all the big names at this wonderful club. Well we were thrilled. We said, "Yes, of course we would love to." We would use the house PA system so all we had to do was turn up, set the props up and perform.

On our opening night we worked with The Searchers. We really couldn't believe it. I was in the same dressing room with the group I'd idolised in the 60's when I went to the Boom Boom Beat Club.

I rang our Eileen the next day and she asked if she could come along to a show. The Searchers were at the club for 6 nights. It was good regular work for us and we were on stage at 9.00pm until 9.45pm. It was perfect. I put Richard to bed before we went to work. I made sure he was asleep. Ann, Malcolm's wife, would come in and baby sit for us. We'd be back home by 10.30 pm and Richard wouldn't even have known we'd been out.

Each week it was a different top of the bill. We worked with Bernard Manning, Frank Carson, Mick Miller, The Drifters, The Grumbleweeds to name but a few. At the weekends Richard went to his grandparents and stayed there. They were brilliant. Richard was no problem and it meant he could spend quality time with his lovely Grandmas and Grandas.

The club was big and it always advertised the acts in the local papers. A full four course meal was provided so the evening was always a great success. It was packed every night because the tickets were the price people could afford. Mind it was always cold inside the club as there was no central heating but there were several calor gas mobile heaters scattered around the club. It didn't bother the audience. There was plenty of cheap drink, good food and excellent entertainment.

One week there was a hypnotist booked, Tony Sands. He was great. Our Eileen was in the audience and he invited her to get up on stage and be hypnotised. Oh dear. It was so funny.

One of the instructions Tony gave Eileen was to imagine all the men in the hall were naked every time she put on these glasses Tony gave her. Eeeh laugh, I couldn't stop.

When she got down from the stage she told me he hadn't hypnotised her at all. She said she just went along with it because she didn't want to embarrass herself. I think she did a very good job in embarrassing herself.

She stood on the stage where she'd never been of late
Her lips shook like jelly on a plate
She'd never seen so many men in the nude
As she was always looked upon as a prude
She was young beautiful and sleek
And seeing all these different shapes made her legs very weak
Now our Eileen stared at all these men with not a stitch or a thong
She thought, "That reminds me I must go and put the kettle on."
She got down in utter dismay and surrender
And thought, "Thank goodness the stage is not for me but for our Brenda!"

The London Palladium

Clive Webb the mad magician, who I mentioned earlier, asked me if I would be his assistant for his magic tricks at the London Palladium!!! Wow! I couldn't believe it.

I was size 8 you see, and I could get into very small spaces such as boxes. I rang me Mam and Dad and told them. They were over the moon. They said that they would look after our Richard while we went down to London. Jacquie and John came with Webby and I.

We had a great weekend. We stayed in a lovely hotel with a balcony. Very posh.

On the day of the show we went to the stage door entrance of the Palladium. I couldn't believe that I was to actually appear at this famous theatre. I had to nip myself.

We had rehearsals and I met my fellow artistes. Mind my dressing room was very tatty, with paint peeling off the walls, but it was clean. I said to Webby that my dressing room was minging. I thought the staff had given me the minging one because I was a nobody. He said that his was the same and that all the dressing rooms were like ours.

I couldn't understand why the big stars put up with such shabby dressing rooms. Even in Clubland we had decent dressing rooms. Oh well here I was in a dressing room where possibly our Cilla had been or Shirley Bassey, Tom Jones or Bett Midler just to name a few. It was a Wow and here I was little Brenda Swainston at the London Palladium.

Dressing room at the London Palladium

LONDON PALLADIUM

PUBLAND VARIETY SHOW 1980

Valid Sunday, 9th November, 1980 only

Backstage Pass

Name ...Brenda... Ref ...Clive Webb...

Authorised by ....

ARTISTE / MUSICIAN / PRESS / STAFF

After rehearsals we went back to the hotel and we all went out for a lovely meal. The evening soon arrived and we set off for the theatre. I was so nervous. I was in my dressing room and I had a bouquet of flowers delivered and a telegram wishing me luck. It was fantastic. Again I had to nip myself, me at the London Palladium. The announcement came over the tannoy,

"Clive Webb and Brenda to the stage please." Oh heck, here we go. I hoped I would get everything right and that I wouldn't let Clive down. The previous act was taking the applause and Webby said to me,"Break a leg Brenda."

"Same to you, Webby with brass knobs on," I replied to him.

Off we went together onto the famous boards of the most famous theatre in the world. When I got into the box on the stage Webby put the blades through the boxes. When he did this I screamed. I got out of the box by knocking the sides and the box fell apart. Webby chased me all around the stage.

Then I got into another box where I was supposed to disappear but I never did and so I ended up with gunge being poured into the top of the large box where I was standing. I was covered in blue gunge. The show went down very well with the audience and Webby and I took our bows to rapturous applause.

We came off stage and I was floating on air. I felt that our show went over so quickly. One minute we were being announced then the next we were taking a bow.

I went back to my dressing room and Webby followed and we opened a bottle of champagne which had been delivered to Clive's dressing room. I got the flowers. After the show there was a party and John and I mixed with the Producers and Directors of the show. We went back to the hotel and I was buzzing with excitement so much I couldn't sleep.

The next day we drove back home and I couldn't wait to tell me Mam and Dad, our Eileen, Malcolm and Ann all about the London Palladium.

The night after I appeared at the London Palladium I worked at a club just outside a place called Greenside, which was near Newcastle. We went on stage and died a death. Nobody laughed. Not one titter. It was a case of 'entertain us, if you can'. At the end of the show I said, "Do you know I appeared at the London Palladium last night." They didn't believe one word I said. Rotten sods. Yeah but I knew I had.

Clive asked me to appear in a few television shows with him such as the Bruce Forsyth Show, Gerry Cottles Circus, where I worked alongside Sacha Distelle. Of course working with Bruce Forsyth was just mind blowing. Again I couldn't wait to tell everyone who I had been working with.

Clive appeared on a television programme called "Tiswas". It was televised on a Saturday morning and it was a children's programme but it became popular with the grown-ups. There was the 'Phantom Flan Flinger' who threw custard pies in every direction possible. Clive joined in the antics along with Chris Tarrant and John Gorman from The Scaffold group. They were famous for 'Lilly the Pink'. John and I were invited to have dinner with these two very famous stars. Once again I was nipping myself and very, very nervous. Clive mixed with the famous regularly so he was used to it.

As part of our act, Krack and Dorn, I thought it would be a good idea to bring 'Tiswas' to the clubs and so I bought cans of artificial custard pie and got members out of the audience to play 'passy the pie', which was basically passy the parcel but with custard pies.

The 'volunteers' would pass the pie, which was on a plate, along their line to the music and when the music stopped the person with the pie would put the pie in the next person's face. It was very funny for the audience but sometimes not so funny for the recipient of the pie, and men would sometimes be a bit too heavy handed. Naughty boys! Most of the time I ended up covered completely with custard pie. I didn't mind it was all part of the fun.

John and I constantly thought of new sketches for the

double act. One new sketch was with the aid of pyrotechnics or explosive flashes. I would spin round and round and turn into wonder woman after impersonating Barbara Streisand, then the flash would go off while I was spinning and I'd put soot on my face which was on a chair then I'd go into Brown Girl in the Ring by Boney M. I wouldn't get away with it now. Oh no no no no!

On one occasion we were working at a social club near Middlesbrough. While setting up I noticed the bingo machine (the ball type) was just below the stage. The type of machine they use for the National Lottery. It was a high stage. I asked the Concert Chairman if it could be moved. I told him what was going to happen and that I was also going to ride a little bike across the stage then leap off the stage on the bike.

"Eeeh it's alright pet I'll get it moved," he said

We started the show and oh dear the bingo machine was still there. Oh no. I had a feeling as to what was going to happen. The explosion went off and a spark got in the bingo machine and set all the balls on fire. Well at first people started to laugh until they realised they hadn't played the bingo. Well there was hell on, mayhem! Then the boo's started.

Committee men were throwing beer over the flames. People were running all over panicking. Fortunately I had my bagpipes (homemade type with a co2 fire extinguisher canister inside) so John put the fire out with that.

Of course we got banned!! Oh well. I even offered to cut up little pieces of paper and put numbers 1-90 on but that didn't go down very well with the committee. John told me to not to joke with them. They were not in the mood for jokes after having the bingo machine set on fire.

We just got the gear out of the club quickly and left without another word. At another club just down the road from that one. We'd already done one spot and it was in the middle of a game of bingo. John and I were sat in the audience. The people were very pleasant and chatty.

The bingo caller and the bingo machine were on stage. Well the balls stopped going up the tube. I knew what was wrong, there was an airlock. I mentioned to John what was wrong and he agreed with my suggestion. So I jumped up on stage moved the metal strip back from the tube and blew down the tube, thereby releasing the airlock and in doing so it would release the balls.

But, you see, I didn't put the metal strip back in its original place and so all the balls shot out of the tube into the air one after another at great speed. There were balls all over the place, on tables and on the floor. People were even trying to catch them!

Again there was hell on and the committee immediately had a meeting about me and banned me for 20 years. 20 years I got!! I went back after the 20 years were up and a committee man who remembered me said, "I hope you're going to behave yourself tonight." I think I did.

I used to impersonate Barbara Woodhouse and had a pretendy dog on a leader made rigid by a wire coat hanger and a dog collar on the end. Apparently you can buy them now. I also impersonated Margaret Thatcher during her reign. I used to say, "A white paper has been issued this morning and I've passed a motion on it." The impersonation of Mrs. Thatcher went well in Conservative Clubs but not so well in Labour Clubs.

While we were in the double act, Krack and Dorn, I used to dress up as an old woman and sit in the audience and heckle my husband, who was on stage. I did this in the group and since it worked well we included it in the double act.

At one club, Gosforth and Coxlodge British Legion. I was in the audience dressed as an old woman. In fact I looked more like a tramp. By the way I don't have to bother dressing up now as an old woman!!

Anyway, next to the club was a mental hospital nicknamed "Over the Wall". Remember, I was in the audience heckling my husband and it was at the beginning of our show. The committee of this club thought I was one of the patients from "Over the Wall"

They must have rang the mental hospital and told the hospital that one of their patients had got into the club again. It must have be a regular occurrence.

A nurse came to the club and came up to me.

"Come on dear I'm going to take you back to the hospital." I didn't know who she was or where she was from. I didn't know about any mental hospital. So I said to her to leave me alone as I was part of the act.

"Come on I've heard this all before I'm taking you back."She replied very sternly,

John saw me being taken away and didn't know what was happening. I mean I might not have got back into the club and been taken to the mental hospital and kept inside forever. I did get back in to the club and got back on stage and carried on with the show. John whispered to me,

"Where the hell have you been?"

"In a mental hospital," I replied. He looked at me in disbelief.

Mind when we finished the show and we got into the dressing room and I told John what had happened and who the lady was in the white coat. John had a bloody good laugh and said that they should have kept me in. Cheeky bugger!

The Miner's Strike

In 1984 the pop culture centred around Michael Jackson, Madonna and Frankie Goes to Hollywood. Leg warmers, shell suits, hot pants and for night time padded shoulders were essential for jackets, dresses or jump suits. Lady Diana had a big influence on fashion of this era as well as the television programme Dynasty starring Joan Collins.

It was also the start of the miner's strike. It was a bad time for a lot of mining families. We used to do shows for the miners' strike fund so that they could buy food for their families. The strike caused great rifts between families too, because some of the men went back to work down the pit in order to support their own families. It tore close relatives apart, some never spoke to each other again.

The village of Sacriston was a pit village and the miners were all on strike. John and I did shows locally to help the families of Sacriston. The police were constantly around the village. They came in their vans and on their horses when there was trouble at the pit gates. By trouble I mean fights between the miners and the police.

The striking pitmen would travel to other pits in the North East to give their fellow miners support.

The strike dominated the news. The fights erupted usually because a pitman had gone back to work. He was looked upon as a 'scab'. The pitmen were strong union men and labour men and were fighting for their 'cause' to keep the pits open and save their jobs. But some miners felt they had to go back to feed their family.

The pitmen who went back to work had trouble following them not only at work, but also outside of work.

Their children were picked on at school by the other pitmen's children and fights between the children broke out in the play yard. Their wives were 'sent to Coventry'. The families' cars were damaged and in some cases even set on fire. It was a very bad time for all the pit villages in Durham and the North East.

Being from a family where my Dad was a miner, I could understand how the pitmen felt, but I could also understand how the miners who went back to work felt. They were fighting for survival.

Unfortunately the pits closed and everyone was out of a job, even the bosses. The scars still remain in those villages.

Granda Bobby

Granda Bobby found some lumps in his neck and on his feet. He went to the doctor, who referred him to the hospital. He was diagnosed with cancer of the lymph glands. We were all devastated.

Bobby and Audrey sold their house in High Shincliffe and bought a house in Bowburn in the colliery houses. The NCB were selling them off. Bobby was still working and still called to see his beloved Richard.

Grandma Audrey and Granda Bobby still babysat Richard at weekends and he stayed over on Saturday nights. John and I would go for Sunday lunch. We'd knock at the door and hide. Grandma would open the door with Richard then shut the door because there was no one there. We'd then knock on the door again when the door would open I'd say, "Booo." We'd giggle and giggle.

Granda Bobby died when Richard was 4 years old.

He was a very brave man and the worst thing that upset him was that he wouldn't see Richard grow up. Grandma Audrey coped as well as she could.

We took Richard every weekend to keep Grandma company. Granda Bobby was a very big miss. Richard adored his Granda. Everyone loved Bobby Woods. He was the kindest man ever. When he came to the clubs to see us perform, even when we first started the group up in 1967, I always dedicated 'Bobby's Girl' to him. It was his song.

Another Caravan

We had a nice touring caravan now with hot water. Eeeh it was lovely getting a wash in running hot water. It was a Compass caravan. My Mam and Dad used to borrow it for little holidays. We'd tow it to some nice place like the Lake District and we'd pitch it up for them. When I booked the site I would ask for a nice location and near the toilet block. The caravan had a toilet but I don't think me Mam liked using it.

They used to take our Richard. Me Mam would sit peacefully in the caravan reading the paper or a book and my Dad would be out with Richard around the camp site, on adventures. How exciting. I was quite envious!

We used the new caravan to tour around clubs in different areas, taking a babysitter with us. We'd park the caravan up on a site. The babysitter stayed with Richard in the caravan while we went to perform. It worked well.

New Neighbours

We had new neighbours now, Marjorie and Billy.

Ann, Malcolm and the girlies moved to Hartlepool into a pub. Malcolm just loved entertaining and Castles, the night club had closed down so the next best thing for Malcolm was to be the master of his own venue. We entertained there a few times and it was great. I missed them and I'm sure Richard missed the girlies.

The new next door neighbours had a son, Gary, who was one year older than our Richard and they had a daughter Gemma who was a year old. They too were good neighbours. Gary played with our Richard which was great. Richard and Gary became great friends.

Again we spent a lot of time down bluebell wood and Gary came with us. Richard and Gary played on their bikes too around the cul-de-sac. There weren't many cars in the street. Their bikes had stabilisers on. I sat on our front door step and watched them.

Richard with his first guitar

Two wheeler bikes on stabilisers are not the safest for children to ride on and unfortunately our Richard fell off his bike while turning a corner. He screamed and screamed, which alerted John. I ran to Richard.

"Stop fussing him", John said, "He's just fallen off his bike."

I got to Richard and his bone in his left arm was sticking out. It was a very bad break.

"Get the car". I shouted to John, "We've got to get to the hospital." John got the car and off we went at speed. A&E was so much better in those days because when a child entered the department he was immediately seen to.

Richard was given pain killers and prepared for X-ray and then sent to the children's ward. After a short while he was operated on and the bone in his arm reset. When he got back to the ward his bed was next to his school friend Alan Clark, who lived on the front street in Sacriston.

"Hello Alan, what are you in hospital for?" I said to him.

"I've been run over again."

"Again?" I asked.

"Yes I'm always getting run over."

Richard recovered well and six weeks later got his plaster removed from his arm.

Another baby

Well, do you know what happened next? I became pregnant again. Richard was 4 by now, and I'd loved every minute of the Richard's four years so I thought I'd like to do that again. Plus I really enjoyed being pregnant.

I blossomed and bloomed again!!! I must have looked the picture of health because I felt it.

There were a few of my neighbours pregnant at the same time as me. Something again in the water or even in the air!

My next door neighbour at the other side, Julie was pregnant, as was Janet who lived at the back of us, also Linda who lived six doors away and Lyn who was Linda's neighbour. We met up during the day comparing our pregnancies and having coffee together. I always thought, "I'm never going to waddle." In fact we all said that we weren't going to waddle. Oh yes we all waddled. Big time. I suppose seeing us all walk up to the school to collect our children, looked quite funny. Like geese waddling around a farm yard.

One night the water mains burst and water gushed and gushed from the top of the estate. The houses were built on the hillside of the valley. So the water ran down the hillside rushing through people's houses flooding them.

"Have all your waters broke at once!" shouted someone.

I still worked around the clubs up to a fortnight before I gave birth. I had to because it was survival. Again we changed the show by taking out the quick changes and this time I said to John that I wasn't keen on riding me bike. So that was taken out of the show.

Superman was very popular; the film had just been released. So I made our Richard a superman outfit. I got some blue little girl tights, red little girl's knickers, a jumper and a cloak which was a red slip cut up the seam and fitted over his head. It looked great. Our Richard loved it. Our Daniel had one too, which our Eileen had made. Our Eileen was outside her front door talking to her neighbour. Daniel ran up the stairs and onto his bedroom window which was open. Daniel was in his Superman outfit.

"Mammy I'm Superman, watch I can fly."

"Daniel!!! Noooo!!!!" shouted our Eileen. A neighbour talked to him from his open window while our Eileen ran up to his bedroom. He didn't jump!!!

It was soon time for the birth and I had been so well during the pregnancy. One day I said to Marjorie my next door neighbour:

"Can you look after our Richard because I'm going into hospital?"

"Oh Brenda of course. Good Luck. Don't worry about Richard he'll be fine."

I'd told Richard that he was going to get a baby brother or baby sister. I think he was looking forward to it. He never said anything. I just assumed he knew there was something in my tummy.

I was sure I was going to have a girl. I had several girls' names picked but nothing definite. John wasn't bothered.

I decided to have an epidural, (I wasn't going through that pain again). This time I was booked in for delivery only. When I had Richard five years previous I was in hospital for ten days.

I got to the labour ward and was directed to the delivery room and I got on the bed. The midwife and I chatted.

"Why don't you try and breathe through the birth?" she asked.

"No way. Breath through the birth, I don't think so", I told her.

The consultant came to see me in the delivery room and asked:

"Do you mind if we film the birth?"

"Why no, do what you like, I have no objections." I said.

I thought that someone would come in with a little Kodak brownie. Oh no a whole film crew came in with the whole shebang.

It was, "lights, camera and action". I thought to myself that I couldn't believe that this was happening. The crew were all young students too. I don't think I was looking my best.

When the anaesthetist came into the delivery room he said,

"Do you know you've just got me out of the pub?" This was all I needed. I hope he knew where to put the needle. I had visions of him holding the needle with his hand wavering trying to focus.

Anyway I was in full labour and the pains were bloody hurting. I screamed to the film director:

"You don't mind if I don't smile at this point". I didn't know if they were going to be there for the long haul and were taking their lights and cameras to another mother in labour. I couldn't have cared less. I also couldn't have cared if it was going to be shown on News at Ten, with Trevor McDonald.

The anaesthetist must have hit the spot because yes and few hours later I painlessly gave birth. The midwife and I were chatting away for ages.

"Brenda I'll just check how you're progressing. Oh my goodness the baby is on its way." About a quarter of an hour later I gave birth. The midwife put the baby on my tummy and said, "You have a wonderful baby boy."

"No. Eeeh well that's lovely. I thought I was having a girl. Another boy. Brilliant." Immediately I thought that having another boy would be great company for Richard.

I, of course, had another appointment with a set of stirrups and Cosmo Smallpiece, together with his needle and cotton.

My new baby boy was taken and put into the nursery until I was nice and tidy and on the ward with all the other new mammies. I had trouble sleeping and asked one of the nurses if she could give me something to help me sleep as I'd been awake all night giving birth. I thought she'd give me some sort of wonder drug. She gave me a cup of drinking chocolate.

John wasn't present at the birth again. He sent his apologies!

Another lovely baby son

PETER WILLIAM WOODS was born 19th September 1984 at 8.00am. Peter William was 7lb 7ozs.

When Richard and his Dad came to see the baby, I was sat again on a rubber ring! Baby was in the perspex cot fast asleep and John lifted Richard for him to see his new baby brother. I said to him, "What are we going to call your baby brother, Richard?"

"Peter." He said that if it was a baby girl the name would be Jane. The name, of course, came from the Peter and Jane books. We had no names picked for a boy so Peter it was.

Later that day John came back to the hospital with Richard to take Peter home with us. The nurse carried Peter to our car I got in the back of the car with Richard next to me and the nurse passed baby Peter to me. We drove back to our home in Sacriston.

Marjorie was there with a bouquet of flowers.

"Did it hurt Brenda?" she asked.

"Why no, I had an epidural."

I kept Richard off school for a week for him to get know his baby brother. We were now a lovely unit. It was brilliant!!!

I breast fed again. I enjoyed the experience; it was the right temperature, it was free and available at all times with no preparation at all. Peter was a pleasure and Richard helped by getting nappies for me. He was also more independent in that he could dress himself and put his own shoes on, which was a great help.

I got back to work two weeks after Peter was born. I felt fantastic. Marjorie was ever so good, so very kind and babysat for us.

Again I told agents that I would work but only perform one spot so that meant I could put the two boys to bed and I would get back home by 10.30pm. It wasn't too late for Marjorie either, because she had her two children Gary and Gemma to see to.

Peter, two days old, with his brother Richard

Another New Addition

John and I got a booking at a pub in Thornaby. We went down really well and at the end of the night the stewardess of the pub brought a box out and put it on top of the bar. I looked inside and there was a puppy. She said that it was the last pup and if no one would have it the pup was going to be put to sleep or drowned. I was horrified and said to John that we could have the puppy. I don't think John was bothered. But I do think he was thinking of the extra work involved in having a puppy as well as two children.

We took the puppy home. I said to Richard the next

morning that there was a surprise waiting for him downstairs. He couldn't wait to see what it was. He was elated when he saw the puppy.

"Mammy a puppy." He was jumping up and down.

"What are we going to call her?" I asked Richard

"Mary." said Richard. I thought it was going to be Jane, after the Peter and Jane books seeing that's how Peter got his name.

She was lovely and everyone loved Mary. She was a cross between a wirehaired fox terrier, a bearded collie and fifty-five other varieties.

She never had a lead and always walked alongside of me, as young as she was.

One day I thought I'll walk to the shops, take Peter and of course our Mary. Mary sat outside Norman's shop next to the pram. I came out of the shop and Mary and I walked back home.

Well when we got back home I said to Mary, "I'm sure I've forgotten something." Oh aye I'd left Peter in his pram outside Norman's shop. Mary and I ran like hell back to the shop to get the pram and, of course, Peter. Fortunately Peter and the pram were still there. We had a casual walk back.

Our Peter, to this day, says he's been scarred by that experience!!!

"Yes Mam you left me outside a shop in me pram and went back home. You took the dog but left me."

Mary even had her own seat in the big four wheel drive car. Her seat was the vanity box between the driver's seat and the passenger seat. I called it her perch.

"Come on Mary get on your perch."

During the day she came everywhere with us in the car sitting proud on her own seat.

176

Mary the dog, with Richard, Catherine and
Daniel with Peter

Opening a Shop or Two

Our street was great. All the girls in the street, who were
pregnant when I was, all had baby boys. So we had a street
full of boys.

Peter was a very good baby and Richard thought he was
great. Richard was in the Cub Scouts and I helped out with
the group. I always took Peter with me on hikes, and on all
the activities I joined in with. John would be at home
watching the television.

John got frustrated just sitting at home and wanted to
start a business. I've always been of the opinion that you
should do what you are best at.

Well after a lot of thought we came up with the idea of
opening a Marks and Spencer seconds shop. We did
research and knew where we could get the stock.

I went to see the Bank Manager and he was willing to

lend us £2000 to open the shop and stock it. It wasn't much but we were willing to give it a go.

We found an empty shop in a small village called Langley Moor. John set about decorating the shop, carpeting it, dressing the window in a way to entice customers into the shop. There were other items to buy such as a till, security, and of course mirrors.

I'd not long had Peter. John wanted to run the shop and I said I'd look after the boys and when he wanted more stock I'd go to collect it. I have such a big mouth for a little person.

John built a cubicle for the ladies to change in and try the clothes on. Then we got the stock on the hangers then on the stands. We'd spent all the £2000. John loved going to the shop. Some days I'd take John to the shop so that I could use the car to go shopping in and get new stock.

It was like juggling soot. I took Richard to school. I had to be back in Sacriston to pick him up at 3 pm. I was also breast feeding Peter. He'd have his naps in the car while I was dashing here and there. I wished at times that I had said to John that I would look after the shop. It would have been a doddle.

Some days John said he needed the car. By this time we had a big Datsun Patrol and it was bright orange. We were noted by our Patrol car. On the days John needed the car I had to get the bus with Peter in a baby buggy. Sometimes I had the shopping on the handles of the buggy and when I lifted Peter out I forgot about the shopping and the buggy would tip over. I'm sure reading this all you ladies have had this happen. It was awful, especially if it was raining or snowing.

I carried shopping on the bus and had to work my day around feeding Peter too. He was a good boy and I'm sure he realised I was harassed to hell. We were still entertaining in the clubs at weekends.

The shop didn't do too well, so I came up with the idea of

selling the clothes around the clubs. I rang a few clubs and asked if they would be interested in holding a fashion show. I told them I would deal with all the publicity. All they would have to do was let us have the room.

We got Janet, one of the girls who was pregnant at the same time as me and lived nearby and another girl called Christine who I knew from nursery. They became our models.

The first show was very, very funny. The 'models' were in the dressing room and I was compere. I announced them and they came out modelling the clothes.

One outfit Christine was wearing when she came out on the 'catwalk' was a bit tight and a button shot off her trousers and hit a lady sitting in the front row. Christine started giggling as did the audience. There was always a good turnout of ladies in the audience. The club was happy and we were happy because we were selling the clothes or should I say getting rid of them. That was the whole point of the fashion shows - trying to break even.

We'd given up the shop so we didn't have the overheads. We got more stock in because the fashion shows were popular. We were still working in the clubs doing our show. It was very hard work, but I suppose enjoyable.

The fashion shows lasted about 6 months in the clubs and then we packed them in. We were doing about one a week.

John was still wanting to start another business and scouring the papers for some other business to start up. We didn't have the money and would have to get another loan.

I was just happy doing the act and looking after and playing with the boys. I was also organising charity evenings for our Richard's school in order to raise money for the school funds. John was bored during the day.

A shop came up for sale in Edmondsley, about a mile

away. It was a general dealers and apart from the post office it was the only shop in the village so John thought it would be a success.

I went to see the bank manager and again he gave us the money to buy stock. Here we go again.

When Richard was at school Peter and I would go to mother and baby groups and have a chat and coffee with other mams. I told John it was too much for me to get the stock for this shop and look after the children.

We were performing at one club and a man asked if I wanted to buy a Renault car for £70.

"Has it got wheels?

"Yes and it's taxed and tested."

"No it hasn't."

"Yes it has," he told me. So, I bought it and gave him the £70 and drove away with a 1960 bright pink hatchback Renault 4. It was brilliant so I christened her Pinky.

The gear stick was mounted on the dashboard. I loved it and I loved being independent because John needed the Datsun Patrol for the shop for getting the stock.

The winters were always bad because Sacriston was built on a hillside. John was fine getting to the shop in the Patrol because it was four wheel drive. 'Pinky' the Renault wasn't, so often I was grounded and had to walk everywhere with the pram, getting the shopping in locally. It was hard work pushing a pram in the snow. I know we had a general dealers shop, but I could buy the food cheaper in Sacriston than get it out of our shop!!

We had the shop in Edmondsley for about a year and made a loss so John sold it for what the stock was worth. Back to where we were again. Just as well we still had our show to fall back on.

A Husky Voice

Now our Peter, he would be about 1 year old. Julie Hopps, she lived next door at the other side, she had a son, Anthony, who was one month younger than our Peter. She said to me one day:

"Brenda have you noticed your Peter's voice? I think it sounds a bit husky." Well I'd never noticed it until then and yes he did have a bit of a husky voice when I listened to him talk.

I made an immediate appointment at the doctors. He got a specialist's appointment immediately. We saw the specialist and he said that he was going to look down Peter's throat.

Our appointment was for the Saturday afternoon of that week. Oh dear, Peter had to have no food. They could have made the appointment for the morning.

Keeping Peter entertained all morning without food was not easy. At this time we had a baby sitter who lived in the village, which was handy. She'd come over to our's. I'd lie with Peter and Richard until they went off to sleep. Then off John and I would go to work.

The specialist examined Peter's throat and said he had laryngitis. His throat was inflamed and was I leaving him crying or screaming? NO WAY! I never left my boys upset. He said that someone was. Oh dear, it was the baby sitter. I was devastated that Peter was being left to cry.

When the advert for the NSPCC comes on the television I can't watch it. We got rid of the babysitter. John and I cut down on the amount of work we were doing and when we did work, the boys went to Grandma and Granda's.

An awful time so let's move on!

John still loved his television. We never went to the cinema because John always said that the film would eventually end up on the television. We had a VHS video now.

I always bought plenty of blank tapes for the films to be recorded over the Christmas period. Our Peter was learning to walk and on Christmas Eve he balanced himself against the screen of the tele – no nappy. I was potty training him, and what did he do? He weed in the video player! Oh dear. I tried to grab Peter before he did it. Too late was the cry. Not a happy Daddy. No recording good films, shops shut, no repair men working.

Not a Happy Christmas for John. Oh heck!! It was a brilliant Christmas for the boys.

Our Richard

During the school summer holidays the council held different activities for the children to get involved in; tennis, cycling, swimming and ice hockey. Durham used to have an ice rink which I frequented in my teens.

Richard wanted to go on the ice hockey course. I took him every day and he loved it. He was so good, he got an award for being the most improved player and his picture was in the Northern Echo. He was smitten.

He played in the garden with a hockey kit we made up from stuff which we had in the attic; the hockey shirt was an old jumper of John's. John made him a hockey stick. The helmet was a toy motorbike helmet and John made the puck out of wood.

So as something special for Christmas we got him a pair of ice hockey boots. We couldn't get the right size, but on Christmas morning I would say Santa was trying to find the right size for him and would send them later.

Richard got his ice hockey boots and understood that Santa would be sending him his size later on in the week and Peter played with the box. Once this happened we went skating every day during the Christmas holidays. I booked in a few skating lessons for him. Richard was loving it. I also took him to an ice hockey match; Durham Ice Rink had its own team they were called the Wasps. They were very good. There was also a junior team called the Midges and Richard wanted to join. He was still playing in the garden with his pretendy hockey outfit. His skating was improving so I talked it over with John and he agreed that he could join the Midges.

Richard and I went to a practice and just watched. As members of the Midges got older, there was always kit for sale such as shirts and shorts, so we got him second hand shorts, a shirt, gloves and we borrowed a helmet and hockey stick. We packed it all up in a large bag I had in the loft. Richard was ecstatic.

He went to practice once a week. I'd take Peter along with us. He enjoyed watching the lads practice.

A friend of mine, called Carol Kears, her two sons were in the Midges too, so that was nice. Once the practice was over Peter used to have a skate on the ice on skates that had two blades with me holding on to him. He loved it too.

Mind hockey was very fast, very competitive and dangerous. Richard got better and he got on really well with all the other members of the team and the leaders. Richard was asked to be on the team but in the reserves. When he was asked he could hardly speak with excitement.

Sometimes he would get on the ice I always worried because the other lads were older and bigger and ice hockey is quite an aggressive game, but Richard held his own and always got a great cheer from the spectators. Eventually he got on the team.

The team had away matches, which was awkward because John and I had work in the clubs to go to. This is where Grandma Audrey helped out and went with Richard. She was very kind. She always said,

"By it's cold at those ice rinks."

Sometimes there were practises held at 6:00 in the morning. Ugh, I'm not a morning person but I did it. John stayed in bed with our Peter.

My Organising Skills

I organised egg and spoon races and sack races, which were held at the end of our cul-de-sac on the football field. On special national days of celebration I'd organise street parties. Going back as far as the Royal Wedding of Charles and Diana, we had a street party where everyone in the street supplied the food. John got dressed up as Charles. We made a Charles mask from a cutting out of a newspaper and I got dressed as Diana in her wedding dress. I didn't need a mask because I had my veil (net curtain) over my face. I bet you thought I was going to say I didn't need a mask because I looked like Lady Diana.

I organised fun runs for all the children on our estate. I bought medals for every child because it wasn't a competition, everyone was a winner. It was lovely to see all the children enjoying themselves and I loved it when I awarded them their medals.

I held charity shows for different organisations, for example, the local schools and children's clubs. They all needed money to help them survive and get essential equipment and toys for the children of Sacriston.

I was always on the streets selling raffle tickets or tickets for a forthcoming show I was organising. I'd walk around the streets in fancy dress to promote the event. It was really good and I enjoyed it so much. I took the local children and my own two boys swimming, running, climbing hills, in fact everywhere.

I was never out of the local newspapers publicising whichever event I was arranging. I organised the Sacriston fun run, which was a run for all the children of the village instead of just our estate. There was no entrance fee; I just needed the child's name so that I knew how many children would be running.

I got roads closed with Police permission and they were involved too. I had St. John's Ambulance there in case of any injuries. We had water stations, all manned by parents. We had a starting point and of course we had a finishing line.

The streets were lined with supporters. It was brilliant. Again, every child got a medal and a certificate. I suppose if I still lived in Sacriston I would be still organising the Sacriston Fun Run.

Our dining room table, which was also used as a table tennis table, was full of tickets, begging letters to companies asking for items to either raffle or auction for the next charity event I was organising. Life was full.

Marie Raincock, the niece of Marjorie Atkinson who used to live next door to us, contracted meningitis. Richard was just a year younger than Marie. I wanted to help her family because Marie was in Newcastle hospital critically ill and her Mam and Dad had no car to get there on a regular basis.

I held a charity show at Witton Gilbert Club and we raised £1000 in one night for Marie. I handed the money over to her Mam and Dad. I thought they could maybe buy a secondhand car with the money, or something to help Marie.

I heard, about a couple of weeks later that Marie was making progress, but that she would be in hospital for some time. We couldn't have raised the money without the help and support from the people of Sacriston and Witton Gilbert.

I helped organise the first Sacriston Carnival. After a lot of research I got the White Helmets, the motor cycle display team from the Royal Marines, to entertain with their riding skills on the school field. They rode through fire, jumped great heights and had about 10 riders balancing on one another all on one bike. They were very good. The spectators loved them. They had seen them on the television and here they were in Sacriston. Everyone commented on how good they were. I just hoped that none of the children copied their stunts while on their bicycles. We had dancers, judo displays and gymnastics. All run to a tight timetable and we had programmes printed for the visitors to the carnival.

Each committee member had a job or volunteered for it. One printed the programmes, one was treasurer, one took the minutes of the meeting, one knew someone who had a jumpy castle, so they organised that.

I was the gofer. Go for this, go for that and go for the other. I was the co-ordinator. I attended the committee meetings and presented the names and telephone numbers of acrobats, judo display teams, rodeo bulls and lots of other acts and had the job of booking it all. I didn't mind.

All the pubs, clubs and shops were all involved in the day. I got wagons with flat trailers from local firms and the village schools, scout group including cubs and other organisations of the village were on the 'floats' dressed in the theme of their choice.

We had the Sacriston brass band leading the wagons in a convoy driving slowly up the front street, which was crowded with people. Everyone was waving and cheering. Bunting was hung across the street lights. All the children were given flags to wave as the procession drove past.

The procession of wagons, followed by the villagers all made their way to the comprehensive school, called Fyndoune, where the carnival was held.

We had jugglers, face painters, rodeo bull rides, and rides for the little ones, jumpy castles and coconut shies. There were cake stalls, homemade wine stalls. Every kind of stall you could think of.

We also had a balloon race. The day took some organising but what a brilliant time was had by all.

Of course, we had to be up so early to get to the school to welcome the White Helmet Display Team and advise them as to which field they were to perform their display in and to direct stallholders as to where to position their stalls.

There was a lot of liaising going on and in those days there was no mobile phones and we couldn't afford those walkie talkie radio handsets so it was usually me running from one area to another making sure everything was ready and on cue.

I was running up and down the street making sure the wagons were all ready and everyone was on their appropriate wagon. I knew I wouldn't be on the wagon on that evening. I was teetotal, but I would need a drink after the day was over.

I was here there every bloody where. People would ask questions and everyone's answer would be, "Oh you'd better see Brenda. She'll know." I even compered the gymnastics.

"Just give me a broom, I'll stick it up my backside and sweep up while I'm on," I said

All the organisers were exhausted but we still had some energy left because there was an evening of entertainment on the Carnival night.

John and I did a show and during the act I sang a song where I changed the words of the Benny Hill hit   'Ernie '. My song was all about prominent figures of the community of Sacriston, people who everyone in the village knew. It was called "Colin" and he Drove the Fastest van in the Sacriston". Colin had the florist shop in the village. The evil looking man was 'Nutty Norm' and he drove old Kelly's van. That was Norman Kelly from the Mace shop.

Both of them, in the song, loved a woman named Fran she lived alone in Lingley Close and she always wanted a man.

They said she was too good for them she was lovely shy
and sleek but Colin got his cocoa there 3 times every week.
She said she'd love a bunch of roses he said, "Alright
sweetheart." And when he finished work one night he
loaded up his van. He said, "Do you want them cellophaned
'cos cellophaned is good." She said, "Colin I don't mind if
they're covered all in mud." And that tickled old Colin.

It went down very well with the audience that night. The
carnival day was the talk of the village for a long time and
everyone said how much they had enjoyed themselves. It
was a fabulous family day out.

My Mam, had had a heart attack and in A&E they had no
defibrillator. They had to get one from Intensive Care. Well
how many patients who'd suffered a heart attack had died?
Well my Mam fortunately didn't but I set about to raise
money for Dryburn Hospital's A&E to get them a defibrillator.

I also helped out at the Infants school: coffee mornings,
painting skirting boards, sanding floors, in fact anything. I'd
do anything to help out. Peter was in the Infants so it meant
I saw him a lot of the time. Richard was in the Junior school;
I was involved with the Juniors but just with the fund raising
and, of course, I was on the governing body as Chairperson
and so I had a lot of meetings to attend too.

John, my husband just let me get on with what I was
happy doing and that was organising things for the village of
Sacriston and helping people. I loved it. Some months later
he did have his beard shaved off for fund raising for the
Infants school.

My family

The boys in the street who were born in the same year as our Peter were growing up nicely. It was lovely because they all grew up and played together; they eventually learned to swim together, learned to ride bikes and started school together.

Richard was now in the Scouts and I became a Scout Leader. Peter came everywhere with us. Carol Kears and Val Wilkinson took turns in holding Peter while I went canoeing, rafting or even abseiling with the Scouts.

Peter behaved really well and everyone loved him. I loved it too because my two boys were with me. Richard enjoyed the Scouts but didn't stay very long. I enjoyed it while he was there because it brought back memories of my Guiding years.

I used to make costumes for Halloween out of black bin-liners. I used mud as make-up for their faces, as well as my own stage makeup. We didn't have the money to do anything else.

Every autumn we collected conkers. On a lovely crisp day I said to the boys,

"I'll get you some conkers today whilst you are at school." I went down to the County Hospital, now a mental institution, as there was a wonderful conker tree in the grounds. I was kicking the dead leaves around when a man came up to me and said, "What are you doing?"

"I'm looking for conkers," I said.

"I've got two in my pocket. Do you want to see them?" I made a hasty retreat.

Richard, Peter and I went conkering at the weekends at various locations and got carrier bags full. It was great. I still love conkering to this very day and so do the boys.

We never had holidays abroad; we couldn't afford it. I used to say to my boys when we were down the wood I'd build a camp.

"You can be anywhere in the world down here." Yes. We'd build Tarzan swings. Richard fell off one and broke his arm!! I knew it was bad when a young lad carried him back to our house. I looked at his arm and the bone was pushing its way out. Oh dear, Dryburn Hospital here we come again.

He had to be operated on, there and then, for the bone to be reset. I waited patiently sitting next to his bed in the children's ward waiting for him to return from his operation. While I was sitting there, another young lad was wheeled in and do you know who it was? It was Alan, the young boy who was in the last time Richard had broken his arm. I said to him,

"Hello Alan how are you?"

"I'm not very well Brenda, I've been run over again." Poor lad. I bet he had notches on his headboard of his bed as to how many times he'd been run over just so that he could keep count.

Our Mary

I went looking for our Richard one day and I went to the house of one of his friends, and of course Mary came with me. When the door opened, their big dog shot out and attacked our Mary by ramming into her. It really hurt her and she limped back home.

I took her to the vets and they x-rayed her. The vet explained to me that the knock had damaged her spine and it was inoperable. He suggested she should be put to sleep. I couldn't believe what he was saying. Our Mary was here with me lying on a bed under sedation and a vet was telling me she was going to die. She'd been a very big part of our lives and everybody's. Me Mam and Dad's, our Eileen's and her family and all the neighbours, everyone loved Mary.

Eeeh she was lovely. Memories of her passed through my mind.

During the winter when it was snowing she used to pull the boys on the sledge. She protected the boys and went everywhere with them. One day sniffing Richard's scent, she made her way up to the school and went into the school play yard. Richard's teacher, Mrs. Robson had said,

"There's a dog in the yard. Does it belong to any of you?" Richard had apparently denied it. He was probably too shy to say anything.

Mary went on holiday with us in our caravan and played in the sand on the beach with the boys. She travelled with me in the patrol car; her seat was right next to me while I was driving.

Our Eileen never wanted any pets. They never had a dog but she regularly borrowed Mary and she'd stay a few days at our Eileen's house.The same with me Mam and Dad. Mary loved me Mam's Yorkshire puddings and me Mam always made an extra Sunday dinner for Mary.

My Dad used to cut Mary's hair and she always ended up looking like a Bedlington terrier. When she'd been staying at me Mam and Dad's I knew Mary would come back home with a new hair style. Sometimes she would come back home looking like a poodle, pompoms and all.

On a visit to Holy Island with me Mam and Dad, Mary ran into a field full of tall grass. When she reappeared she was green. She was literally covered from head to toe in stickle jacks, which I think are seeds. She looked so funny and it took us ages to get the seeds out of her hair. In the end my Dad cut her hair to get rid of them.

We holidayed in Whitby every year in the caravan and we all loved it, including Mary. They were good times. Peter had a pair of Doc Martin boots. Would he take them off? No! He even wore them with his swimming trunks.

We had an inflatable dinghy and in Whitby we used to

stay in a little cove called Saltwick Bay. In fact it's the same place our Eileen and I used to holiday in a caravan with our parents. Anyway the sea was always very calm and we had life jackets and John would take the boys and, of course, Mary out in the dinghy.

We'd also make a campfire on the beach and have our dinner there. Mary would run into the sea with the boys and together they would have a brilliant time.

Whitby has a Jurassic coastline. We went fossil hunting and still do to this day, just like conkering. I have kept all the fossils and they have become my treasures.

We also went on holiday one year to Bournemouth at a Haven park. The weather was great and the boys and I spent a lot of the time in the pool and went horse riding.

But the best activity I enjoyed and I'm sure the boys did was crabbing on the quayside. I bought the boys a crab line and they lowered it into the murky water. I told them to be gentle and not to tug on it and just let the crabs attach themselves to the line. It worked brilliantly. Then the hard job was to get the crabs into the bucket of water. Actually, the bucket wasn't big enough. We could have done with a pail! They caught hundreds and the sight of them scurrying about when the bucket got tipped over caused quite a scene. Passers-by stopped to watch them. When the crabs went back into the water Richard and Peter once again set about catching more. Probably the same ones. The crabs probably thought, "Oh here we go again."

Another dog

When I got back home from the vets without Mary it was so very hard for me to tell the boys that Mary had died. It was very sad. The boys cried for days, so I thought we must get another dog. It might make loosing Mary a bit easier for the boys. Mary couldn't be replaced but we were used to having a dog.

My Dad rang me and said that there was a dog running around Bowburn and he thought it was a stray. I went over to Bowburn and told the village police that I would have her. They said that I could have her if I could catch her. Apparently she was a bit of a wild one.

She was a Jack Russell dog and I eventually caught her and took her home to show the boys. We called her Tebby because that was the only word she seemed to recognise. We didn't know what her original name was so we tried all sorts of words and names to see if she responded to any so Tebby was the word.

She was wild, nothing like our Mary. One night Tebby was circling round and round as if she was going to have a whoopsie on the carpet.

"Take her out on her lead along the field and see if she does anything." I said to John.

"On his return he said, "No she's done nothing." Do you know she went behind the chair and she gave birth to one puppy? That's what was wrong; she was trying to give birth and I sent her out with John for a walk. That was the last thing she wanted to do. Poor Tebby.

We called the puppy Poppy. Tebby occasionally escaped from our house if the door had been left open by mistake. She would have been roaming around the wood and obviously met up with a boy dog.

Poppy was a Jack Russell crossed with whippet. Jack Russell body and whippet legs; She couldn't half run!! Anyway Poppy the puppy was born. So now we had two dogs, Tebby and Poppy. Tebby was still a bit hyper and Poppy copied her mother so they were very mischievous.

One day Tebby got out and ran away. We never saw her again. We never found out what happened to her. We posted signs up on telegraph posts asking if anyone should find her to return her to us, but we never heard anything.

It's Magic

At this time to make more money I became a children's entertainer (magician), not a very good one I hasten to add. Clive Webb told me what tricks to buy, one was a dovepan.

I advertised myself as a magician in places such as the swimming baths of local villages, post offices, doctors' surgeries and local shops. In fact, anywhere where there were plenty of people.

I also rang agents and work started to come in. I entertained at children's Christmas parties, at schools and even in the social clubs. There was plenty of work and the money wasn't bad.

I received a call from Olly at Air's office in Spennymoor (agents). Olly asked if I could come to their house and entertain his two boys.

"Well Yes." I said. "Can I bring my two boys too?"

"Yes of course," Olly said. I thought to myself, "Um, no hamster." Molly the hamster had just died. I used Molly the hamster in one of my tricks. I also used to let the children hold Molly. They loved it. Because she had died, I thought about what I could put into the dove pan instead of Molly. Then it came to me, I'd use Poppy the puppy.

I packed everything and put Poppy in the basket. The boys got in the car and off we went to Olly's house.

When we got to Olly's house all the children were sitting nicely on the floor. They were young, aged from three years to six years old. I started setting the magic tricks up. I put Poppy in the lid of the dove pan (it's a trick) she was still very tiny. The children couldn't see what I was doing.

Whilst setting up I thought, "Oh no I've no lighter fuel to bake the cake." I asked Olly if he had any lighter fuel.

"No" he said, "but I've got some petrol."

"Aww that'll do," I said.

I started the show and did a few tricks with ribbons and dice. Then I said to the children,

"We're going to bake a cake --- Ooooohhhhhh." I started making the cake, putting flour, eggs, milk etc in the pan.

"Now boys and girls we're going to bake the cake." A lot of Ooooooooooohs and AAAAAAAAAhhhhhhhs at this point in order to get an atmosphere!!!

"Get the petrol." I said to Olly. Upon which I poured it into the pan and lit it. Well it was like bonfire night. Some of the petrol dripped on to the carpet which caught fire. I jumped up and down on the carpet and then my sock caught fire. Olly ran in with a bucket of water to put the fire out on the carpet and me out!!!! He threw the bucket of water over me. It was total mayhem. There was plenty of noise from Olly, well he was shouting and his wife Ann she was shouting. I was shouting, "Me sock's on fire."

All the children just sat there quietly watching an inferno. Probably thinking, "Ohhh this is a different type of magic show." Then I thought POPPY!!! Poppy the puppy was still in the pan. I quickly got her out of the pan. She came out of the ordeal unscathed and the children gave her a round of applause!!!! And for my next trick!!!

I packed the magic in after that.

Not a Good Day

That same day my Mam had a heart attack. I was coming back home, and as I turned in to our estate, another car was turning out and we clipped each other. He knocked the front of my car; in fact it just broke the front driver's side indicator. I knocked his back driver's side side-light. I said that it was knock for knock, but the driver of the other car had other ideas. He said that it was my fault and he said he had witnesses.

"Where" I asked? He said that his mate would have seen it as he was always looking out of his lounge window. He lived opposite. On getting out of his car he took a piece of chalk from his top pocket and proceeded to mark around where my tyres were on the road.

"Well it's obvious you've done this before." I said to him. He wasn't amused. I went back home and told John. He went straight down to the man's house to have a word with him but it made no difference. He got a full re-spray out of me. Oh what a day.

My Mam survived the heart attack. She had a pacing wire inserted into her heart. She was in hospital for about 2 weeks. When I told me Mam about the magic show she laughed and laughed. They say, "Laughter is a good medicine."

Just very recently I went into a shop to get my microphone mended. I asked the lady behind the counter whether it could be repaired, and if so when it would be ready.

"Oh it'll be ready tomorrow." She said.

"Do you want my name?"

"Oh no, I know who you are. You're Brenda who set fire to my Uncle Olly's carpet." At the time of talking to her she would be about 35 years old!

"Oh," I said, "Were you traumatised by what happened?"

"No, but I think Uncle Olly was." What a reputation I have!

More Pets

Apart from hamsters as pets we had two goldfish, two hens, two dogs, a rabbit called Roger and a guinea pig called Wendy. The hens laid our fresh eggs. The rabbit, hamster and guinea pig were house animals and the hens roamed the garden but if the patio door was open they'd pop into the house too. Yes, we had free range eggs delivered to our door personally.

I got the hens from old Joe, who was in his nineties, he lived two doors away from us and he bred hens. He was only too happy to give me two of his Silkies.

Oh and at one time we had a white tame rat. John drew the line to the rat running around the house.

Roger the rabbit sometimes appeared in our show, Krack and Dorn. John used to do the trick where he'd put Roger in a box, wave the magic wand, and then drop the four sides of the box until it was flat. Roger wasn't keen and he got a bit too fat for the box. Many a time, after John took the applause and was walking off the stage, Roger would stick his head out of the sides of the flat box. I thought it was funny but John said it was embarrassing. So the trick got dropped using Roger the rabbit.

Music to my Ears

Richard came in from school one day and said,
"I'm going to play the clarinet."

"Oh that's great," I said. A week or so went by and I never heard anything about Richard learning to play the clarinet.

I was Chairperson of the Governors of both schools, Infants and Juniors. So I rang the Head Teacher of the Juniors and told him the story about Richard. He said that he would look into it. He came back to me and said that Richard had heard the clarinet being played in school and had walked into the classroom and had said to the teacher that he'd like to play the clarinet.

Well Richard, as I have mentioned, was a very, very shy

197

boy and it must have taken a lot of courage for him to walk into another classroom and speak to a teacher.

Both of my boys during their childhood were shy and very well behaved. Anyway the Head Teacher rang me and said that Richard hadn't been selected for musical instrument tuition, but that the clarinet teacher was prepared to give Richard a chance and gave him a clarinet to borrow.

I wonder how many more children missed out of playing an instrument because of that test. Richard was a lucky one. I don't think the exam exists now which is just as well.

Richard took to the clarinet like a fish to water and so did Poppy (you remember Poppy, the Jack Russell crossed with a whippet). When Richard practiced his clarinet in the house, which was most nights after school, Poppy used to sing along with him, her head held back, you get the picture? AaaaawwwoooooooAaaawwwwwooooAaaaaawwwooooooooo. That was Stranger on the Shore by Acker Bilk!!!

John used to shout up "Will you all stop that racket?" Huh I don't think so, that's our son learning his trade, a budding superstar!! And Poppy was too.

I bought Richard his own clarinet. He passed grade after grade and was in the District Wind Band and County Wind Band.

In our house we always had instruments in the dining room, for example, a drum kit, a keyboard, clarinet and guitar. We were popular with the neighbours! Well Julie next door never complained.

I recorded Richard playing Stranger on the Shore with Peter announcing and dedicating it to Granda Alfie, Grandma Cathy and Grandma Audrey. Whenever I hear Stranger on the Shore played on the clarinet it always makes me cry. Nice memories.

Life in the Street

We had sold the shop at Edmondsley by this time so John was back in the house in his chair watching the television or in the garage. Peter loved being in the garage with his Dad, making boxes for our sound equipment or props, just I suppose, generally tinkering on.

Richard and Peter both ice skated. Richard had his hockey and Peter did speed skating. They were both excellent swimmers too. I used to stitch their badges onto their swimming trunks every time they came rushing home telling me they'd passed another swimming test. They both got their two-mile certificates.

Richard and Peter loved their bikes too and went cycling with Granda Alfie. My Dad took them all over on their bikes to places where he took Eileen and me when we were little. Still today Richard and Peter go cycling together.

Life was good in the street (Valley View). Everyone got on with each other and we'd help each other out when need be. John and I often had barbeques in our garden. John did all the cooking. We invited everyone in the street as well as all the children. It was brilliant.

The street was home to boys and girls of similar ages and they all got on well together and played in the street or down the wood in all weathers. There was no sitting in front of computers because no-one had one!

Peter

Peter and his friend Anthony, together with Richard used to put on shows in our garden. They'd rehearse the show and have full dress rehearsal. They'd dress up in costumes from our loft. These outfits were from our act but we no longer used them.

They'd go around the estate and sell tickets. The garden was always full of children. Then they'd put on a performance. The curtains of our patio windows acted as the stage curtains where Peter, Anthony would do their quick changes. They wore grass skirts, wigs, dresses and Peter came out as yes....ET. Richard would be dressed as Darth Vader.

The money they made went to the local hospital children's ward. It was a wonderful happy time. They all grew up together.

Eeeh I used to always have a gang of children as well as my own, with me. Sometimes we'd get back to our house from a day out and we'd be all filthy from riding our bikes through all the puddles. It was brilliant fun.

I used to put each child in our bath before I returned them to their parents in one piece. We went on adventures up on the fells and down the wood or at a local park.

I also would hold toy swaps on our front lawn. Children often get fed up of playing with their same old toys, so I'd put up the pasting board we used for decorating and displayed all the toys which Richard and Peter were fed up with. Other children brought their toys too, with their parent's permission, of course.

Although one little lad brought a Tonka truck without asking his Mam and she came running up and said to her son, "Hey you're not swapping that, I paid good money for that toy and you only got it a couple of months ago for Christmas

"But I thought Santa brought it for me," the little lad replied. He wanted to swap it for a Darth Vader laser torch. The little toy swaps on our garden were a great success.

A garden full of children waiting to be entertained by Peter and Anthony

Mother's Day with Peter

At the bottom of the estate there was a small farm with a horse we named Geordie. We used to go and feed him often.

During the winter the ponds used to freeze over and so we'd get our ice boots out and go skating. I still had my own pair of ice skates I had from my teenage years.

In the summer months, down in the wood I would build all the children a camp, one each. It was hard work but worth it. I told them to go and ask their Mammies for some food i.e. beans and bread. I'd build a fire and cook the beans and toast the bread. No-one was poisoned. I'd also black their faces up with charcoal. They went back home at night time dirty and tired but happy.

On a lot of occasions I'd take a car full of children to a place called Hill End in the Dales, which was a magical place. There was nothing there except hills and a river, but we'd climb the hills and look for fluorspar, which years ago had been mined there. We also walked along the river bank, then have a picnic and, of course, feed the sheep. One sheep tried to get into our car. I would have let it, but I thought John wouldn't agree to a sheep living with us. Again we went home totally exhausted, the children and me! I always slept well.

John often had garage clear out days. This is where he would chuck out items he didn't need. I would take it all to the local tip. I always took the boys with me. More often than not I'd take back more than I went with. John used to go mad. He'd say, "What rubbish have you brought back with you this time?" You see he was a chucker outer and I was a hoarder. I never chucked stuff out. My theory is 'it'll come in handy one day', and it usually does.

Peter once asked me, "Mammy where was I when Richard was a baby?" I was quiet for a moment in thought and I was about to reply when Peter said, "I know I was in the loft."

Anyway John knew what I was like, and knowing I was going to bring a load of stuff back with me, well he should have gone to the tip himself. Also at the tip there was always good stuff that people had thrown out: bikes, scooters, skate boards, roller blades, hoola hoops, dolls prams, prams for babies, and buggies for toddlers. Yes, you name it and it was usually there.

The men who worked at the tip had all the items which they could make a bob or two on, all displayed nicely. Our Peter got his very first bike from the tip. I don't think he knew it at the time. He will now, when he reads this.

Bonfire night was always great too. This is another time I asked John to clear the garage out and any rubbish went on the bonfire.

The children of the street would go around the doors asking for anything they could put on the fire. Bonfire night always attracted a good crowd and we made it into quite a party. We adults had a wine or two, or a beer. I'd make a Guy out of John's old clothes and a mask that we no longer used in the act. I remember one year it was Elvis who was on top of the bonfire. Then, of course, the fireworks.I relived my childhood with my children. It was brilliant.

Changes

John and I were still in the double act, but I could tell he was getting fed up. I still loved entertaining. We'd got rid of both the shops and so John did all the cooking and ironing and things. Nowadays, he would be called a 'house-husband'. He said that he didn't mind. I hated housework and loved being involved with my boys. But by this time John was talking about getting a real job. Being a double act and working together I'm sure kept us together.

A job was advertised for a position as manager of a

timber department with a firm called J. G. Archibald in Durham. John applied for the job and was successful. He loved it and settled into the job really well. He liked everyone he worked with, he liked the job and he was happy. It was just what he was looking for. He was no longer happy being in the double act so we talked it over and we both came to a decision.

Next Stage – Brenda Collins

It was decided that I would continue to entertain, but as a comedy vocalist. It was the end of the double act, Krack and Dorn. I felt very sad, but I wanted to carry on and entertain and I knew I could easily put a show together singing and telling jokes in between the songs.

I discussed it with John Wray, an agent. He came up with the name Bette Collins. Well, I didn't like that. My name was Brenda Woods. He said that Woods, which was my married name didn't have the right ring to it.

Anyway I became Brenda Collins. Aye, I was back to singing. My first night was so different. Here I was setting the equipment up on my own. In fact I had to learn how to set the equipment up because John always did it previously. Carrying it up fire escapes was an awful chore too.

If I worked with another act I would sometimes ask them if I could use their equipment just to save me carrying mine in. I'd always buy them a drink if they agreed.

Getting changed in the dressing room on my own and walking out on stage all by myself facing an audience was a new experience.

When I was in the group and in the duo with John, if the night wasn't going too well I could turn to one of the lads or to John. I would say without moving my lips, "I can't wait to get off this stage." Now I had no one to lean on, no one to strike the equipment down with, no one to talk to on the way back home, to discuss the evening's performance.

The only time I'd suffered big time with nerves before I went out on stage was when I was very young, in my teens. I was nervous now; dry mouthed and my heart going ten to the dozen before I went out onto the big lonely stage. If the night was good then it wasn't too bad, but when it was a hard night, it wasn't very good and it was awful driving back home.

I went out entertaining two or three evenings a week. John stayed at home and looked after the boys.

Richard was having piano lessons with Mrs Wadge. I'd leave the money and say to John, "Now don't forget to take Richard to piano lesson." He never took him when I was at work. I always made sure Richard went for his piano lessons as it was important, you see. It wasn't to John.

John and I were drifting apart. I'd get in from a club late at night. John would be in bed because he had to be up early for work the next morning. It's a good true saying, "People who play together stay together." It was obvious the double act kept us together. We were really drifting apart now.

I used to go for morning coffee at Linda Murphy's and also to Lyn's house. I wasn't happy and I don't think John was either. Richard was about 13 or 14 and Peter about 8 years old. I used to say,"John do you want to come with me tonight." "What do I want to come and see you for?" We spent less and less time together. It was very sad. We'd been married for 23 years.

I can joke now and say, "We bought a water bed and drifted apart," but it was true. John found a friend called Jennifer, who also worked at Archibalds', who he could talk to and who he eventually married. My two boys stayed between John and myself.

At this time I was staying at a caravan park near

Durham, called Finchale Abbey. I'd bought an old caravan, but I decorated it and it was alright. The caravan park was beautiful and the boys found plenty of things to do to entertain themselves, like swimming, building Tarzan swings and climbing trees.

My sister Eileen helped me with looking after the boys at weekends when I had to go to work. It wasn't a good time for the boys, John or me, but we got through it.

John was still living in the house at Valley View. However we eventually got round to discussing the future and after that John moved to a nearby village with Jennifer and I was back to Valley View with the boys.

I have wonderful memories of my life in Sacriston and being totally involved with the people of the village.

Me Mam

Me Mam was the driving force during my early years of singing in the chapel and choirs. She was quiet. Not like me Dad. She was always there for when I needed advice.

My Mam had celebrated her 80th birthday and a few months later she wasn't very well. Her toes weren't healing up after a visit from a chiropodist. While cutting her toe nails, he made her big toe bleed. I rang her GP and she was admitted into hospital in Durham.

The boys and I were in Whitby on a little holiday for a couple of days. Our Eileen was on holiday in Turkey.

We asked the Doctor if it was alright for us all to go on holiday. Would me Mam be alright? The Doctor said it was fine and assured us they would take care of her. The hospital did lots and lots of tests. Me Mam was very chirpy.

She had a brilliant sense of humour. I'm sure I got my sense of humour from me Mam. She always had lots of visitors while she was in hospital. I visited Mam everyday while Eileen was abroad.

One day I went she was very upset. Something was very wrong. She was always chatting with the other patients. This day was different. I went to see the nurse and she said that the Registrar had told my Mam that if the treatment which she was receiving didn't work, then they were going to amputate her leg.

Me Mam was 80 years old and it was a terrible shock to her. She was very, very loving and also a very independent person. I suppose she couldn't imagine relying on others and being trapped in the bungalow with my Dad.

My Dad would care for her, but she enjoyed going to the WI, Mothers Union and to Church regularly as well as going on mystery trips run by the Community Centre in Bowburn. She used to say she was sure that the trip was a mystery to the driver too. I said that we could get one of those mobility scooters for her. The only trouble there was my Dad wouldn't trust her driving it on the roads so he would have to ride shotgun on the back of the scooter with her.

The next day when I went to see her she was on oxygen. Oh dear, then the next day she was even worse and so on. Her body had given up. Each day she deteriorated.

I spoke to our Eileen and recommended that she returned home from Turkey. I told her that our Mam was dying. Eileen couldn't believe it because me Mam was really chirpy when she left for her holiday and looking forward to getting back home to the bungalow.

Eileen said that she would make arrangements to return home as soon as possible. Me Mam wasn't eating, it was awful.

She stayed conscious until our Eileen got back. I met Eileen from Newcastle airport and we made our way to the hospital.Mam held our hands and said that we'd been good girls, that she'd been proud of us and that she'd had a good life. We then watched her slip into unconsciousness.

After work every night I called into the hospital to see her. She was just the size of a little doll and her features changed. Oh dear it was awful to see her like this.

My Mam passed away a few days later. My Dad was heart broken. He would be on his own, Eileen and I didn't know how he'd cope. My Mam had always done all the household tasks such as paying the bills, cooking and cleaning. So it was up to us to support him during this difficult time. We thought he would feel very vulnerable and maybe frightened of all the letters and bills but I'm sure he'd know that our Eileen and I would look after him.

The day before the funeral Mrs. Jordan, me Mam's friend who she went to church with and whose daughter our dog, Tiger, had bitten the day before my wedding day, asked me if I had a photograph of me Mam and herself. I said to her that I would go into me Mam and Dad's bedroom and look through the photo albums. I shouted to my Dad, "I'm just going into your bedroom to look for a photo of me Mam and Mrs. Jordan."

"Aye." he shouted. When I went into the bedroom there on the double bed, right in the middle was a photograph of me Mam and Mrs. Jordan. I couldn't believe it. Eeeh I looked upwards and said,

"It's alright Mam I've found it." I went into the sitting room and gave Mrs. Jordan the photograph. She said,

"By Brenda that didn't take long to find." I didn't try to explain just in case she didn't believe in things like that.

The funeral service was held at me Mam's church just down the road from their bungalow. The hearse came to the bungalow and we all walked behind to the church. It was a terrible feeling knowing that me Mam was in that car in front of us.

Eileen and I walked with me Dad and, of course, our families were there all walking behind us. John even turned up to pay his respects which was very nice of him.

The church was packed. It was a very sad day. It was 31st August, 1993 when me Mam passed away.

She had always been there for me, caring and loving, helping me learn words and supporting me in every way possible, even saying a prayer while down on her knees scrubbing the kitchen floor hoping it would help for me to pass my driving test.

I miss me Mam so very much but I'm sure she's not far from me still looking after me.

I was asked to perform at a local hospital called Earls House. It's a hospital for the mentally ill or patients with Alzheimer's. While I was singing I looked over to a lady sitting in a chair. She was elderly and didn't look very well. When I looked more carefully I thought to myself, "I'm sure that's Mrs. Smith." Mrs. Smith was the Doctor's wife who lived in Shincliffe, who my Mam worked for cleaning their house. After my show I asked one of the nurses if the lady was Mrs. Smith. The nurse said that she was. Well the first thing that came into my head was to ring me Mam and tell her that Mrs. Smith was a patient in Earls House. Well a split second after that thought, I knew I couldn't ring me Mam and what a shock that was for me realising I couldn't ring me Mam to tell her. The mind plays strange tricks at times.

I went up to Mrs. Smith and told her that I was Mrs Swainston's daughter Brenda. She nodded and smiled. I mentioned our Eileen and told her that me Mam had recently died. She nodded as if she knew.

When I said to her that I remembered her with fondness and I told her that me Mam thought the world of her. She again smiled then she went off to sleep, maybe to dream of the years me Mam worked for her.

Life Without Me Mam

Poppy, our Jack Russell went to live with my Dad to keep him company. Eileen and I thought it was a good idea and it would give my Dad a reason to get him up out of bed on a morning and take Poppy for a walk.

They became soulmates, never apart. When my Dad went on his bike Poppy ran alongside. Everyone in Bowburn knew my Dad and of course they got to know Poppy.

My dad with Poppy

Eileen and I saw to all Dad's business regarding letters and bills. I'd drop dinners off and he liked doing his own shopping at Asda or in Durham. He coped very well. He did his own washing and always, weather permitting hung his clothes on the washing line. He was very proud of how he kept his house and himself clean. He must have missed me

Mam terribly, as we all did. My Dad also had his neighbours to keep him company and to keep an eye on him. He had the phone and our telephone numbers next to it, so he could reach us anytime if he needed anything.

He'd go for his bike rides and after a long ride would sit on a seat by the side of the road and watch the traffic go by, while drinking his can of Mackeson, which he always carried in the bag at the back of his bike. He would also sit; smoke his pipe and wave to passers-by in their cars.

The Metro Centre

I was working at the Metro Centre Gateshead during school holidays. Richard and Peter would sometimes come along with me. An agent first sent me as a children's entertainer. Karen Carr, the marketing Manager, asked if I'd do some promotional work: putting smiles on customer's faces while giving out balloons or leaflets.

I always dressed in different costumes depending on the theme. One week it could be nautical, another pirates or clowns.

I was Noddy one week, driving my little car with Big Ears next to me, all around the malls; then a clown the next. Every week was different.

Karen and I got on really well – we had the same sense of humour. She asked me to go to Oslo in Norway with a team from the Marketing Department. We took my little car and I drove around the streets (on the paths) of Oslo promoting the Metro Centre.

Karen and I laughed and laughed all the time we were there, acting like two naughty school girls. I think we got on people's nerves.

At the Metro Centre, Karen asked me to perform in a

pantomime, Snow White and the Seven Dwarfs. I was Dopey (a bit typecast). It was great because I had no words to learn just facial expressions. It was good fun.

We also put together a Mr. and Mrs. Show. I was the hostess with my sticky-out dress and high heels. Could I hell walk in those shoes, I walked like Dick Emery on a good day.

A young man called Ian Fraser took the part as Derek Batey. We opened the show with the song It Takes Two. I'm useless at learning words. I could get the first bit right, but could I hell learn the other verses.

So I made it up as I went along.

Trouble was that Ian had to make the next line rhyme. I wasn't the most popular person- so we went into a quiet room and rehearsed and rehearsed. I got it right in rehearsal but when we went back on stage I forgot everything and made the verses up again and in the end Ian was singing about a parrot. Ian was not happy!!! I've worked with him since the show and I think he has forgiven me.

The BBC was staging Children in Need at the Metro Centre. I was asked to be the link person and fill-in between filming. The whole centre was packed.

There were acts who had been auditioned to perform in front of the cameras. I was also the warm-up comedian and it was up to me to get the audience 'in the mood' and buzzing.

When an act was on stage I'd make sure the next one was ready to go on stage to perform at the right time. Nerves were high. I was to liaise with the Director and Producer. They would cue me and then I would cue everyone else who was involved with the show. I did this as well as getting the audience to respond at the right time when we went live and entertaining them between televised slots.

I worked non-stop from 2.00pm – 2.00am the next morning. I was shattered. All the invited guests had been in the Management Suite drinking, so they were well tipsy. I worked so hard my muscles ached.

I left the Metro Centre that night walking through the quiet Malls. I left everyone to enjoy the success of the event. I was so tired. I got a lovely letter from the BBC thanking me for all my hard work. Phew!! I was totally exhausted.

My time at the Metro Centre was very happy. I met quite a few celebrities. For a number of years I was there to switch on the Christmas lights. One year it was with Mr. Blobby. I'm such a name dropper! I also met a lovely lady called Hannah Hauxwell.

I noticed the other day that my photograph with Mr. Blobby was up on a wall with big stars who switched on the Christmas Lights.

Sometimes I would work for ten hours at the Metro Centre, go home for tea then drive over to a holiday park in Filey, North Yorkshire. Occasionally, if I was staying over for a show at another holiday park, the boys would come with me. It was often foggy over the Yorkshire Moors and on our way back home Richard would say, "Do you know your way back Mam? Will you be alright driving in this fog?"

"Of course Richard," I'd reply upon which he would fall asleep. Peter would already be asleep.

I never did the BBC Children in Need show again. It was too exhausting, plus I started accepting work abroad as working holidays. I would entertain for a couple of nights on a holiday complex, say in Lanzarote. Food was paid for and the flights where too. It meant I could take my two boys with me. On one occasion while entertaining in Lanzarote I worked with Senita. Yes the Senita who was connected with Simon Cowell.

A Single Mam

The boys and I just got on with life. Richard was playing guitar now. Peter got interested in playing the drums, (like his Dad). I worked hard bringing up the boys on my own most of the time. Again it was like juggling soot!!

Peter loved riding his BMX bike so I always knew where he was. Richard by this time was old enough to look after Peter for me while I was at work.

Richard asked to go on a skiing holiday with the school. He was a very active young lad and it was hard work but I got the money together for him to go.

He'd been away for about 5 days when my telephone rang and it was one of the teachers who had gone with the party of children skiing.

"Hello Brenda, are you sitting down?" he asked.

"No but I will, what's wrong." "Well Richard has had an accident on the slopes and has snapped two bones in his right leg."

"Oh my goodness," I said, "How is Richard?"

"He's in hospital and they've operated on him. He's out of theatre now and he's come round from the anaesthetic. Do you want to speak to him?"

"Yes of course I do."

I spoke to Richard and he said that when he fell the ski should have detached itself from his boot, but it didn't thereby breaking his leg. Oh my goodness I thought poor Richard. The whole party was due back home in 4 days so the teachers had decided Richard should return as well.

I was there at the airport waiting for Richard. He came through the doors of arrivals in a wheelchair with his leg sticking right out in front of him. He was smiling; so obviously no pain there. He had a plaster on his leg which was split to allow for swelling while flying. I was instructed to take him to our local hospital immediately, which I did.

When we got there he was X-rayed then they put another plaster over the top of the one he already had on. His leg was double the weight. He couldn't walk so he was in a wheelchair and I had to lift him everywhere. I'm only little and it was hard work. Every time I lifted him I'd knock his leg on a door frame or anything which was in the way.

Trying to get him into the car was a horrendous task. I'm only 4 feet 10 inches and trying to carry a teenager with a plaster cast on his leg was not easy.

"Mam!" Richard would shout, "That hurt."

"I'm so sorry," was my reply.

He was off school for three weeks after which he could go to school on crutches.

Anyway Richard survived the ordeal; it was a terrible time for him and he was so glad when it came to the day of the removal of the plaster casts (plural).

It was nearly time for Richard to leave school. He got a place at New College, Durham for a NVQ Level 3 and HNC Course in popular music. He pursued lessons on the guitar and he was very good.

Richard got a new set of friends at college who were all fellow musicians. They would often put on a concert together in college and I loved going to see them perform.

Peter loved the drums and went for private lessons every week. He too was very good. As I said earlier we had a drum kit set up in the house and Peter used to practice playing every day. It was great; I encouraged him as much as I could.

By this time our neighbours Julie and Geoff had moved and new neighbours moved in. They didn't like the sound of drums. Well not many people do when that's all you can hear is bang bang, bang, thud thud thud. Julie and Geoff had been wonderful neighbours and very understanding. Peter loved the drums –our new neighbours didn't!!

They complained to us on a few occasions but I suppose enough was enough and reported Peter and me to the Council for noise pollution. Oh dear we were in trouble. I'd never been in trouble ever in my life, nor had our Peter.

Marjorie and Billy from the other side of us had moved too so the street wasn't the same. How sad. Valley View had changed. It wasn't the happy place it use to be.

Everyone Keeping Busy

Brenda Collins was still going down well in the clubs and holiday parks. I only worked in venues where I could get back to the boys.

I started to change my show from stand up to visual, reverting a little back to mime just like John and I did. I'd always looked like Cilla so I impersonated her, opening my show with one of her songs. I brought back ET and 'I Who Have Nothing'. That's a sketch where my tummy blows up as I sing the song. Little by little I added more as months went by.

John had always done the editing and I couldn't do it. So I asked Kevin, who used to live in North Terrace, if he could help me. He was only too willing.

Richard had joined a local band as a guitarist. He was still at college so it was pocket money for him.

I still paid him for looking after Peter when he could. My Dad and our Eileen helped me when our Richard was working with the band. Again it was a hard slog working, keeping house and looking after the boys.

By this time Richard had passed his driving test. I used to take him out practicing well before he was 17 on disused roads so that when he was 17 and his test came around he was a very able driver.

My Dad's Temper

My Dad was doing well. He kept busy by riding his bike, shopping, gardening or watching television. He still cut his friends' hair. He also cleaned his neighbours' windows. Years ago he would sweep chimneys too. He was a Jack of all trades. He loved his garden and instead of live flowers growing in the garden he had plastic flowers. It meant no matter what season his garden was always colourful. It was also full of gnomes.

I went to see him every day and he'd ring me beforehand and say, "Bring your camera Brenda; I've bought some new flowers while I was in Durham."

Our Eileen rang me up one day.

"Has me Dad been on the telephone?" She asked.

"No, why?"

"Well." She said, "He won't be ringing you because he's in hospital with broken ribs."

"Oh dear," I said, "Has he fallen off his bike?" He was at this stage of his life 90 years old.

"No, he's been fighting!!!!!"

Here's how it all happened. My Dad used to get the free Asda bus from Bowburn to Stockton to do his shopping. It was a lovely day out for him and he loved chatting up the Asda staff (especially the women); he was a total flirt. They loved him and he loved them. They'd help him if he had difficulty with anything he couldn't understand.

He'd do a full week's shop and even have a bit of lunch in the cafe. Perfect. On the way back in the bus each week my Dad always got up first to get off the bus maybe a mile away from his intended stop.

This particular Saturday another elderly man got up first. My Dad said to him that he always got up first.

The man said, "No, not today Alfie."

Oh dear. The man told my Dad that if he didn't shut up he'd hit him over the head with a whisky bottle. Well that was it; my Dad saw red and the fight started. Not a verbal fight but with fists. This is two elderly men who should have known better! Oh my goodness.

It got so bad the bus driver had to stop the bus to get them off and they finished the fight on the grass. My Mam would have been horrified. In fact it would never have happened if my Mam had been there. My Dad always had a temper but my Mam always calmed him down.

I went to see my Dad in hospital and he was still seething.

"I'll do it again." he said.

"Now Dad," I said "No you wouldn't." to which he replied, "Yes I bloody would."

A few months later my Dad had recovered and was back on his bike, riding miles and miles daily. Weather permitting, of course.

Our Richard rang me one day and said,

"Mam has the Jehovah's Witness been on the phone to you or Auntie Eileen?" The Jehovah's Witness lived next door to my Dad.

"No."

"Well," Richard said, "She's trying to get hold of you or Auntie Eileen,"

"Oh." I said, "Why, what's happened?"

"Well." said Richard. "Granda's been arrested."

"Oh no!" I shouted. "He's attacked the man at the top of his street." (He's on two sticks and my Dad had attacked him before over a gate being shut.) My Dad liked the communal gate open and the man on sticks liked it shut.

I rang our Eileen. Our Eileen's a bit posher than me. We're quite the opposite to each other. I said to her.

"Are you sitting down?"

"No," she said.

"Well you should."

"Why?"

"He's been arrested."

"Who?"

"Who do you think?" I asked.

"Oh no, not me Dad!"

"Yes." I replied.

I told her what had happened.

"Where is he now?"

"They've taken him to Durham Police Station. She said she'd have to get her husband off the golf course and get in touch with her daughter Catherine and son Daniel and we'd all meet up in Durham. I said that I'd get in touch with our Richard and get our Peter out of bed. I shouted to our Peter.

"Your Granda's been arrested. We're all meeting up in Durham to get him out of the cells."

Peter responded, "Ok Mam," as if it were an everyday occurrence.

I rang my friend and told her because I was supposed to

meet up with her. Whilst I was on the phone to her I had a
call waiting. It was our Richard and he said,
"Mam Stop, Mam Stop." Wait for it ... "April Fool!"
"Richard, ye beggar." Eeeh. It was a total gotcha!
I had to quickly ring our Eileen and tell her not to go any
further. Eeeh we were all relieved that our Dad was still
sitting at home in his rocking chair, smoking his pipe and
watching the television with Poppy. You see my Dad was
very capable of being arrested.

In his nineties his wardrobe consisted of denim jeans
(torn at the knee) bomber jacket and a baseball cap with one
of me Mam's brooches pinned in!!! Eileen hated his taste in
fashion but my Dad loved it.

He was by this time the oldest man in Bowburn and was
invited to the Bowburn Carnival celebrating the village's
centenary. He and the youngest baby boy were there to cut
the Bowburn centenary cake. Everyone knew Alfie. He was
quite a celebrity. He still came along with me when I was
working in a local club.

Richard had moved out of Valley View and was living
with the band so there was just Peter and I. We had Sharon
and George on one side as neighbours and-Pam and Keith,
on the other side, as new neighbours. Both couples were
very friendly.

Peter was well into his motocross – riding motorbikes
leaping over heights. Peter was to race at a two day event
in Crook, County Durham. I was working on the Saturday
night at Primrose Valley, North Yorkshire.

I said to Peter that I would take him for the first day
racing on the Saturday and I would stay with him because I
was marshalling. Marshalling wasn't hard work at all, but we
all got covered in mud. We stood there holding our flags
and when a rider came skidding past on his motor bike the
mud would fly into the air and spatter the marshal from head
to toe. After the race about twelve of us, who had been

marshals, would all make our way back to the marquee the best we could. By this time the mud had hardened on every part of our bodies and so it was very difficult to bend any of our limbs. My friend, who does crafts, said we looked and walked like a dried mud encrusted parade of 'mummies' and daddies straight from the cast of Michael Jackson's 'Thriller'.

After getting cleaned up I said I would take him (our Peter, not Michael Jackson) home and bring him back the next morning (Sunday) for the racing.

Marion who lived at the end of our street said that Peter could stay over and sleep in their caravan. Michael, Marion's son, was also racing. Peter was over the moon that he was sleeping over in Michael's caravan.

Just before I left the course Peter said,

"What about my disco clothes Mam?" There was to be a disco on the Saturday night. I said that I would ring his Dad and ask him to drop them off to him. I rang John and said that Peter's clothes were in a bin liner in the lounge at Valley View.

When I got back to Valley View, there were my neighbours at the gate.

"Ohhh hello Brenda." said Pam, who was Scottish.

"Oh Hello Pam."

"John's been."

"What?" I said.

"Aayyye, John's been."

"No." I said.

"Aye he's been and he carried out an orange bag."

"No not an orange bag?" I said.

"Aye, it was an orange bag." John had taken the charity bag up to Peter for his disco clothes. There were lamp shades, shoes belonging to me, some of my Dad's clothes. Well I thought he'll have to go to the disco as a standard lamp!!!

I rang Peter and told him that his Dad had picked up the

wrong bag and he wasn't happy at all. You see John had got there before me and assumed the orange bag was for Peter, as that was the only bag there. Well John would have to come back and get the bag with Peter's clothes in. He never liked to put himself out - well this time he was going to have to!!!

Peter was alright about it and had a wonderful weekend. He even won a trophy. That's my boy! He was growing up nicely and had some lovely friends; friends who are still good friends today.

Another Dog

Richard rang me one day and said,
"Mam I've rescued a dog from someone's garden, where it's been left tied up when the weather has been minus four degrees. I've been to the police and they said that it was ok for me to rescue it. I told them that you would look after it. It's a very friendly dog."
"So I'm getting a dog to look after?"
"Yes." said Richard.
"But Richard, I'm hardly in the house on a night time." I said. Upon which Richard said,
"Well Peter can look after the dog." I shouted upstairs to Peter.
"We're getting a dog."
"Oh no." Peter said, "Why?"
"Because our Richard has rescued one and he's told the police that I will look after it."
"Why doesn't he look after it?" Our Peter pleaded.
"Oh I don't know. I just said I would because I'm anything for a peaceful life."
"It's not going to be peaceful with a strange dog in the house." Our Peter said. And do you know he was right.

Richard brought the dog to us and it was a beautiful dog. I later found out that she was a Bearded Collie. Richard told me that her name was Holly.

"Well hello Holly, welcome to your new home." I said.

Peter just looked at her. Peter was a teenager and a young man of few words. I think all mothers of teenagers will know what I mean.

Holly settled in nice, in fact she was a pleasure. One day I looked at her tummy and thought I'm sure she looks pregnant. I made an appointment at the vets and they said that they thought she was coming out of a pregnancy.

Oh no, how wrong they were. Holly was very pregnant and went into labour on my bed.

Peter was playing with her at the time, when out pops a puppy.

"Maaammmm. Holly has just had a puppy. Oh and another one. Oh and another one. Oh and another one."

I was downstairs but ran up to see Holly in labour. Peter put the new babies to Holly for their first feed.

Holly gave birth to eight puppies. Yes, eight. I couldn't believe it but there they were, like tiny mice-looking puppies. Mother and babies were doing well.

Eeeh if someone had said to me that there would be nine dogs in our house I would have said, "No bloody way." But oh yes here they were all nine of them.

Holly was a good Mammy. When I was away at work at night Peter kept an eye on them.

A friend of mine Alan Wormold made a nursing box for mother and her eight bairns. But as they got older Holly found it difficult to feed them and she was bleeding and very sore. So I took over the feeding. Not personally but by a syringe and puppy milk I bought from the vets.

When I got back from work I'd give them all a feed, then again through the night. I ended up sleeping on the settee so I could hear them cry for a feed. I'd feed one then put it down, then the next, then the next. More often than not I forgot which ones I'd fed so I got a cardboard box and lined it with newspapers and when I'd fed one; in it went into the box. Hey, I was a dab hand at it but I was very, very tired.

Peter got fed up of looking after them and feeding them too. We had newspaper from one end of the through lounge and dining room to the other. Everywhere was covered with puppy poo and wee. It was everywhere.When the pups woke up through the night they would start yapping and I would say, "Shhhhhh, "flapping my hands at them, "bloody shhhhhh."

Then they would start climbing the curtains and running up and down the lounge in fact running and yapping all over.

"Oh please just shhhhhh the neighbours will hear."

When they were six weeks old I started looking for good homes for them. I was desperate, but it was difficult. A local dog rescue home said that they would get good homes for all the pups on the condition Holly could stay at the rescue centre and be a surrogate mother and feed some puppies whose mother had abandoned them. I agreed because I was so, so tired and desperate to find good homes for the puppies. They were such hard work.

Kevin, the lad who puts my ideas for my show together, he and his wife, Christine were looking for a mature dog. Not a puppy. So I said to them that when Holly gets out of the rescue centre they would be very welcome to have her. I knew they would deck her with diamonds and they would give her a wonderful home and lots of their time. Time I didn't have.

Holly got out of the rescue centre and Kevin and Christine took her home to their house. I was so pleased and so was our Peter. We were both relieved.

Loneliness

Because I was carrying more props and doing more quick changes I got friends to come along and help me. I also enjoyed their company. It can get very lonely when you're travelling on your own.

In the days of the duo John and I had each other and at the end of a booking and driving home even if you don't speak, it's still nice to have someone there. Even better if you've had a bad night and the show hadn't gone as well as it should have. It's comforting to talk the evening's events over and trying to convince ourselves that it wasn't our fault and that it was the audience's fault.

I was working on the holiday parks on the east coast of Yorkshire. I had a two day run. Peter was staying at friends and so I asked a friend of mine to come along with me. I was so much happier when I had company. The first show was in Scarborough. I was top of the bill at a hotel and my name was up in 'chalk'.

We did a bit of shopping during the day. I'm always looking around joke shops and even charity shops getting ideas for new sketches. Also I'm always on the lookout for nice wigs.

We were staying in Scarborough I said to my friend:

"Pop into that off licence and get a bottle of wine for tonight after the show, I'll sit outside here." I had all the bags from the shopping. I was holding the TV Times. It was a really hot day so I just plonked myself down on the pavement. Well do you know what happened? Someone stopped and gave me £1. They thought the TV Times was The Big Issue and they said,

"It's better if you have a sign." The cheeky B---er. I was top of the bill in Scarborough!!

When I told our Eileen she was not amused and asked what I was wearing? I told her it was my nice warm jumper.

"Get rid of that bloody jumper." She said. I wished I'd never told her because I liked that jumper.

"In fact," she said, "Get rid of all your old jumpers and buy some new ones. I have some you can have."

"Oh good," I thought, "Our Eileen's going to give me some of her jumpers it'll save me buying some." Her clothes are always designer always the best. Eeeh there's never a dull moment.

Fellow Artistes

While working around the clubs I have met some lovely entertainers. Mind some were a pain in the backside.

I was working in a club in South Shields and the concert room was upstairs. There were two acts on that night myself and a singer. The singer was to open the show and I was to follow. While he was on stage he thought he was so clever by putting the microphone down on a chair and he burst into opera. I wasn't on immediately after him; there was to be a break for the bingo, then it was me. So I sat in the audience to watch him.

It was a hot summer night, so all the windows and doors were open. The concert room was upstairs; the fire escape door was open too. While singing his operatic song backed by the organist and drummer he made his way through the emergency doors to the fire escape stairs. He stood there and started to throw his voice into the concert room. Well he must have thrown it a bit too hard because the fire escape doors slammed shut on him, leaving him outside the club at the top of the stairs. By the time he got down the fire escape and back up the stairs into the concert room and threw again his operatic voice the bingo had started and all the audience had their heads down marking their bingo books. On its own number ... silly sod.

He was well put out, so he packed up all his equipment and departed. Meanwhile...two fat ladies 88 and so the bingo carried on.

While working in a club I was appearing with another comedy act and we had to perform two spots each. His first one didn't go too well so he said to me, "I'm getting out of here."

There was a window in the dressing room, so he opened it and pushed through first his suit bag then his speakers, which he'd taken down during the bingo behind closed curtains.

While he was pushing the gear through the window, unknown to him a policeman was watching it all from his patrol car. When the act had finally got everything through the window, including himself, he shouted, "Bye Brenda, see you again sometime." Then off he went.

I went back on stage and as I was singing, here he comes back into the concert room with his suit bag over his arm. The policeman in the patrol car had thought he was a robber and the stuff he was shoving through the window was his spoils.

Anyway the policeman took him back into the club and spoke to a committee man to confirm that he wasn't a robber, but the comedian who had just been on stage. His plan of trying to escape backfired and he was made to go back on stage.

Clubland in a village became the hub. Fathers were proud to make their sons members as soon as they became of age. Of course Catholic clubs were regularly attended by the priest and when this happened, if the priest was laughing at the artiste on stage, then everyone laughed at the artiste and a good night was had by all.

A now famous act called Chubby Brown was always getting into bother at Catholic clubs for being too blue. I was always squeaky clean in the Catholic clubs.

Clubland was a big industry employing lots and lots of people. The beer flowed because it was cheap and it even had its own brewery called Federation. Unfortunately there aren't many clubs left.

People's drinking habits have changed and I believe once my generation are gone then so will the clubs, which is sad because the clubs were a venue for acts just starting a career in music or comedy.

They was plenty of work in the clubs and an act was doing something they enjoyed and getting paid for it. Where will up and coming artistes go now? Clubland has developed some very famous entertainers. It was a brilliant time for me working in this industry.

Organists and drummers used to be resident at clubs in order to accompany the artistes. All acts had their music or dots as they were called. An organist was happily playing away during an interval when all of a sudden he slumped across the organ. Because his body was slumped across the two keyboards the noise was horrendous, Derrrrrrrrrrrrr.

"Unplug him!" someone shouted.

"It's not him it's the bloody organ that wants unplugging." Shouted another.

"What's happened to him the silly sod? Come on Harry get playing." Were some of the comments.

Inspection by the Concert Chairman confirmed that poor Harry had gone to the big concert room in the sky. He had died. The Concert Chairman announced this to the audience:

"Harry's dead."The audience's attention was abruptly brought to this poor man's plight and there was a gasp.

The audience were now concerned as to what was going to happen next. The committee had an emergency meeting and the police were called. It was agreed to cover Harry over with the organ cover while they waited for a doctor to arrive to certify him dead.

The Concert Chairman announced that a game of bingo would be played to fill the time in and he would call the numbers very quietly in order to show respect to poor Harry.

Bingo, of course, ruled a club. No one ever dared talk during a game. If they did they would get the "Shush" from everyone. If they continued to talk someone playing would pipe up:

"Come on we're playing for bloody money here, shut up." Then the caller would say,

"If you want to talk go into the lounge."

Acts appearing at the club would always be welcomed to play the game, but it really wasn't allowed for the act to win. Oh no, and if they did that was it. They were doomed. When it was their turn to go back on stage their popularity had ceased to exist.

Lyn, my friend, once won the bingo and the club refused to pay me. I fought my case through Equity but still didn't get my money. And I'm still getting the poisoned darts from the back of my neck!

The prize money was, most of the time, very good, and that's what attracted members and visitors to the clubs - bingo. It was sometimes maybe £50 a line and £100 for a full house. If there was a jackpot it would be even greater.

An Angel

I was off to one of the Canary Islands to work and when I set off for the airport "The Angel of The North" wasn't there. When I came back it was. Oh my goodness what a sight to behold!!

As I passed it P.P Arnold was on the radio singing Just Call Me Angel of the Morning. What timing?

"Heck." I said, "Well I must put this in my act but how would I go about it, being a one woman show?"

You see if I get an idea for my show, I like to get it into my show as soon as possible. The thoughts of the logistics were racing. I would have to have a base colour, that would be brown. Brown trousers and brown socks to begin with. Now, how to get the body of the statue? A brown ribbed jumper, yes.

Now the head. At first I thought maybe thick women's tights. So off I trot to a department store's hosiery department and I ask the assistant for some thick tights.

"Oh yes, come this way." She showed me the product and I asked if I could try them on!! I put them doubled-up on my head. I think she thought I was going to rob the store.

"Oh dear," she went in a high-pitched voice.

"Don't worry I'm the Angel of The North, I'm putting together the costume."

Anyway the tights were too thin. My whole face could be seen through the material. In the meantime I was thinking about the wings. They had to be light, so foam was the obvious answer. Then came the panels of the wings. I came up with the idea of knitted panels. Yes. I had to find someone who could knit. I couldn't. Then I thought of Ann Jones from the infants' school and asked her to knit the panels for me.

I still hadn't solved the problem of the head. Then it came to me – yes, a balaclava helmet but completely knitted-in so it formed a head. A lady who worked at the local garage knit me a couple of balaclavas! Yes the sketch was coming together, I had the outfit.

The next part was to go into the recording studio. So off I went to Kevin's. You see I sit with him and tell him where to start and where to stop the sketch. Just as John and I did all those years ago except now it was on a computer. I always have to allow time between each sketch to either put costumes on, or take them off. It's all to do with timing.

Harry Potter Lookalike

As well as holiday parks I still worked in the Working Men's Clubs. I was asked by an agent to go to a club. It was a mid week show so that was good. Daniel a friend was helping on this occasion.

When I arrived at the club I discovered it was an 'all male' audience. It was good money so I thought, "Oh let's just do it." Daniel set the equipment up and I prepared my props. I knew I'd have my work cut out. When it's an all male audience I get nervous.

I started my show and, of course, I had my hecklers. Over the years I've learned all the one liners and learned how to deal with them. One heckler was a young lad, a Harry Potter lookalike.

The older men in the audience were goading him to heckle me. Really, he had no idea, he was so naive. He was fodder to me. The more he shouted at me the more the men laughed at him. I felt sorry for him because he was getting upset and got up and started shouting at me whilst walking away. He was walking backwards and therefore wasn't looking where he was going and when he turned round he smashed into a pillar and knocked his glasses skew-whiff. Poor lad, the audience were in hysterics.

When he came back into the audience I made a lot of him and said how nice a person he was and how rotten his mates were behaving.

There was a raffle during the interval and the older men gave Harry Potter lookalike a bottle of bubbly to give to me. It wasn't even theirs to give away. It was someone else's prize from the raffle. Anyway Harry came up to me and gave me the beautiful bottle with a bow on it.

"Eeeh," I said, "Thank you very much" and apologised for making fun of him and I hoped he hadn't been offended.

A few months later my friend, Lyn, rang and said have

you got Sylvia (an acquaintance) a present for her birthday. Well I hadn't. Then I thought of that bottle of bubbly. It looked the part. It had a big bow around its neck. So I gave it to Sylvia. I never noticed but it still had the raffle ticket attached. Oh dear me, 'Too late' was the cry. There are times when you wish the floor would swallow you up. I do, however, believe in recycling!!

Thieves Operate in this Area

I went to Makro to do a bit shopping one day. I was still living at Valley View with our Peter. I told Peter where I was going.

When I got there I locked my car, put the keys in my handbag, collected a trolley and then entered the store to do my shopping.

I completed my shopping and put my bag on top of the shopping in the trolley. WRONG! Coming out of Makro a car came right along side of me. I thought it was someone who knew me and were playing silly b...... No, an arm came out of the driver's window and picked up my bag from the top of the trolley and drove off.

I screamed and screamed.

"He's got my bag." No cameras at Makro. In fact I still don't think they have any now.

The police arrived. The thief had my bag with my phone, keys to my car and house, work diary, purse with credit cards, discs of my show, fee from the previous night. Bloody everything.

The police sent a car to my home. Already the thieves had rang my home and told Peter they had my handbag. I suppose they were checking to see if anyone was in and if not they would have gone into my home and robbed that.

It was like a bad dream. I had the locks changed that

day, which cost about £300. Each night Peter and I barricaded ourselves in. It was awful. Peter slept with a baseball bat next to him.

They also had my diary, but fortunately I always keep a duplicate of where I'm working. I rang a friend who had a radio show to announce that if the robbers were listening for them to return my discs of my show.

Kevin, who has the recording studio, had a copy of my show. So I was alright there, I could still work.

A week or so later I received a phone call. The caller asked "Is that the lass who's lost or had her handbag stolen? Are you Brenda?"

"Yes I am," I replied.

"Well I've found some of your belongings. Do you want to come and pick them up?"

"Yes." He told me the address and off I went with a friend.

A man with rolled up shirt sleeves stood in front of his detached house gates. I couldn't take my eyes off his right arm. That was the arm that came out of the car window and snatched my handbag from my trolley. "That's the robber." I said to my friend.

"No."

"Yes it is."

"Oh my goodness." she said. "Don't go in, phone the police."

"No." I said, "I'm going in."   Sounds like a plot from a film!!!

My friend said she would time me and that if time was ticking too much she would ring the police.

"Ok." I said. I also rang our Eileen and told her what had happened. She told me not to go in and ring the police. I told her I was going in.

"Hello Brenda." The man said to me

"Hello." He had a pit bull terrier with him sitting by his

side on a lead.

"Come into the house."

A large lady with blonde hair sat at the table near the window. She was a large version of Bette Lynch from Coronation Street.

"Sit down Brenda." She spoke to me as if she'd known me for years. I sat down. She leaned across to the window ledge.

"Now those discs you were asking for. Well my son found them."

She also said that she didn't have my purse but had my driving licence and credit cards.

"No keys or diary?" I asked.

"No I haven't got those."

The woman asked if I wanted a cup of tea. I said that I wanted to go because I was due back on stage. She said that it was nice meeting me. They both came to the door, watched me get in my car and waved bye-bye.

"Bye bye Brenda."

"Let's get out of here quick." I said to my friend. It was a scary experience. We drove back to the club. I rang our Eileen and told her what had happened

They thought they were doing me a favour by giving me my discs back. I never take my bag with me into Makro now. In fact it was a very long time before I went back to that store. I think years ago bags used to be banned from the store. Maybe they should be banned again.

Benidorm

Peter had passed his driving test at 17 like Richard. I took him out well before his 17th birthday round disused roads. He had a little Mini, which was brilliant to look at, but was always breaking down. We were forever getting towed back by the AA. In fact I was put on their Christmas card list.

It was coming up to Peter's 18th and I asked our Peter what he fancied doing for his birthday. Gosh 18, doesn't time fly.

I got some work over in Benidorm. A fellow act called Ronnie Oliver was already working there and he organised for me to work in a couple of the bars in Benidorm.

Peter said that he'd love to go to Benidorm and invited two friends to celebrate his birthday. I took a friend too to help me with my show and also it was company for me while the lads were celebrating.

We stayed at the Presidente Hotel, very plush with open air swimming pools on the roof and ground floor. It was lovely. I hardly saw the boys.

I said earlier Richard was living with the band and his life revolved around them. I asked if he wanted to join us but declined as he was working away. The band did a lot of travelling around the country. He was very busy so no problem.

I was working at a bar called Morgan's Tavern. The venue was shaped like a boat. Well the outside was.

From the hotel we used to set off for work at 11.30pm because I wasn't on stage until 1.30am. The boys were out on the town somewhere. I didn't like to think about it. Peter was l8 and they were out enjoying themselves. As long as they didn't get into trouble.

Anyway we came out of the hotel. I was carrying my Angel of The North wings and my friend was pulling a case full of the props. A lady was in the foyer and we said good night to each other and we went out of the front door and off to work. Remember this was at 11.30 at night.

The next night there were about 4 ladies in the foyer. I said, "Goodnight." They all said, "Goodnight." Well the next night the foyer was chocker block (full) with ladies, about 12 of them had turned up. We got out of the lift and I heard one of them say, "Here they are, here they are." I bet her lips never moved as she nudged the lady next to her with folded arms. I said,

"Good-night," upon which they all said, (all 12 of them),

"Goodnight." Eeeh well we giggled when we got out of the hotel.

The next morning at breakfast a man said to me:

"Did you make much money last night?"

"Yes, you should come and see me." Me thinking he should come and see my show at Morgan's Tavern. NO – Do you know what they thought we were - Ladies of the Night!!!! They thought my Angel of the North wings were our beds to flop down on the beach!!!!

The next night I appeared at the Presidente Hotel cabaret venue and guess who was in the audience? Yes, all those women and their husbands. I heard one woman say,

"Hey that's her with the two beds." It was a good night everyone enjoyed themselves and we all had a good laugh.

Peter and his friends also had a great time, although I don't think they remember much of it!!! Who cares, it was his 18th birthday.

I returned to Benidorm a few years later and it had changed. The bar in which I worked wanted me to swear even when there were children in. No thank you - I can do without that!

Also because I was the new kid on the block on my first night of entertaining, other comedians from other bars would stand at the back of the venue jotting down all my gags. They didn't care as long as they got some new jokes for their show.

A lady one night came up to me after I'd finished my performance and said that she'd just been to a bar up the road before she came to see me and the comedy act there had told all my jokes. Sods! They couldn't be bothered to do the research themselves it was easier for them to copy another act's gags.

Holidays

Guests or passengers often ask,
"Where do you go for your holidays?"
Well myself and a friend went on a Nile cruise holiday. Ann Watson, a lovely lady, had recommended it so off we went.

We soon gathered a gang to knock around with, all of whom had the same sense of humour. Other passengers on the cruise avoided us. Some were envious of the fun we were having.

We used to have Egyptian lessons on the deck. We made all the words up. I was the teacher and "our gang" were the pupils. Well we laughed and laughed until we ached. Again passengers moved away from us but we didn't care. We were having a great time.

One day we were having lunch and having meat, we always had meat, what kind of meat we never found out but we ate it.

My phone rang at the table.
"Is that Brenda Collins?"
"Yes," I said.
"Can you do a show for us on Friday night?" the caller said.
"I'm sorry but I'm on a Nile cruise."

"You're not, what's it like?" "Is it good?" So I told them how great it was and that we'd been to The Valley of the Kings, been to the temples, rode a camel on the Sahara, where I became Florence of Arabia. "Can you come the following Friday?" asked the caller.

"If you can hold on I will run down for my diary." I put my phone down on the dinner table and ran as fast as I could, explaining to my fellow diners that I had a possible booking in the offing.

"Yes I can, yes I can work next Friday."

"Oh that's good," said the caller, "Can you be a belly dancer?" Well I put the phone down and I stood up and turned around and saw that it was a fellow gang member ringing me up from the other side of the dining room on the boat. It was a total gotcha!!! The place was in an uproar because everyone except my friend and I were in on it. Eeeeehhh the rotten b...ers.

I made my mind up there and then that I was going to get them back some way or another. Oh yes I was!!!!! Big Time!!!!

There were some very intelligent passengers on the Nile Cruise (none of them in our gang!). Some carried books with them and referred to them now and again. We didn't. So I had to think what I could do to get them back.

I thought and thought then I thought ...yes I will be a belly dancer.

Before we came on the cruise I bought lots of lollies, pens, pencils, sweeties, which the Egyptian children called booboos. I bought them for the children to give to them on our excusions.

I discussed my plan with our guide and he was up for it. On the last night of the tour there was to be a presentation to the couple who had paid the most attention, joined in the role play and answered the most questions posed by Salla, our guide, during the cruise. Well our gang knew it would be none of them. Or would it?

It was the evening of the presentation. Everyone was anxious as to who would win the prize and what it would be. It was, of course, going to Janet and her husband, the couple who rang me for me to be a belly dancer.

I got into my belly dancer costume; I put pens, pencils, lollies and booboos down my skirt waistband and my bra then I hid under a sheet in reception. Salla was nearby to give me the cue.

My friend was with all the gang who had enquired where I was. She replied to them that I wasn't very well and was on the toilet!!! I was under the sheet so that no one would notice me. Yeah!!!

When the music started I was to come into the room and belly dance all the way to the winners of the tour. That would be Janet and Brian, who would least expect it. See.

While I was under the sheet my bra snapped and all the lollies, pens, pencils, booboos fell out onto the floor. I shouted (in a whisper)

"Salla, Salla, me bra's snapped. Come over here."

"But Miss Brenda I know nothing about brassieres," replied Salla.

"Never mind that, it's time you learned. Now just put your hand up the sheet and fasten my bra."

"But no Miss Brenda."

"Salla just DO IT."

Well what did he do? He put his hand up the sheet I handed him the two fasteners of my bra and what did he do? He tied my bra in a knot. My boobs were up to my chin!!! Anyway I put the lollies and pens and pencils all back into position and off I went into the room full of people.

It was a really good night and Janet and Brian were gob smacked that they received the prize although I do believe there were a lot of disappointed couples!!!

Salla was a good guide and a very nice person. There

was another guide on the tour who wasn't very nice or very good and people defected from his group into ours because we were having a fab time.

The next day, before we left, our gang went on camels for a little ride. We thought it would be like on the donkeys at Scarborough. Oh no, we got on the camels and a boy slapped the backside of the camel and off we went galloping across the Sahara. Eeeeh we hung on, clinging to the camel's neck.

Janet's camel was called Titanic. She wasn't very happy and neither was her camel. I think he had the 'hump'!

It was great fun. After the journey, Janet said that she had hated every minute of that ride across the Sahara.

During one of the excursions, in fact all the excursions were to temples. We were all 'templed' out. I mean it was wonderful but our brains could only take so much in. So we decided to move away from one of our tours. This was in Luxor. Our group decided we'd make our way back to the boat.

When we left the boat on the morning it was moored not far away from the temple. There were armed guards everywhere. This was our plan of action.

I'd move first away from the group and hide behind a pillar, then the next would move and so on until we were all hiding behind pillars in the temple. I mean these pillars are about the height of a 4 storey building. We were like Japanese snipers on a mission. The armed guards must have watched us with thoughts of "What the hell are they up to?" It's a wonder we weren't arrested. We thought we would make our way to the boat and have dinner first. Yes first, because we were usually always last for our dinners. I wonder why?

The cruise ships all moor up side by side with their reception areas next to each other. So if you were midstream, you had to walk through all the receptions of the other ships to get to your ship. The last one was usually ours because it was the smallest. The ships were linked by gangplanks. So off we went through where we thought our ship was moored. Well it was there when we left it that morning.

Oh dear we went through the ships expecting to find ours at the end but it wasn't there. We went through rows and rows of ships but they had moved ours. We had no idea where to. So we went searching and searching until it came near the time for us to sail. We were well and truly lost.

The ship sent a search party out to find us via the horse and trap men.

"You the lost people you must get to your ship it is going to sail," they shouted to us,

"Where is our ship?"

"It is over there Miss." So many of the horse and trap men shouted this to us so we got into a couple of carriages, there were about 10 of us, so we took up quite a few horse and traps. All of the locals knew about us. In fact I think the whole of Egypt knew about us!!

We got back to the ship and we were the talk of the place. Nothing new there then!! That night we got no dinner at all.

You see if we had stayed with the guide, Salla, he would have taken us straight back to our ship. We were all on the naughty step that night. In fact every night we were on the naughty step!!!!

When we got our meals our table was right next to the toaster. Passengers would come and put their bread into the toaster then forget about it. We would shout, all of us:

"Toast ready," a few minutes later...

"Toast ready." a few minutes later....

"Toast burning, toast burning." Then....

"Toast burnt."

Well we used to laugh and laugh until our sides really

hurt. We laughed when we met up in the morning until it was time to go to bed. It was a wonderful cruise with a wonderful gang of people. It was great!!!!

I never thought that in a few more years I would be cruising around the world entertaining passengers and even going to Egypt working on a cruise.

Naughty Soldiers

I got a phone call from an agent, I'm freelance you see, asking if I would fly to Padderborn, Germany for one night and entertain the soldiers. I told him that I would only go if it was Officers' or Sergeants' mess. He said that it was one or the other.

So we flew out. A car picked us up from the airport in Germany and took us to the venue. It was Christmas time.

Oh we thought, "We'll see the Christmas markets. Lovely."

We got to the venue and a sergeant came into my dressing room.

"Hello Brenda, can you be ready as soon as possible as we're running late."

"Yes, no problem." I didn't get a chance to see the audience because everything was a bit of a rush. The sergeant then proceeded to tell me that there were 500 squaddies in the audience who knew I was female. They were all armed with pork pies from the buffet and were out to get me. The last act, a man, only lasted 10 minutes on stage then they pied him!!! Well how do you think I felt about that? I wanted to go home. Why should I put up with 500 boys full of testosterone and all out to get ME?

Yes me, little Brenda, who never hurt anyone. They were out to get me for their own fun!!! NO WAY. I'd been in entertainment for long enough and why should I put up with this sort of behaviour? I didn't have to put up with it. I wasn't going to stand there and let young'uns throw pies at me. NO WAY!!!! I don't even like pork pies.

My friend said:

"Brenda we're here, go out there and show them'...'
Then I thought,

"Right.... I will go out there and show the little b...ers, even though they were all over 6 feet tall. I'm not frightened of them!!! No way..."

I started the show with a Cilla song. There was some reaction, maybe not of a good kind...murmurings such as, 'Oh it's a middle aged woman trying to make us laugh, go on then try.' So in the middle of the song I said:

"If you don't wave your arms or join in I will … bleep bleep pick on you." I had to give them the shock factor. One lad shouted back,

"Cilla doesn't swear."

"Well this one does." I felt terrible doing it but it had to be done.

I thought to myself, "Oh dear what am I doing up here?" Then I said to myself, "Brenda just get on with it and show them who the boss really is."

You see entertaining is at first like a cricket match. How does the bowler pitch the ball? How am I going to treat this audience? Give me the WMC audience, a Warner's audience, a cruise audience anything other than the one I was facing. These were like animals out for the kill, with pork pies and they were out to get me!!! Ughhhhhh!!!

I had hecklers, some easy to deal with, but one in particular was a cheeky chappy. He thought he was clever, cleverer than me. Huh!! Now it became like a tennis match. He was whacking the insults to me and I was whacking the one-liners in return. In between I still carried on with jokes. NO PIES YET!!!!

My young heckler went to the toilet. I still carried on telling the jokes.

It was the time in the show where I get a young man out of the audience and the heckler's disappearance to the toilet had come at the best time because no way did I want him up on stage. I dressed the 'volunteer' up and he entered into the fun of the sketch. Remember all of this audience of young soldiers were full of alcohol. NO PIES YET!!!

The young soldier started to do the strip tease to the stripper music; by the way the young heckler was still in the toilet! Anyway the young soldier loved the attention he was getting to taking the dress off, which I'd dressed him in. Da da de de Da da de da......when who should make his appearance from the toilets but Mighty Mouth. Oh dear – oh dear he was mad; he wasn't happy at all. Oh no. You see he saw the young soldier doing what he thought he should have been doing. Anyway the young soldier made his way back to his seat to cheers and applause which was deafening.

Mighty Mouth was coming down the aisle towards me. He was angry, in fact if looks could kill. I'd be on the front line. And, of course, I was.

He roared at the audience to get their attention. The room fell silent. He looked at me and I looked at him. I said,

"Yes, can I help?" upon which he turned his back to me, dropped his trousers and pants and mooned at me (showed me his backside).

"Young man," I said "pull your trousers up get back into that toilet and wipe your arse properly."

He stayed in the bent over position for a few moments. There was a deathly silence – then the audience erupted. Everyone laughed like mad 'at' the bully. His time had come.

He pulled his trousers up and went back to his seat. I bet he was seething mad. At this point I told the audience to drop the pies, which they did. They obeyed ME! I was applauded and got a standing ovation from everyone. Well nearly everyone. I don't think Mighty Mouth stood up. But he did come to my dressing room with a stein of beer.

He said to me that no one ever got the better of him, and then said, "Well done." I took it as a compliment. All in all I was on stage for about one hour and a half but I never, never ever want an audience like that in front of me again. I may not be as lucky the next time.

Life Ticking Over

Richard was in the band and, of course, I was here there and everywhere.

Our Peter was employed as a welder but fancied training as a plasterer. He got an interview with a local firm and landed himself an apprenticeship to train as a plasterer. Peter would be about 20 years old and Richard 25. They were both fine, good looking young men.

The boys hardly ever saw their Dad. So sad. I did go and see him and told him he should see his boys, his sons. His reply was:

"They know where I am." His loss.

My Dad was still doing well. Still riding his bike, Poppy running alongside, both of them popular characters of the village.

My Dad loved to come along with me when I was working locally. He never sat and watched me on stage, he always watched the audience. At the end of the evening he'd get a lady up to dance. He loved it. He was such a flirt.

I had a booking at a club in a local village. My Dad sat in the front of my van. Lyn, my friend, was in the back of the van with all the equipment. Dad didn't know she was there.

We arrived at the venue and I told my Dad that I was going to get the doors open at the back of the building.

While I was doing this Lyn had said to my Dad,

"Hello Alfie." She thought he knew she was in the back of the van. She said again,

"Hello Alfie, it's me."

"Who?"

"It's me Alfie, Lyn."

"Oh Aye, Eeeh Hello Lyn." I think he thought he'd had a spiritual visit. After that whenever my Dad got into the van to go to a club he'd say, "Are you in there Lyn?" And bang the side of the van, just to make sure.

He used to think the sat-nav voice was Lyn telling me how to get to the club.

"Is that Lyn?" he'd say,

"No Dad it's the sat nav".

"Oh Aye, by Lyn's clever knowing all the roads." I never tried to convince him that it wasn't Lyn, but the sat nav. My dad was the oldest groupie in the UK.

The Waitress from Hell

I had a call from my accountant, Phil. My accountant's office is in a small town called Crook. How amazing is that?

He asked me if I'd ever done any waitressing.

"You're joking, no never. I wouldn't know what to do. I'm absolutely useless at anything like that."

"Well." he said, "I've booked The Helm Park Hotel for our annual works Christmas function and I want you to be a waitress there, then to do your show straight after the waitressing." He said that it would be silver service.

Oh my goodness, me a waitress. Anyway I agreed because I thought it could be fun if done properly. I gave it some thought on how I would work it – not to be too OTT and too obvious a plant.

I went for a meeting with the manager of the hotel. He was very nice and very up for the gottcha. We came up with the plan of action. I thought, "This is going to be good."

Only a few people were in on the plan.

Well the evening arrived and the manager gave me my uniform and I had a badge. My name for the evening was Lisa and I was a trainee sent by the Job Centre. I had a hair clip in to keep my fringe from my eyes. I had fish net tights and sandshoes (plimsolls). I wasn't as immaculate as the other waitresses but I wasn't scruffy, oh no.

I was introduced to the head waitress and my fellow waitresses, who were all in on "it". We were all lined up in front of the guests. The hotel manager welcomed everyone and introduced each waitress in turn. When it came to my name being called out by the manager I did a curtsey. After all the introductions he wished all the guests Bon Appetite.

Off we went. It was full steam ahead. Starters, "Who's for melon, who's for soup, who's for fish (smoked salmon)."

I told the guests I served that I'd been sent by the Social to help the hotel out during the busy season and I hoped they would keep me on permanent.

During the course of the dinner I dropped the odd folk and wiped it on my apron then put it back on the table as if it was normal for me to do that. I also gave an old man a cuddle and told him he was a cheeky old bugger.

All the time I made sure I wasn't too over the top. I played the part of a middle aged woman just happy to get a job at Christmas.

I told them my veins were killing me and that I was dying for a fag. I said that I might pop out for a sly drag and would they come out and let me know if the boss comes into the room. I also told them I'd brought my slippers for when my feet started aching. I carried my fags in my pinny (apron) pocket.

On my way to have a smoke (by the way I don't smoke) a young man passed me and I turned round and nipped his bottom, making sure people saw.

"Hey she's just nipped my arse."

"No I didn't," I replied" it was her." And I pointed to a very posh lady. Well she got up and went straight to the manager.

"If you don't get rid of her, that woman, the standard of your hotel will drastically drop. She's a disgrace,"

There was a screen where the coffee facilities were situated,'staff only', and all of us waitresses kept going behind there to get our laughs out and come from behind the screen with a straight face.

While the posh woman was ranting and raving it gave me a chance to go into another room next to the dining room and turn into Cilla Black. I came out on stage while guests were just finishing their coffee.

Everyone applauded and laughed. Oh my goodness I loved every minute of it. It was an amazing evening. I hope everyone felt the same. I know the waitresses did and the hotel manager did too.

Do you know I was never offered the job permanently!! Huh!!

About a year later the manager offered me another job comedy waitressing but this time it was a buffet. It was just as good, and just as good fun for me and for the guests.

A Christmas Letter

It was Christmas week and one morning I opened my mail. There was a brown envelope so I left that until last.

When I eventually opened it and read it my heart sank. I had to sit down. Oh dear, what have I done? What am I to do? Oh dear I've done nothing wrong. Who's done this to me and why?

All of these questions ran through my head. I felt sick. I needed to speak to someone fast. I needed to speak to my accountant, Phil. He'd know what to do. The letter said I was to be investigated by the Inland Revenue.

They had picked two years and they wanted everything, bank statements, receipts, bank books, paying in books – everything that applied to those two years.

Oh my goodness, oh dear me. What was going to happen? I thought to myself that I had nothing to feel guilty about. I'd paid my taxes since I started work at the age of 16.

Jack Brandes, our first manager, always told us to pay our taxes by putting some money away each week. This was years ago when I was in the group and, of course, we were self-employed and when we turned professional we had to register for VAT.

I used to do the accounts for all the lads in the group and put all the invoices in an onion string bag (orange type).

Well we got a visit from a Customs and Excise Inspector and he asked to see some invoices.

"They're all in there," I said, handing him the onion bag.

We'd had a late night the night before so I said to the Inspector that I was going for a lie down. I hoped he didn't mind. I knew the inspector as he was in the Scouts, also a Queen's Scout and of course I was a Queen's Guide.

"Go and have a lie down and I'll look through the invoices."

He was on hours because when I eventually woke it was tea time. He had arrived at 9 o'clock in the morning. When I went down stairs he was still there.

"Eeeh," I said, "Are you still here?"

He suggested I should get a wire coat hanger, open it out into a straight piece of wire and put a bit of wood at the bottom. Then as I receive invoices place them on the coat hanger and they will be in date order. "Well what a good idea."I thought to myself.

Do you know I still use that system to this day? I've only

just found out from a couple of passengers from a cruise, who were Customs and Excise Officers that that lovely Queen's Scout had recently died. He was a very kind person. Nice Lad.

Getting back to my investigation. Well all my invoices were on a coat hanger and I sent this, along with statements and things to Phil, my accountant.

What did he do? He sent the coat-hanger to the Inspector of Taxes. I didn't know this until my "Interview"

Do you know? That's what Ken Dodd and I have in common. We have big teeth, won't get off stage and have been investigated by the Inland Revenue!!!!

The meeting was held at my accountant's office. My accountant, Phil, is confined to an electric wheelchair.

It came to the day of my interview. Oh dear. Phil told me not to be nervous and told me to sit on a chair which was in the corner of his office.

"Oh no Phil, I'm not sitting in the naughty corner, I'm sitting next to you for support and help when I most need it."

I pulled my chair up to Phil's electric chair. The phone rang to advise Phil that the inspectors had arrived and Phil duly asked the receptionist to show them to his office. The inspectors came in and I stood up.

"Hello." I said. "I'm Brenda." "Yes we know who you are." the man said. It was a man and a woman and they were very serious. He told me to sit down.

"Now." he said, "We want you to tell us all about yourself, and how you got started entertaining. We want you to tell us everything. Just relax." Well I did and I leaned on Phil's electric chair arm. My chair had no arms. Phil's chair wasn't in lock position and what did it do? The chair started moving, going backwards. I daresay Phil never locked his chair because he didn't think anyone would lean on the controls. Oh dear it was serious. His chair didn't move very fast but it was moving.

I was no good because I didn't know which buttons to press. I jumped up and tried to stop the chair. The chair with Phil in it was heading for the window. Oh no!! I stood rigid and bit my bottom lip. What was going to happen? The inspectors just looked on in disbelief.

Phil at the very last moment before the chair went through the window got the chair in the forward mode and moved the chair up to the desk. Phew, Eeeehhhh. The lady inspector, I noticed when I got back to my chair, was down at her bag. She was down there for a while. The man inspector said,

"Can you come up now from your bag?"

"Of course."She said.

When we'd all recovered from the incident the man asked:

"Now what's this invoice for a lampshade"?

"Well now."I said, "that's for when it's hot and I put it on my head and say: 'By, it's cooler in the shade'! You see I think of ideas and go out and buy the items to make up the sketch and to make it funny." We were on ages chatting about different props I'd bought, including football bladders for when my tummy gets blown up by a car foot pump.

We were on ages chatting about my life. I told them funny situations which had happened.

Then we got onto star signs. Both were very interested. I asked the man what his star sign was. He said that he was a Capricorn.

"Oooooooh." I said, "Can I tell you something?"

"Yes, please do."

"Now you give 200% but you also expect everyone else to. Am I right?"

"Yes." He said. And the lady inspector said,

"Eeeh mind you do."

"And," I said. "You must stop taking work home with you, you work too hard."

"Yes I do." He said in agreement. He said that his mother always warned him that he was in line for a heart attack if he kept taking work home with him. The inspectors told me at the end of the two and a half hour interview that they had never had an interview like mine – full of laughter. I told them that I too had never had an interview like it either!!

A Chinese Meal

I was still working very hard, in holiday parks, clubs and anything that came my way. I had to work nearly every night in order to survive.

Richard was still living with the band so I had only Peter to look after. He went to his Dad's now and again. Peter and I managed by sharing the bills. It worked well. By this time Peter had a girlfriend, Kathryn who was lovely.

I'd paid into a private pension and on the last forecast it indicated that in total I'd lost £11,000. I ended up with £3,000 lump sum. I was not a happy person.

During my interview with the Inland Revenue the man asked,

"Where did you go for your holidays?"

My boys and I had been abroad quite a bit, but it was always working holidays. The flights, accommodation and food were all paid for; all I had to do was entertain for two nights. It was great because my boys could take a couple of friends with them.

My answer to the question by the inspector was – wait for it, "China." He said, "China." I said, "Yes China." He said, "And how could you afford China?" I told him that he could see from my statements I saved £100 per month which went into a pension and after years of saving all that was left was £3,000 and I wasn't going to lose that! They'd got enough out of me.

I rang my friend and said, "I need a break." She needed a break too, as she had just lost her husband.

"Oh yes, where are you going?"

"China." I said,

"China!!!" she said.

"Yes, China, and you are coming with me so pack your bags we're going tomorrow. My friend, Ann had been and she said it was great. So, bags packed and off we went to Heathrow by coach.

The journey by coach was most entertaining. We sat near the back of the coach next to the toilet. A lady came by and went to the toilet. It was obvious the door lock didn't work properly. When the bus turned a tight corner, the toilet door flung open and there she was this lady holding onto the door handle with her knickers around her ankles.

We couldn't stop laughing because when the bus straightened up, she as able to shut the door and have some privacy. I hope you can picture the scene. A few hours later up the aisle she came again to have another go.

A young lad behind us was trying to shut the curtains. He tugged and tugged until the whole rail came adrift from the window. He, my friend and I ended up with the curtain covering us. He apologised. He was very embarrassed.

Anyway we got to Heathrow and went through to the departure lounge. We sat with people who we would spend the next 18 days with. Ummm.

We looked at this bunch of people; a very big bunch, and we started to pick "our gang" like we did in Egypt. They're not in our gang, they're not, they're definitely not. Do you know all the ones who we said were not, ended up on our gang because we all had the similar sense of humour (the gutter)!!!

We flew out on a massive jumbo, massive it was. We sat next to a lovely Welsh couple, a retired teacher and her husband. She was called Rosalynn.

Unknown to us our tour guides were in the seats directly in front of us. They were all suffering from a hangover and were trying to sleep it off before landing in China. Well we didn't know that at the time.

Settling into the flight Rosalynn, her husband, Lyn and myself started sharing stories with each other and so the laughter started.

We'd go for a little walk around the plane for a bit of exercise. We did aerobics at the back of the plane, bending and lifting our knees one at a time.

One lady was leaning against a door.

"Oh be careful" I told her "that's the outside toilet." After a good laugh doing the aerobics we made our way back to our seats.

There was a big screen right at the front of the plane; in fact it was right in front of us, because we were at the front of the plane too. A film started with English subtitles. The actors spoke Chinese. We decided to make up our story line for this film and not take any notice of the subtitles. We called it "The Fag." because after every scene a Chinese couple would have a cigarette.

I started the story off, all the time looking at what was happening in the film, and then it was Rosalynn's turn then her husband's and then Lyn's. Then back to me. We were putting our version of the film together. We couldn't talk for laughing. We giggled and giggled.

By the time the film finished we were half way through the flight, which was good. We did chair aerobics. Then we went to the back of the plane to do some stand up aerobics. Some of the passengers who saw that we were having fun came to join in.

We were up and down the aisles getting more people involved. The more people that got involved the more we laughed and they did too. Anyway, soon an announcement came over that we were due to land. Well that flight went over quickly. Rosalynn and her husband hoped that they were in the same group as us. We hoped so too.

At this point four very, very, very disgruntled girls looked over the backs of their seats at us. They were staring at us. We looked at them and they stared back at us. We wondered, "What's wrong with them?"

The girl, who we found out later to be the head of the tour guides said, "You four are to be separated. We are your tour guides and we haven't slept a wink. We are very tired and very angry." Ooooooohhh. We wondered what had rattled their cages? We looked at them in all innocence. We hadn't done anything wrong. What had made them so upset? We just looked at them like school children, wondering what we had done wrong.

These four tour guides were not going to forgive us – not for a long time. Oh dear. On the naughty step again.

We got off the plane and went through security, which was very health conscious because of the SARS virus. We met up with our tour guides and we were put into groups of three coaches. Rosalynn and her husband were not on our coach. We were sad about that. We were obviously the naughty girls and were to be kept an eye on.

Our coach filled up and our Chinese tour guide got on and introduced himself as Ho. Well it couldn't have been scripted because we all shouted, "Hi Ho." What more did we want, our passengers on our coach we all bonded and we became – Yes, The Naughty Coach!!!

We sang songs, we sent each other presents up and down the coach, usually tooth brushes or shower caps, chop sticks, and shower gel which we got free from the the Holiday Inn Hotel.

Our English tour guide kept an eye on Lyn and me. I didn't tell a soul what I did for a living. I just said that I worked on a night time.

Suzanne our guide guessed, "You're a nurse."

"No try again."

"You're a waitress."

"No try again."

"You're a lady of the night." I ended up telling our tour guides what I did for a living. They didn't believe me at first. No one ever does.

When passengers or guests who haven't seen me ask what I do and I say that I'm a comedian. They usually make a little laugh and say, "Yeah." They never believe me and still don't until they see me appear on stage and then it's:

"Eeeh it's that woman we were talking to."

We went on a cruise up the Yangtze as part of the tour and we were split up into tables, of course, our table became the very noisy table from morning until night. We laughed all day. You see our table was full of lively and colourful characters.

We did Ti Chi on a morning. Well the ladies of our gang did. The men just walked around us laughing. We told them to go away.

There was one evening of entertainment on this little boat and that was Chinese dancing, which was very good.

While we were in China the food was horrible, I couldn't eat most of it, in fact I couldn't eat any of it. I just stuck to crisps and biscuits. While we were on the boat the food was very westernised and it was lovely. At least I got something to eat while we were on there. The food elsewhere was, believe me, vile. I lost a stone in one week.

While we were on the boat I told our gang what my job was, so we got together in a cabin, all 8 of us, and we put together a Blind Date show. The contestants were all from our gang. We had a Bob the Builder, a drummer, two gay men and a gay air steward. Sophia was the lovely girl looking for a Blind Date. Poor lass.

Our four tour guides, who had all forgiven us by this time, knew what we were up to and even encouraged us.

It was a comedy version of Blind Date. We had "Our Graham" and the music was just the rest of the gang going Da de da de da de dede. Yes well.

It was the night of the show. Everyone was nervous especially me. I'd borrowed someone's curling tongs to do my hair because I hadn't brought my Carmen rollers, which I got when I was 21. Do you know I still use them to make myself look like Cilla?

Anyway we were all in costume, which we'd put together by beg, steal or borrow. The audience were made up of all the other coaches, who incidentally weren't keen on us. Mainly because we were always laughing and usually I was the instigator.

None of the audience knew what the entertainment for that evening was and when I came out as Cilla Black they all got a shock because only our coach knew what I did for a living.

It was a great evening and the audience roared with laughter. All our gang remembered their lines, except me. I kept saying, "And it's make your mind up time", when it wasn't!!

We had a sing along at the end of the show and do you know the other passengers from the other coaches even started talking to me. Well that was a first!!! It was a great night and I do believe everyone enjoyed themselves, especially our gang.

We went to see the Terracotta Army. Lyn and I were told to keep moving because they were stock taking. Cheek!!

We also went to the Great Wall of China. It was all so fabulous. Again our gang laughed and laughed.

A few passengers went down with chest infections, I still couldn't eat the food even though we were back on land by this time.

We went on a tour on the Yangtze in a sampan and our Captain with his 'steer board' (a large oar) started singing.

His voice echoed around the Gorges. OhhhhZinnnnChingggDaaaa (this is his singing in Chinese). When he finished the song he spat into the river. He got a round of applause for that. I thought to myself I must remember to spit when I finish a song.

Well we got back to Beijing and we were told by Ho that under no circumstances must we go into Hotel No 2.

You see the hotel was split into three hotels: No 1; No 2; and No 3. These were all linked by tunnels which were full of shops and places to eat. It was lovely. Ho repeated,

"Under no circumstances must you go into Hotel No 2, anyway you will not get in because it is heavily guarded because the Emperor's sister is staying in Hotel No 2." All this in his best broken English.

Lyn and I went looking around the shops in the tunnels of Hotel No 1 when all of a sudden a Chinese woman with black hair (I think they all have black hair), anyway, hers was tied in a bun. She wore a black dress. She said, "HaaaarrrrraChaaaraaa Chi ReeeeHaaaarrrrra" or words to that effect.

We didn't know what she was saying and we looked at her with blank faces. But we knew she wasn't very happy.

All of a sudden armed guards came towards us, marching at the double. I was told, in Chinese, (I was getting the gist by this time of what the woman was meaning), to get behind the front guard. A guard was behind me, then Lyn and then a guard behind her.

"We've really done it now," said Lyn. We had no idea where they were taking us. We thought we were going to be put in prison and the key thrown away and we were never to be seen again! The Chinese lady said something, which must have meant quick march because off we went marching at the double. These guards all had guns and I bet they were loaded.

We were taken into reception, and there in reception

was everyone: our tour guides, our gang and our guide, Ho. "Where the hell have you two been?" Suzanne said, Need she have asked?

They looked at the armed guards then again to us. The Chinese lady said something to Ho which was something like. "We found them in Hotel No 2." We said that we hadn't seen any restrictions and we didn't know we were in Hotel No 2. Anyway, we got out and weren't locked up!! Our tour guides looked at us in a way that implied 'what more did they expect from us two'.

I thought to myself, "Oh well we're on the naughty step again." We thoroughly enjoyed our trip to China and met up with some wonderful people, our tour guides. A holiday never to be forgotten.

Hospital for My Dad

When my Dad was 90 years old he rang me up and said, "I have to go to the hospital. I have an appointment." I went through to pick him and dropped him off at the hospital. I said to him,

"Do you know where you have to go because I can come with you?" I said.

"Why aye I know where I'm going, if I get lost I'll ask someone."

Eileen and I thought he was being examined for a claim for compensation with the NCB. Some of his friends had got some money from the Coal Board. He had told me he was going to try and get some money. I said to him that he wouldn't get any because he was fitter than the doctors. Not many doctors would be able to ride 4 miles every day when they reached the age of 90.

Well a few days later I got a telephone call from the hospital asking me to bring my Dad to the hospital and they suggested I accompany him. His appointment was with a Miss Green.

I went to collect him from his bungalow and off we went to the hospital and we checked into reception.

"My Dad is here to see a Miss Green."

"Oh yes, Miss Green", the receptionist replied, "The Consultant Surgeon." Surgeon! Oh dear me I didn't expect this.

We went into an office and faced a young, slightly built lady. We shook hands and she asked us to take a seat. My Dad was as charming as ever, always smiling, (for the women).

"Mr. Swainston you have bowel cancer." I don't think he took it in because he never flinched, he just kept smiling." Because you are so fit for a 90 year old we are going to operate and remove the cancer."

"What's she saying?" my Dad said. I told him.

"You have to have an operation, you're going into hospital." She said that she would be operating on him that week.

"Oh my goodness."

We left the hospital and I again said to my Dad that he was going into hospital for an operation.

"Aye, alright. I heard what you said the first time."

I rang our Eileen and told her the news. She got him some new pyjamas and some toiletries. I said I'd look after Poppy. He went into hospital two days later; it was as quick as that.

We went to see him on the day before his operation and eeeh he was enjoying himself – flirting with all the nurses and chatting to the other patients. He was having a great time. He loved the company and he said the food was lovely. He'd had cake and custard and it was really nice. We often gave him cake and custard he never told us it was nice!

He also loved touching young nurses' bottoms. Very naughty. Eileen and I told him it was very wrong. He just grinned and said that he only touched their arms.

"No you didn't." I'd say.

The sister in charge of the ward said that he had even touched her bottom. I said, "I'm sorry I can only apologise for his behaviour. "Well we are trained for that sort of thing!!" she replied.

The day after his admission he had his operation. Eileen and I went to see him. I said to our Eileen, "Well the operation should calm him down." Eileen said that she wondered if it was worth going in because he would be heavily sedated.

Anyway we went into the hospital. We stood outside intensive care and then rang the bell, a nurse came and we asked for Alfred Swainston. "Oh Alfie, yes come on in." We were expecting to see him zonked out. Oh no not Alfie – I mean, he'd just had major surgery and here he was sitting up chatting away to the nurses. All the intensive care nurses said that he was a tonic - just what they needed. All the other patients in the other beds were all out for the count.

He was transferred onto the medical ward and I took in a photograph of Poppy so that he could show all his new friends his wonderful dog. He was chuffed to bits.

He enjoyed his stay in hospital but missed smoking his pipe. Yes, he was still smoking a pipe at 90. When I worked abroad he'd say, "Bring us some baccy back will you?"

If there was a discipline policy in the hospital my Dad would have always been on the naughty step! And why not?

Miss Green, the Consultant who operated on my Dad said that it was his healthy lifestyle that contributed to her operating on him and his speedy recovery. He ate steak pies; in fact he bloody loved them. Bacon sandwiches, fish and chips, oh and of course cake and custard.

He went for rehabilitation for a few weeks and then they

allowed him home. He was to get extra care from Social Services. After a while he soon forgot he'd even been in hospital and he was back on his bike, stopping off now and again for a smoke of his pipe and a drink, waving to passers-by.

During the autumn months he collected blackberries which grew at the back of his bungalow. He gave them to his neighbours, whose wives always baked him blackberry pies.

Our Eileen used to go mad with his behaviour and his attire. He was still wearing his denims, split at the knee, a bomber jacket and of course the baseball cap.   Sometimes the cap had a picture of Spiderman or one of me Mam's brooches.

Remember our Eileen is a Mrs. Bouquet replica!!!

Next Stage - Cruising

I got a phone call from an agent asking if I would like to go on a cruise to the Red Sea in Egypt. Oh, and if I did well, I would get more cruises. Wow!

Oh my goodness. I couldn't believe it, me going to work on a cruise. I was told by the agent that it was a Thomson Cruise and it would be on a ship called The Celebration. I would be flown out to greet the ship in Egypt.

Oh dear, what was I going to do? I had to think fast and put two shows together suitable for cruises, not holiday parks or social clubs. My friend and I set about changing my show completely, changing the costumes and the props as well as the sketches and, of course, the songs. It was going to be hard work but we set about the task.

I also wanted film work to feature in my two shows. I had to find someone who could help me there as well as Kevin to do all the studio work. We put a script together and researched for film and picture material for one of my songs The Working Man. This song is all about young men who worked down the mines.

We worked from morning till night, as we had a deadline to meet. I also wanted some film work to highlight nostalgia. How our lives were in the 50s, 60s and 70s. Again a lot of research had to be done. Lyn made all the costumes while I was in the recording studio.

I learnt the words to new songs while I was travelling in the car. Then came rehearsals and dress rehearsals. It was hard, hard work but we did it.

Then I had to find someone who I could take with me to assist with my costume changes and also to assist with the technical side of my show.

Clive Webb's ex-wife, Jacquie said she would come with me. So I went down to Cardiff, took all the props, costumes, sound system and tracks in order to train Jacquie to be my stage manager. She had to learn how to get me in and out of costumes in seconds and in the correct order. Jacquie was enthusiastic and so was I. Jacquie learned fast and she had the same sense of humour, so she would be a good companion.

The time came for us to fly out and join the ship. Jacquie came up to Newcastle Airport and there we were with four suitcases between us. We were feeling very nervous.

We landed in Sharm el Sheikh and we were greeted by men in white frocks and scone-like hats all asking for English pounds.

A coach was at the airport to transfer us to the ship. We got to the ship and when we first saw it we both went wow. ,

"Well here we go Bren." said Jacquie.

"Yeah, here we go."

We were given a nice cabin and there was a letter asking me to meet the cruise director at 2.00pm to discuss my shows. My cruise director was a gentleman called David Bradshaw and he was very nice. He welcomed us both on board and hoped we'd settle in. He told me the days of my shows. I was still running through words in my head of new songs and, of course, the running order of the new shows. Oh my goodness.

Well the night of my first show came. I was so nervous that my top lip stuck to my gum. I was still learning the order of all the jokes. Jacquie was as nervous as I was. Eeeeeh.

David announced me.

"Welcome on stage Brenda Collins. And Brenda who are you going to be tonight?" Out I went onto that big stage with about 500 passengers sitting in front of me. I was frightened, nervous and scared all at the same time.

Once I sang my opening song I settled into my routines. Jacquie was there in the wings, ready and all prepared to get me into the costumes. The quick changes went very smoothly.

In one evening, I had to perform my number one show twice for the passengers from each of the two dinner sittings. My first show went really well.

I came off stage on a high. Weeeeeee!!! Then I had to do it all over again; this meant coming down from the 'high' and preparing myself mentally for the second show as well as preparing the props on stage and back stage again.

It all went well. Both shows were a success with the passengers. David came to me at the end of the evening and said he had already put in a glowing report about me. Well, I was skipping and dancing. I was over the moon.

I rang my Dad the next day and told him that my show had gone down well.

"Well done Brenda. Well done," he said.

For my next evening's performance, which was about four days after my first one, I only had to do half an hour and that too went really, really well. I loved every minute of it. In fact I didn't want my show to end.

During the week I was asked to be part of the Call My Bluff team. Oh dear. I was given the words and so Jacquie and I got down to working out our own answers. They had a list of scripted ones but we thought we'd do our own. Of course it was all about ancient Egypt. My first question was the meaning of 'Tut'.

Here's how it went on the night of the game show:

"It's not Tut it's Tutem, Tutem Carmen, and he was the mobile hairdresser in Egypt for the Pharoes of the land. He travelled around on a camel. He was the Teasy-Weasy of the Egyptian world. He even combed the locks of Cleopatra on her barge, this was before the asp. He also invented the first heated rollers thousands of years ago. Hence the name 'Carmen'.

Wearing my Carmen rollers I got for my 21st birthday

My second word was Pylon. Here's how this one went:

"Well again, it's not Pylon but Pylonny Donegan, who was the Egyptian minstrel. He wrote songs such as My Old Man's a Pharaoh; He wears a Pharaoh's hat. All his songs, in order to remember them, were inscribed in the tombs of Egypt and even got into the Egyptian charts of that time. We laughed and laughed until we wet ourselves and I think some of the passengers did too. Jacquie was brilliant and we had a great time on The Celebration in Egypt.

When I got back home the agent rang me up and told me that I had been given 8 more cruises for that year. Weeeeeeeeee!!!!!! I set about fine tuning my two shows and working on more routines.

My next cruise was in 4 weeks time so I had to get cracking.

My two boys were both pleased for me. My next cruise was Norway, cruising around the Fjords. I went over to my Dad's and told him I was off on another cruise.

"Where are you going this time?"

"Norway."

"Oh well maybe you'll get somewhere next year." He thought I said, "Nowhere." I tried to explain. My Dad had selective hearing, and so do I!!

This time Lyn, my friend, came with me. We sailed from Newcastle, which was great. Better than flying. It was an amazing cruise. The passengers were fantastic. We went on a couple of the tours one was to a glacier. Wow. We were very excited about going to see a glacier, as were all the passengers.

I had been on stage the night before, so all the passengers knew who I was. It was nice walking up to the glacier chatting to different passengers. We got to the glacier and it was spectacular, an amazing sight.

On the way back down I walked with a lady who was a hairdresser. We chattered and chattered. I didn't say who I was and she never mentioned it. I just presumed she hadn't been to the show. I had my multi coloured Norwegian hat on and sunglasses so maybe she didn't recognise me.

Well on the way down two men passed us. They were on their way up to the glacier.

"By Brenda you were good last night."

"Thank you," I replied "I did enjoy myself too." A little further on some other men passed us and said,

"Hey Brenda do you know we didn't want last night to end, we were enjoying ourselves so much, and you were so good."

"Eeeh." I said, "I didn't want it to end either, but I'll be doing it again on Sunday night.

Well, we got down to the bottom of the mountain and she apparently said to her friend, who was walking with Lyn.

"I don't know who the hell the woman is who I've been walking and talking to but she's very popular with the men."Her friend said, "That's little Brenda who was on stage last night you daft b---er."

A very popular tour in Norway is on the Flam Railway; Lyn and I were asked to be tour guides or escorts and carry the Thomson paddles. We were given the responsibility of counting all our passengers and had a form to fill in of the events of the day and if there were any accidents. I hoped there wouldn't be any accidents and I hoped I wouldn't lose anyone.

I counted my lot onto the train and I was in charge of carriage number one. Lyn was in charge of carriage number 2 and other Thomson staff were in charge of the other carriages. Everything was going well. Everybody was enjoying the beautiful scenery, when all of a sudden the train came to a halt. Now, some passengers had come on this cruise because of this Flam Railway tour. They had saved all their money to come on the cruise purely for this. There was nobody of any official capacity to let us know what was happening.

Passengers were wondering when we were going to get started and what the problem was. We sat and we sat, then the message came through that we were to go back to the port. We were not going any further because there was a power cut further up the line.

"What are you going to do about it?" a lady said to me. So I got our carriage singing. What a jolly lot our carriage was. I went into Lyn's carriage and a man said to me,

"Don't even think about it." The atmosphere in that carriage just went as flat as a pancake. Ohhh. I felt awful. But I picked myself up and went into carriage no. 3 and got them singing, as I did with the rest of the carriages. To get back to my carriage I had to pass through no. 2 I wasn't looking forward to it at all. I came to the seats where the man sat and his wife said to him:

"Go on. Go on tell Brenda."

"I'm sorry Brenda, I was just disappointed." He said, "It's alright I understand. Now is everybody ready to sing?"

"Yes." Everyone shouted.

So off we reversed back to the port singing "She'll be Coming Round the Mountain When she Comes, Toot Toot".

The excursion staff and some of Thomson's management were at the railway station waiting for us, expecting trouble and prepared for a battle on their hands. We all got off the train in high spirits.

Of course, everyone was compensated and I was told I had done a good job. Thank you very much. I'm much obliged. I never lost anyone either.

One of the companies I worked for is called Peel and they are based in Skipton, Yorkshire. They arrange all the entertainment for Thomson ships.

Kathy from their office rang me.

"The Baltic Cruise is a two week cruise and you're on the second week so we're flying you out from Heathrow to Helsinki to join the ship." I was to put our day and evening clothes cases on the ship before it sailed the week before from Newcastle. All we had to carry on the flight was the two prop cases. That was fine by me. It was to do with the weight allowance on the aeroplane from Newcastle to Heathrow.

We got a BA plane from Newcastle and landed at Terminal 5 Heathrow. We got off the plane and waited at the carousel. We waited 40 minutes for our cases to come around on the carousel. Time was ticking, so I asked someone where we got the plane for Helsinki. They said to just to go upstairs.

We went upstairs and asked a woman the same question and she said "Oh no it's Terminal 1 you need. There's a coach downstairs."

"A coach we thought." We went downstairs got to the coach and asked a young man about us boarding the coach for Terminal 1.

"Oh no you'd be better off getting the tube." "The tube we thought."

"Where's the tube?"

"Just down the escalator. You'd better run though because it's due to go." So off we ran for the tube, running down the escalator with our cases and Angel of the North wings, which were in a bag.

The tube was in the station so we boarded and asked these lovely ladies the way to Terminal 1. They said that when the train stops they'd point us in the right direction and to run as fast as we could.

When we stopped the ladies said, "Now run that way." Well we ran and ran as fast as we could with two suitcases, a bag containing the Angel of the North wings, and two kit bags on our backs. We eventually got to the check-in exhausted but pleased and smiling that we got there in time. It was 9.30am. The check in didn't close until 9.45am.

But the smile was soon wiped from our faces. The man at the desk said, "You're too late I've closed the check-in." Lyn said, "That's not right you're not supposed to close yet." He said, "Well I have and you might as well make your way back to Newcastle." "What?" I said. He said, "You heard I'm not opening the gate."

I told him that I wanted to see his superior immediately. He said that he was the superior officer.

I was in a state of shock. I said to him that we had to get to Helsinki to meet up with a ship and he said he knew all that.

A man walked towards us with a badge on, so I asked him in desperation if he could help us. He asked what was wrong and I told him what the man on the check-in desk had said and how rude he was. He went straight to the man on the desk and asked why he had closed the gate and told him that it wasn't due to close for 10 minutes. He also asked why he had spoken to us in an impolite manner. He didn't answer.

The man with the badge asked the check-in man to move; the badge-man got behind the computer and tap, tap, tapped at the keyboard and then asked us to put our cases on the belt. We did just that and he gave us our boarding passes and told us we must run as fast as we could because the gate would be closing soon. We smiled at the nice man with the badge and said to him how grateful we were. He smiled back and said,

"My pleasure ladies. Now run."

So off we went, this time without our cases, through security, missing all the spraying of the perfumes. We got to the gate and what do you know? The plane was just landing. Eeeh all that running.

Anyway we got on the plane and guess what? The

plane sat on the tarmac for two hours. Yes, two hours. No one had any idea why we were delayed.

When we eventually got to Helsinki airport it was announced that the plane had lost its parking bay at the airport, due to the late arrival. So we waited and waited.

I know it's not allowed, but I got my phone down from the overhead locker and decided to ring the Cruise Director to let him know the situation. He told me that as soon as we got our cases from the carousel to ring him.

We eventually found a parking bay, got off the plane as quickly as we could, then made our way to get our cases. As we were lifting the cases off the carousel my phone rang.

It was Cruise Director.

"I'm sorry Brenda but we're going without you."

"What?" I pleaded and told him we had our cases and I could see the driver holding a piece of paper with my name on it, it was the car waiting for us to take us to the ship.

"I'm sorry but the Captain has decided to go."

Well we got to the car and I said to the driver,

"Please drive as fast as you can and get us to the ship. The ship is going to go without us." The driver was on a mission and the car squealed through the streets of Helsinki. We got to the port only to see The Celebration sail slowly away. Our hearts sank as deep as the Baltic.

"What do we do now?" I said to the driver, "You go to Estonia?"

The ship was going to St. Petersburg but we couldn't go there as we had no papers for entry.

"How do we get to Estonia?"

"I'll take you to the ferry port and from there you will catch the ferry to Estonia."

He took us and just dropped us off and drove away. We stood there not knowing exactly what was happening. We were in a daze.

I went up to the ticket office and asked for two tickets to

Tallinn, the capital of Estonia.

"I'm sorry but we are closed the ferry has been cancelled," the girl said.

"Eh, what? What are we to do now?"

We looked at her with faces in shock. She said that there was another ferry port a mile away, but she said that we must run as fast as we can because it may be leaving soon.

Can you believe it? So off we bloody go again, pulling two suitcases, a large tent type bag with the wings in and back packs running through the cobbled streets of Helsinki. When we arrived we were out of breath to say the least. I mean we're not olympic standard runners and we both carry a bit weight apart from our luggage!

I staggered up to the ticket booth and asked for two tickets to Tallinn. The girl said, "Yes, of course, and may I suggest that you stay the night on board because the ferry is docking very late at night and it's not good for two ladies to be wandering the streets searching for accommodation."

The girl also asked if we'd like a meal on board.

"Yes please."

"Oh and by the way," she said, "If you have a meal all the drinks are free."

"Yyyyyyeessssss!" We said. We had a lovely meal and the wine was wonderful. We drank as much wine as we were allowed before they turned the tap off. It was in a big urn and I think the staff were watching how much we were drinking. I'm sure they knew we could have easily drunk the lot.

Our cabin had bunk beds. I had to have the top bunk because I was the only one able to get up there. The bunks had straps to fasten you in while we were sailing. By the way it was a brand new ship; we heard later that the other one sank! The Baltic must get rough especially with belts to strap you in.

272

Eeeehhh I slept lovely that night, with the help of the wine, only to be woken by knocking on the door.

"Please hurry, get up get up." So we leapt out of bed and I struggled down the ladders from the top bunk. Got ready and out of the cabin. What was all the rush for? We had no idea

Then an announcement came over the tannoy:

"Would Brenda Woods, me, make her way as quickly as possible to reception." Oh no, so off we were again. We tried some doors to the outside deck but they were all locked.

"Oh hell we're on our way back to Helsinki" we thought. We eventually found our way to reception with the help from other passengers. They assisted with the carrying of the cases up the stairs as the lifts weren't working. You can see the picture can't you?

At the reception they told us we had docked last night in Tallinn and that the port agent was waiting for us. We breathed a sigh of relief. We disembarked and met up with the agent and he took us to a lovely hotel where we would stay for three days until the ship docked.

Then we thought, "Oh no. We have no clothes, no toiletries, no nowt except the props". You see, what seemed a lifetime ago, but was only one week; we had put our daytime clothes on the ship at Newcastle.

I thought, "Come on Brenda be positive." I could wear the River Dance outfit and Lyn could wear The Angel of the North for when we went down for breakfast!

The next day we bought some clothes from a local market. There was an alcohol warehouse for the Scandinavians to buy their cheap drink. We took advantage of their samples.

"Yes very nice, thank you."

We had a fab time in Tallinn. Then on the third day the Cruise Director rang me and said,

"Where are you Brenda?"

"Where am I?" I said, "I'm in Tallinn waiting for the ship."

"Well we'll be docking in about one hour. Can you make your way to the docks?"

"Yes of course I'll be there." We didn't have to run either. We had a whole hour to get there.

Apparently the Captain got into a bit of bother for not waiting for us. Anyway we boarded the ship and what a tale we had to tell.

Zat iz er Table

When working on the ships prior to my show I have a rehearsal with the technicians. I have everything for my shows scripted, so that they can follow the sketches and know exactly what is happening.

In the early days of working on the cruises there was a technician, a Frenchman. He was also a stage manager. My stage manager sees to all my props and sets them on stage according to my plans. I put them in the right order backstage. I need everything set regimentally because of timing. Everything has to run smoothly.

For my second show I require a long table with a cloth and skirt to ensure that the props I have at the back of the table can't be seen by the audience. My stage manager said to Joel, "Where is Brenda's table?"

"Zatizertableu." pointing to a small round table.

"No." said Lyn "Zat is not ertableau." She ended up talking like Joel with a French accent.

"Zat is ertableau," he said, pointing to a small round table.

"No Joel zatiz not her tableau because Brenda needs a big long tableau." I kept out of it. And so it went on until my big long tableau finally arrived with the help from the Cruise

274

Director. He told Joel that he must get me a long table.

When I first started working on the cruises my show used to over-run, which used to infuriate technicians. On one occasion the Cruise Director said, "Just do as long as you want Brenda there's nothing on anywhere else apart from you." So I over-ran.

The technician was Joel again. Ooohhh! And after about 50 minutes into my show he was on the intercom backstage shouting at the Cruise Director.

"I vant overtime, I vant overtime."

The next time I went on that ship and Joel was the technician he said, "I 'ope she as a vatch!!" I think he has left the company now. I 'ope not because ov me!!!

My opening to my first show is an impression of Cilla Black. Cruise Director announces:

"Welcome on stage Brenda Collins, and Brenda, who are you going to be tonight?" I come out on stage and say,

"Tonight I'm going to be Cilla Black."

A technician got the wrong button one night and instead of a Cilla song to open, he pressed The National Anthem. God Save Our Queen. I'm sure Cilla would have been chuffed at that!

On one ship I'd just come off stage and there was a knock on my dressing room door. I shouted, "Come in."

A man came in and introduced himself.

"I'm Cilla Black's producer of Blind Date."

"Well oh my goodness." I thought. He said that he'd never seen anyone impersonate Cilla as well as I had. He said that when I came on stage he had to look twice.

"Can I feel your hair?" He asked.

"You can feel anything you like."

"Umm your hair is a lot thicker than Cilla's." I thought, "Well that's a plus."

We were in Barbados with the ship, The Destiny. My sister text me asking where I was. I texted back, "In

Barbados."

"Where in Barbados?" came her response.

"In a bar having half a lager."

"Are you in a restaurant?"

"No, in a bar having half a lager."

Her friend had text her asking "Where is your Brenda. Is she in a restaurant in Barbados?" Eileen had replied to her that I was in Barbados but in a small bar having half a lager. Norma text back and said," Oh well it must be 'the' Cilla Black in this restaurant." My claim to fame!

Imagine if we (Cilla and I) were ever in the same place at the same time I wonder what we'd say? Maybe, "And what's your name and where're do you come from?"

A lot of people ask whether I have ever met Cilla I haven't, but I did go to see her in panto in Liverpool to see if I was "doing it right". It was a bit scary sitting in the audience and watching someone who, when I looked in the mirror, looked like me!!!!! In the panto she was very good. In fact, she held the panto together. I admire her very much and good luck to you Cilla. I wonder if she knows about me?????? I do meet a lot of passengers who live near her, so who knows? And a lot of people who grew up with her.

When I'm on a ship my poster goes up in the billing area next to the theatre and I sometimes hear, "Oh Cilla Black is on board." I smile and think "Eeeh that's me they're talking about." When I do come out on stage as Cilla there's always a gasp – Oohhhhhhhh. If that's how you write a gasp!

We were on The Emerald, a lovely ship with a lovely crew. The Maitre d' was a very, very tall man called Adrian. Normally, when I say to the audience, "I need a man" I look for a man sitting high in his chair. I know then that he is tall, although some men do slouch.

On one cruise one man was slouching and I said,

"Are you unemployed and on drugs, like simvastatins?" I turned to him and he said, "I am employed and I am a G.P."

276

Oh dear. At that point we all started singing, "Oh Doctor I'm in trouble, Oh Goodness Gracious me. My heart goes bum de di bum de di bum de di bum de di bum de di bum bum bum!!!!!

Anyway I asked my Cruise Director if I could use the Maitre d', Adrian? He must have been nearly 7 feet tall. He said he'd have to ask the Hotel Manager. Well everything was OK'd. Sometimes for health and safety reasons, if the sea is a bit rough, I do ask maybe the Deputy Cruise Director to help me.

Well getting back to the evening in question. On board there was a young man called Mark. He was about 15-16 years old and he suffered from, I think, cerebral palsy.

On this particular night I had asked Adrian to stand near the door so I could see him when I made my selection. Well Mark was stood next to Adrian. When I said:

"The viewers have decided it's you." I pointed to Adrian. Mark thought I was pointing to him and he came on stage along with Adrian. I said to Mark,

"Would you like to sit down here with this nice man who was sitting in the front row?" Mark said,

"No, I'm staying on stage with you."

"Oh." I said. "Well just sit there on my chair while I talk to this nice man in a uniform (Adrian). Adrian said,

"Get out of that one if you can?" Oh my goodness, what was I going to do?

"Right." Adrian did the routine of getting into the dress and left the stage still wearing the dress and wig to the music of The Stripper. Mark was still on stage sitting on my chair. He was still laughing at Adrian, the Maitre d', who was wearing a dress and blonde wig.

"Do you know any clean jokes?" I said to Mark.

"Yes." He said. So he told a joke then I told a joke and so on. He became a star overnight. Everyone loved Mark. He even got a standing ovation in the karaoke and even did some presenting with the Cruise Director. It was a very memorable cruise.

The ships have become part of my life, and the crew and of course the passengers. A lot of the passengers still keep in touch. I love chatting to them.

An officer called Maria, who I first met on a little ship called The Calypso, was sitting with my stage manager in a lounge on board. She was waiting to see me because she was disembarking the next day to go home. Both were sitting near the door of the lounge so they could see me coming through the Clipper Bar.

My stage manager said she had a running commentary from Maria when she saw me coming into the Clipper Bar. It was like this. (In broken English accent)

"O, ere she is Miss Brendaaaa. Oh dear table number one she kneel down. Oh she get up now. Oh yes she is coming now. Oh no table number two, Oh dear me, they get a chair for her. Oh no man sit in chair. Oh Miss Brendaaa sit on man knee. Oh now she get up. Oh table number three she say good evening and smiles nicely. Oh no table number four they make room for Miss Brendaaa and buy her a drink. Lots of laughter going on on table number four. Oh Miss Brendaaa picks up her drink. She is moving closer. Only three more tables to go. Come on Miss Brendaaa. Oh no table number five stop her. She smiles and laughs with them.   Oh well I not seeing Miss Brendaa for tonight. I say goodnight to Miss Brendaaaa on my way out." Maria did just that. I apologised to her and she said that she understood. Maria, what a lovely lady. I wonder where she is now. I wonder if she is still on Thomson cruises.

We were on The Celebration and had docked in Aqaba in Jordan. On the coach taking us back to the ship after doing a bit of shopping, we met a lovely couple; a man and wife from Manchester. We got chatting and she told me how she'd broken her two ankles in Egypt, was operated on in an

Egyptian hospital then flown home.

I asked her how she'd got on the plane and her husband said that she was hoisted up along with the meals container!!

"Were you plastered?" (Me thinking plaster of Paris) She replied,

"Oh no it was just lunch time." She thought I meant, "Were you plastered i.e. drunk." Eeeh it was so funny we laughed and laughed. Well we did - I don't think she got it.

Sue Stewart, another lovely lady, and another Thomson Manager. Well, this particular day we were cruising around the Adriatic. There was a knock on my cabin door. It was my cabin steward

"Hello Miss Brenda."

"Hello." He held a tray carrying two glasses, a bottle of wine and an envelope.

"I have to wait for a reply Miss Brenda."

"Oh well you had better come in and have a seat." The letter was written on Thomson letterhead. "Oh heck, I thought. What's this all about? It was from Sue, Thomson's Manager and it read.

Dear Brenda,

On behalf of Thomson Cruises, I am very sorry that I have cause to write to you on rather a sensitive subject.

I have just had a meeting with our Bar Manager and Provision Manager and they have raised some concerns which I feel I must pass on to you.

It has become apparent that we have to refuse some of our passengers red wine as, since your arrival, our stocks seem to be depleting at a speedier that normal rate.

Whilst I am not suggesting that your red wine consumption is excessive, might I point out that ordinarily our stocks are sufficient for over 1000 passengers and since your arrival, we are fast running out...

Could I suggest that a martini may be quite nice, or a cocktail of the day on occasion?

Either way, I have managed to save you a bottle before we run out altogether... I do hope you will enjoy!!!!

Additionally I wondered might you care to join me for dinner one night before you leave us.

Yours sincerely
Sue Stewart, Thomson Manager

We did have dinner and the bottle of wine was very nice, very nice indeed.

Thank you Sue

On one of our Thomson cruises, to thank me for all the hard work I had done for the company, they upgraded me into a suite. I couldn't believe it when I got on board and was making my way to my usual cabin and one of the crew said, "Oh no Miss Brenda you are not in that cabin on this cruise you are in a cabin on deck 8."

"Deck 8." I said, "But that's for all the posh folk."

Thank you very much Thomson Cruises.

Again on The Celebration in 2011 a young presenter called Lee Brannaghan became friends with us. He used to come to our cabin for a chat often after the shows. It was lovely.

The night after my show Lee, unknown to me, had been asking my stage manager for some of my clothes. Oooohhhh? She'd asked why, because my clothes would be too small for him, if he was going to wear them. So she gave him some of hers. Ummm weird.

The Cruise Director was a lovely man called Bram Lorenz. He and I got on really well.

On this particular night my stage manager told me to stay in the show lounge for a while longer. I wondered why but then it didn't bother me as I would just chat to the passengers, which I loved doing. No problem. Anyway I thought, I'd just go up to Liberty's where all the game shows were held.

Do you know what I saw? It was Lee dressed up with a ginger wig, big teeth, my stage manager's clothes on and impersonating me!!! Bram said,

"Right Brenda, what are the scores?" Lee, as me, said, (and I don't talk like this)!!!! " ShhWellMmmBramVtheshhhcoresgare."

I shouted, "Excuse me, I'm Brenda."

"No Madam", Bram said, "I don't know who you are but this is Brenda Collins. Who are you anyway?"

"I'm Brenda Collins."

"No." Bram said, "This is the Beautiful BrendaCollins." "GsssetShhhhecurity, Ssshhheeeee 's an hhimposterrrr", shouted Lee.

I tried to get Lee off the stage and hit him with my handbag. The audience were in hysterics. It was hilarious and very well thought out by Lee. It was great that Bram went along with the gotcha. Apparently, when starting the game show, he had said. "Ladies and gentlemen welcome on stage your Guest Comedy Vocalist Miss Brenda Collins and Lee had come out in full outfit kneeling with his shoes attached to his knees. I wished I had seen it!!!

Well done Lee and, of course, Bram. Two wonderful young gentlemen.

After my following show in the Show Lounge I went onto the deck because there was a party going on. Lee was dressed in the Thomson dog outfit or character. I was at the bar talking to some passengers when Thomson the dog (Lee) came over to me and tried to "mount my leg."

"Lee, get off the passengers are watching." I said. I heard a man say to his mate,

"Hey look there's Thomson the dog trying to hump Cilla

Black!!!!!" Eeeeeh, what can I say?? I don't think Thomson's Manager would have approved if she had witnessed it. Just as well she wasn't there!!!!

The crew on the ships have been amazing. They are always there to help and I've been invited to their wonderful parties. Another story later on.

Andy Barr and Paula from Shorex Department (they book all the excursions) and Lisa, the social hostess asked me to join them for dinner. It was my birthday.

During dinner I was asked if I was scared of heights. I said, "No." They asked me to meet them at the gangplank at 9.00am the next morning. Oh I thought I must be going up on the cable car or in one of those baskets where young men pull you down a hill.

We, me and my stage manager, were in Madeira you see. I said to her, "If I can't get into one of those baskets and get pulled down the hill, I'm going to find a wheelie bin."

Anyway the next morning arrived and there we were at the bottom of the gangplank. Andy and Paula were waiting.

"Come this way Brenda." We went round the corner and do you know what? There was a helicopter waiting!!!!!

Oh my Goodness!!! What could I say but, "Eeeeeeeehhhhhhhh!!!!!!" We got in the helicopter and it flew us across the Island of Madeira. It was a Wow. We felt like "The Whirly Birds," if any reader can remember that programme on the television. I think it was in black and white. That's how long ago it was. You see getting older means we all have some wonderful memories and that's why I'm writing mine down!!!!!!..........

While having a coffee in one of the ship's lounges, I saw a bar waiter walking past the window pushing a trolley full of drink, bottles of whiskey, vodka, beer and of course, cokes etcetera etcetera.

He was offering passengers a drink. I thought to myself, I could do that. After my coffee I went to see Miss Sue,

Thomson's Manager and mentioned it to her. She thought it was a great idea but she said, "Why don't we put you in every crew uniform, excluding the Captain's?"

Sue contacted the Hotel Manager and he was only too willing to supply the uniforms. We were to do the dressing up the next day, which was a day at sea.

Sue organised a photographer to follow me around. The photographs were to be put on a calendar to give away to passengers.

The day came. I was so excited. My uniforms were in Sue's office.

My first uniform was reception; a very smart white uniform with epaulets on the shoulders. Actually I looked like an officer.

I took up my position behind reception and said to a passenger "Can I help you?" The only trouble was I couldn't see over the counter, it was so high, and the passenger could hear a voice but could only see my ginger hair above the counter. I hope you can visualise the picture. Well I did my stint there, and then Sue whispered, "Right next uniform." Upon which I ran from behind the reception and back into the office to get into my next outfit, which was housekeeping, together with marigold gloves, yellow ones.

Again the photographer followed me. I had my bucket, duster, vacuum cleaner and a chocolate to put on the pillows in the cabins. Mustn't forget them.

I made the bed, in a fashion, then had a go at cleaning the toilet and then a Hoover round. Sue shouted in a whisper, "Right next uniform." Back into her office for another quick change.

This time I was serving behind the buffet in the lido. The passengers didn't know what was happening at first, and then they clicked. I served them their food. Of course, I had experience of serving food from The Helm Park Hotel, if you remember?

I did washing up, cocktail making, at which I was rubbish. I even stacked the sun beds with a little help from a lovely Egyptian lad whose job it was to stack them.

On the evening came my main job. The one I suggested in the first place. Yes the trolley full of drinks!!!!!

I got into the smart uniform with a waistcoat and tie, and then I got my trolley. First job was on the deck. I pushed it around and offered passengers drinks.

The whiskey bottle was full of apple juice and the vodka and Bacardi was water. The passengers weren't aware of this because they ordered the drink from me but they never got to drink it. I did. I even served a table full of officers from Chief Engineer to Staff Captain. They weren't in on it and I think the Staff Captain was ready to give me my p45!!!

By the time I went into Hemingway's I was a bit tipsy, or so the passengers thought, but of course it was just water or apple juice I was drinking. One man asked for a whiskey for himself and a Bacardi for his wife. I poured both into the same glass and then I drank them.

"Hey ye little bugger," he said. Eeeeh I never want to drink apple juice again.

I really enjoyed that day and I'm sure the passengers did. It was such fun going from uniform to uniform and job to job. I hope the crew enjoyed it as much as I did.

I showed the pictures to a young man called James; he was part of the show team at Warner's Hotel, Nidd Hall in Harrogate. He asked for the one of me in the housekeeping uniform cleaning the toilet out with my marigolds on. He told me he had it pinned up in his bathroom and every morning when he got up to go to the toilet he'd say, "Good morning beautiful Brenda."

When we arrived back home from one of the cruises, on checking the props, we realised we'd left the blow-up doll which I use in my show. We left her underneath my bed in the cabin. I had to immediately telephone the ship to advise them of the situation and get someone down to my cabin quickly to retrieve the doll before any passenger went into the cabin and looked under the bed. Just imagine?

Irene, another friend came with me on The Dream. She was fully trained up before we went on the cruise. Anyone I take with me on a cruise, I have to really get on well with them because I'm with them 24/7. Irene is one of those people. We did the first show and it went down really well, as did the second. Christine and Malcolm, our friends, were also on that cruise. They're from a small town near to where I live so it was nice. They came down to the stage after the show and offered to help us carry the prop cases up to our cabin on deck 10.

The blow up doll wasn't quite deflated, so Irene laid her over the suit case to go down properly over night. We'd had a glass of wine so off we went to sleep.

I got up during the night to go to the toilet and when I got up our door was wide open. I thought maybe Christine and Malcolm hadn't shut it properly. I also thought anyone passing our cabin would have seen the blow up doll lying limp and deflated across the case which would make their minds boggle.

I asked Christine the next day and she said that she had shut the door.

"Was it open?"

"Of course it was, Irene and I could have been raped and pillaged."

The next night I said to Irene, "You shut and lock the door to make sure it is secure," which she did. We had just settled down and we were lying quietly in our beds when the door shot open at great speed. We both sat up in bed and said,

"What was that?"

The sea was as calm as a pond, so it wasn't the sea that forcefully opened it. It really was flung open. We both got up and looked up and down the corridor. There was no one there. Oh my goodness, what had made that happen? We secured the door by jamming our suitcases up against it then went off to sleep. The next morning we told Christine and Malcolm and they said that they had heard a woman had died two days ago on our deck. Two days later we saw her being taken off the ship.

We also met Gillian Thow, Operations Manager for Thomson Cruises. She was walking with the Captain of the ship. She said to Captain, "Have you met Brenda, Captain?" I was honoured.

Our Ladies Club

Irene is a terrific cook and at her home she often holds dinner parties. It's always just for women but sometimes the odd husband turns up and we all make him feel very welcome.

We've decided that we're all going into the same home for the elderly and we have given ourselves specific jobs in the home. Irene, of course, is the cook. I'm the bingo caller and head of entertainments. Christine is the craft lady. Elizabeth is head of the library. Mary is in charge of the flowers. Pauline is the nurse. Lyn is the cleaner. Jill is the lady who will fill all the forms in for us in order to get the right benefits. Norma is the lady who will look after our diet because she's always on one and goes to Slimming World every week and knows everything there is to know about syns.

We've got a name for our club. Irene makes an awesome lemon posset for sweet. One night she announced that she'd made these lemon possets and I thought she'd said that they were called lemon gussets hence our club is called the Gusset Club.

286

Back to Cruises

I've met some wonderful passengers. Ray and Mavis, Pauline and Ray, both couples I am still in touch with. They, along with six other couples turned up for my 60th birthday. They actually booked the cruise, knowing it was my birthday. Eeeh how lovely was that?

I asked my boys to come with me on the cruise and Thomson's said they could come on at a very, very cheap price, which I was willing to pay. Both boys said that they would lose too much money and it was awkward for them to take time off work. Anyway we could celebrate when I got back or even before I went. Our Eileen and Steve didn't get on my birthday cruise but came on a one later on. Pauline and Ray were on that one too.

We all had dinner together and on one night we did lookalikes. I was Cilla, our Eileen was Denise Welsh, because she had the same hairstyle. Steve was the England football manager at the time Fabio somebody or other. Ray was David Blunkett, because he looks like him, but didn't have the dog. Lyn was Pam Ferris and Pauline was Terry Wogan because she said someone had mentioned she resembled him!!!

We ordered a bottle of Chateauneuf du Pape while having dinner. Steve said he'd order one, then Pauline and Ray ordered one. This was during the course of the meal.

At the end of the meal we got the bill and the wine per bottle was £55 and so came to a staggering £165. If we'd known that we wouldn't have ordered it or we would not have swallowed it as quick or let it pass through our kidneys as fast either.

The reason we ordered it was that Lyn had sampled some and someone who knew about wines had said that it was a very good wine. Well if it was good enough to be a sampler in the shop Wine Cellar it was good enough for us.

I bet it wasn't £55 a bottle in Wine Cellar. Oh well you live and learn. Next time we'll look at the wine list and maybe go for the house wine.

On the same ship we tendered up to go into Montenegro. On the way back to the ship I got chatting to a couple of lovely ladies. This was on the tender. They were sitting behind me and so I was kneeling on my seat so that I could face them. It was easier for me to talk to them. I told them that once we got sailing there was going to be a sale on in the shop on board. Some items would be half price; this included cigarettes, bottles of spirits and the sale would be for one evening only.

The next day everything would go back to the usual prices. I told them to get stashed up with the spirits and the cigarettes because these sorts of sales don't happen very often. I think they were impressed.

We were approaching the ship and I said to the ladies, "Do you work?" They both replied, "Oh yes, we work for H.M. Customs and Excise at Newcastle Airport." I said, "Oh that's nice and slipped back down in my seat!!!! Eeeh.

When I was on stage I told the passengers the story of what had happened. They fell about laughing. The two ladies in question were sat at the front of the audience they laughed too. I must have been fodder to them when I was going on about how cheap the fags and booze were and for them to get stocked up.

I like to join in the activities on board and Bram, Cruise Director, asked if I'd like to be in the game "I'm an Entertainer or I'm a Crew Member Get Me Out of Here".

The game was held on the sun deck around the swimming pool. Well I had my housekeeping uniform on again with the yellow marigolds, a brown straight wig and orange sunglasses.

We were on the deck so while we were waiting for the Cruise Director to start the game I collected some drinking glasses on my tray. I think some of the passengers whose empty glasses I'd collected really thought I was from the Philippines. One lady shouted, "Excuse me Miss you've forgotten one." Maybe she hadn't been into any of my shows or maybe she didn't recognise me.

The Cruise Director arrived and announced each team member. We each said who we were and where we were from. I said I was Blenda from the Philippines and worked in housekeeping. There was a big cheer from the passengers.

I'm a Crew Member - Get me out of here!

The game started. There were two teams. I was in the one with a member of the bar staff, a member of the show team and a one from housekeeping.

First it was the relay swim. I was the first off. I jumped in the pool and swam on my back (I'm better on my back). A passenger said I went so fast that I should have been in the 2012 Olympics.

I got back to the side of the pool and was dragged out by my swimming costume. Then it was my next team mate's turn, a member of the bar staff. Well he stood at the pool edge just looking at the water. He stood looking for bl...dy ages at the water. I thought to myself. "This is a race." So I pushed him in. Oh dear he couldn't swim he was splashing around so I jumped in to help him but like I said I'm only good on my back in the water.

He eventually got dragged out of the pool. By the way, our team didn't win. It was good fun. Well not for that poor lad. I don't think he joined in any more games after that.

But one day a few months later I did speak to him in one of the lounges and he said, "Miss Brenda I am learning to swim."

I have heard that they don't do that game anymore. It is quite competitive. On another occasion, it was the same game but a different ship, I was again in the team with the bar staff. The opposing team were the show team, the dancers and singers on board.

When it came to my turn I had to jump in the pool to retrieve an inflatable whale, get the whale and swim with it to the side, get out of the pool and make my way to my seat.

All was going well and I was in the lead. I got the whale and was making my way back to the side of the pool when all of a sudden a member of the opposing team started pushing me under the water so that they could get the whale from me. Every time I came up for air I shouted,

"That's not fair." splutter, splutter, splutter. It happened a few times.

On the last time a passenger pushed back the chairs and dived into the pool and dragged the offending team member off me. This meant I could get to the whale and make my way safely to the side of the pool. Other passengers were there to drag me out of the pool and a little lad got the whale and passed it to me when I got to my seat, exhausted and bedraggled.

The member of the show team who I was up against really wanted to win because his Mam and Grandma were around the poolside supporting him. Do you know he could have drowned me all for a bloody blow up whale. Other passengers had a right go at him for trying to drown me.

Warner Hotels

When not on the cruises I work at Warner Hotels. They are lovely; in fact they are just like a cruise ship but on land. I work there regularly and so know all the staff very well. Also passengers who I've met on cruises often come to see me at one of the hotels, which is lovely.

On one particular night at Nidd Hall, I was staying over because I was working at Thoresby Hall the next day. During my show I said I was from Durham and I mentioned the village of Bowburn where I grew up. At the end of my show I went in to the bar area for a glass of wine. A lady came up to me and said that she grew up in West Cornforth, which is not far from Bowburn. In fact, my Dad used to work at the pit there when I was little girl.

The lady asked me if I knew certain boys who went to Bowburn Modern School. She mentioned their names and I said that I knew them but they were older than me, but my sister used to knock around with them when she was at school. In fact, I think she went out with most of the lads she mentioned.

The lady asked me to join her company for a drink, which I did. We chattered and chattered then I noticed this lady was flicking through her camera.

"I met a lady from your village when I was in Memphis in

2009. I wonder if you know of her". She turned the camera screen to me and guess who I saw in the picture --- it was our Eileen, my sister. Well you could have knocked me over with a feather. Eeeh fancy that. Eeeh it's a small world. Isn't it?

I just love entertaining on the ships and in the Warner Hotels. I feel that the passengers, guests and I are all under the same umbrella. We are of a similar age and have a similar sense of humour.

I feel that no matter how funny a joke is if an audience doesn't like you, or haven't warmed to you, then you have no chance of making them laugh.

My show is very visual, using lots of props. I love making people laugh by funny walks, pulling faces and dressing up in silly costumes. I suppose I'm a clown.

A few famous artistes have influenced me during my career or I think they are brilliant. First of all Hylda Baker with her innuendos and getting her words mixed up. I'm sure at our age we do the same and so can relate to Hylda's humour. For example when she said, "I went to the doctors. He had his horoscope round his neck. He examined me and said that I might have a coronary trombonist."

Of course her stooge, Cynthia, makes a good prop for Hylda to fire her humour at.

I impersonate Hylda when I get a tall man out of the audience and dress him up in a frock. I try to get the voice right and her movements. I feel Hylda and I are very similar.

Ken Dodd is another act who I admire. His humour is silly, clean fun and is non offensive. Ken Dodd and I also have a lot in common. We have big hair, big teeth and we've both been investigated by the Inland Revenue!!!

I've always had the opinion that I'm only as good as the people sitting in front of me. If they like me and have the same sense of humour then I know I can bond with them.

I just love making people laugh. When I come off stage

from a show where I've enjoyed myself, it's a fantastic exhilarating feeling.

During all the years I've been entertaining I've never stopped working. The work just keeps coming in. I think it was Frank Carson who said, "If you're not working, then work on your act." and that's what I've always done right from the very beginning.

Just recently I got a phone call offering me eleven world cruises. An agent said, "You've done well Brenda even our best comedian has only got two cruises."

"Well I must be doing something right," I replied.

At Home

Do you know, I also enjoy being at home? My friend who I've known for 30 years and who was my neighbour in Valley View and was one of the ladies who was pregnant at the same time as me, she moved to live in a cottage near Sedgefield.

She goes to Australia every year and this particular time she went for three months. I was looking for somewhere to live so I moved into her house. I rang her and asked her and she agreed. I didn't think it was going to be permanent but I'm still there.

It's a cottage in the countryside of County Durham. It's brilliant. The cottage is situated next to woodland and has an open fire so Richard, who lives about 5 minutes away, Lyn and I go out in the woodland logging. Collecting logs and storing them in crates in the garden making sure we have logs for when the weather gets really cold.

Richard has a chain saw and we saw up the dead logs lying about the wood. He has the easy job of sawing while we do all the labouring; carrying all the sawn logs in the wheelbarrow to the cottage ready for chopping and bagging.

When Richard can't find the time to help us we have a 20 inch bench saw in the yard so we are never stuck. Who needs to go to a gym?

While at home I constantly wear my wellies and my waxy coat. We plant the garden with vegetables. When I wasn't so busy we kept six hens and had fresh eggs every day. I'm so busy now that we had to send the hens to a retirement home: Finchale Abbey, where years ago I used to live in a caravan.

As a fertilizer we go to Whitby and collect seaweed from the beach. When we get it home we put it in a big drum next to the greenhouse, cover the seaweed with water and during the winter months constantly stir the mixture.

When it comes to the potatoes and all the other vegetables, once sown I water them well in with the seaweed mixture. Hey the veg are brilliant and have an amazing taste. You see – free fertilizer.

I'm a very thrifty person. The fire in the lounge doesn't have a back boiler. I wish it had. The central heating is run by LPG, which is very good but I try to save on energy.

When I put the hot water bottles in my bed I heat the water on the fire by boiling a kettle. Just as me Mam and Dad did. I haven't got round to cooking chips on the coal fire yet! Our Eileen often says, "You're turning into me Dad."

Our Eileen's grandchildren, Mila and Isaac come to the cottage and stay over. I love taking them up the wood, building camps, taking them on adventures and having a picnic. They just love it.

When we've finished playing I put the fire on and they sit and watch a film while I toast teacakes on the fire. Absolute heaven! I heat the water and put hot water bottles in their beds too. The cottage is cold but when the fire is on it's lovely and cosy.

While travelling around in the car we're always on the lookout for wood lying around. We were on our way to an auction house in Leyburn, North Yorkshire. On our journey we travelled through Catterick Camp. We passed a small copse of trees and in amongst them, lying on the ground were sawn off pieces of logs. We thought we'd reached heaven.

We pulled up alongside the copse and started to make a plan of action because we could hear the sound of guns in the distance. We'd seen the sign that we were on a tank range so the gun fire we heard was from the tanks. I think Catterick is always either on amber alert or sometimes red alert depending on the political unrest in the world. This of course didn't come into our plan of action. We were after those logs and we meant to get them.

We clambered over some barbed wire and then manoeuvred our way around the trees. We got to the logs and I was the furthest away, so started throwing the logs one at a time to Lyn who then proceeded to throw them nearer my car. It was relay.

I ran a little way but tripped on a stick. Now if you can picture this. The stick lifted upwards with my foot still attached so when the stick was upright and my foot was again still attached, it looked and I felt as if I was flying. I was suspended in the air until the stick decided to move forward. It seemed to take forever.

Lyn at this time watched me fly through the air in slow motion. Of course a Tena lady would have come in handy because she couldn't stop laughing.

Once I'd got down from the stick, I brushed myself clean of leaves and began to shift the logs. The plan was to move closer to the car, Lyn would get next to the car and I'd throw them to her and then she'd load them into the boot.

All was going well. A few cars passed us but they didn't bother us and there was still gun fire in the distance. After every throw of a log we'd duck behind a tree for camouflage. I suppose we looked like two female middle aged Japanese snipers on a mission and the mission was still going well until a Military Police Land Rover pulled up and two Military Policemen got out with their guns. Oh hell here we go again....

Lyn was the nearest to them. I hid behind a tree. So she went up to them. I peeped now and again to check on whether she was being arrested. No, all was well so far, they weren't pointing any guns.

After a few minutes I peeped again and thankfully they were driving away.

"You can come out now, they've gone." Lyn shouted. I went up to the car and asked in a sheepish voice,

"What did they say?"

Lyn, as you can imagine, wasn't very happy for me leaving the encounter all up to her. She said that we could take the logs we had and then get on our way.

The Police had explained that we were in a restricted area because the tanks and shells could come our way at any time. They also said that some military personnel had reported suspicious goings on in woodland. Eeeh why it was just us getting the logs. Oh well the logs were great and burned beautifully.

There is a greenhouse in the garden and Lyn tends to that. She was watering the tomatoes on this particular day when the weather was about 28 degrees.

She asked me to turn the outside tap on, which I did.

"Ouch, turn the water off" she shouted,

"What's wrong?"

"That water is so hot you can't touch it."

"Oh is it," I thought.

Immediately I went into the kitchen and opened the window. Got the hose pipe and turned the tap on and put the water into the bowl in the sink and I washed up with that water. I thought to myself, "Hey this is solar heating, people pay thousands of pounds for this. If the hot weather keeps up I may even have a shower!"

We do have to get coal for the winter in order to keep the fire on overnight. I knew of a pit heap, where coal used to be tipped when the mines were open. I said to Lyn that it would be free coal. She was up for it.

So off we trot, equipped with bags, gloves and a shovel to the big heap which was maybe the size of a small hill. They are called 'slag heaps'.

We got there and we clambered up. On our way up we found bits of coal which we rolled down the hill, to be collected and bagged later.

This is what poor people did years and years ago because they couldn't afford to buy the coal to keep their houses warm so they went 'scratting for coal' on the slag heaps. So this is what we were doing.

While halfway up the heap another car turned up and a man got out. He left his car door open while he got his shovel and bags out and do you know who was singing on his stereo in his car? Bloody me!

Oh dear me I could have hidden. I wanted to hide with shame. Here I was, 'international cabaret act' of the cruises, looking for coal up a 'slag heap'. Our Eileen would have gone mad. I never have told her. She knows now !!!!

Anyway I got down from the heap and the man recognised me.

"Well hello Brenda, I've got your CD on in the car."

"I know I heard it," I said with my head bowed. Eee how embarrassing was that. I haven't been back.

Because of the coal the chimney often has to be cleaned. The cottage belongs to a farm and the farm labourer always comes over with the brushes to clean the chimney.

Two of the labourers arrived one year in a low loader. One of the lads was in the bucket of the low loader and the other drove and raised the bucket so that the lad, John, could get on top of the roof and push the brushes downwards to clean the chimney. They said it was the easiest way to do it.

I stood outside watching while Lyn went inside to tape up the fireplace with an old sheet. Unfortunately she didn't get the job done quick enough. The brushes went down and pushed all the soot into the hearth. John, the labourer and I went round to the back door. We didn't know Lyn hadn't had time to tape up the fire place. She came to the backdoor and what a sight to behold.

She'd been kneeling down in front of the fireplace when whoooooooshhh down came the soot. She was as black as the ace of spades. All you could see were the whites of her eyes and white teeth and a red tongue when she shouted in anger.

She was mad, mad as hell and she showed it by snarling at John and telling him how stupid he was. The more she snarled and showed her teeth the more John wanted to laugh but I kicked him and said,

"I wouldn't if I were you."

Not only was Lyn covered from head to toe in soot but the lounge was too and a new carpet had been fitted not so long ago.

John started to apologise but it wasn't enough. I told John he'd better go because there would have been a murder or even two because I think Lyn was blaming me too. But I never did anything!

She did look funny though. A bit like the Black and White Minstrel Show but the characters in that show were happy.

Any Old Bricks

It was during the time of old hospitals being demolished and new University hospitals being built. A mental hospital near the cottage was being demolished and Lyn wanted a brick path in the garden.

"There'll be loads of bricks at Winterton, the mental hospital", I said. So we went and had a drive out to the site and saw the Site Foreman. He said that we could have as many bricks as we wanted but to come with a truck, hard hats and gloves on a day which wasn't as busy, which he said would be Wednesday.

We went to see Bette, our landlord and she told us to see Cliff and Terrence, her two sons and ask them if we could borrow a Land Rover truck and a couple of hard hats. Job's a good 'un.

So on the following Wednesday off we went to the site of Winterton Hospital. The foreman directed us to the place which would be safe for us.

We stopped the truck and started to load it up with bricks. I found a brick with 'Lumley Brickworks' printed on it. I shouted to Lyn,

"Hey look at this brick, it's got Lumley Brickworks on it." Our Eileen lived in Great Lumley and the brickworks no longer existed. I shouted that I was going to carry this brick very carefully to the truck in case it broke. I placed it carefully on the back of the truck.

"Hey Brenda, I've found one with Lumley Brickworks on and the address."

"Oh you be careful with that one," I said.

We found more and loaded them gently onto the truck. Walking very carefully, taking care not to drop one, (a brick) or trip up.

This went on for a while. We found more bricks with different brickworks printed on them. Taking care all the time, and carrying one at a time, as if they were made of porcelain.

We filled the truck with the bricks, mind it took ages, but we felt very gratified and pleased with ourselves, especially getting the Lumley Brickworks bricks.

I couldn't wait to tell our Eileen. I hope she would be as pleased as we were. What do you think? I rang her before we got to the Site Foreman to thank him. She said,

"Brenda it's only a brick."

"Only a brick." Huh.

On leaving the site the foreman came to us and said,

"Have you got all you want?"

"Yes thank you very much," Was our reply. We were just driving out and he shouted,

"Are you ex-patients of the mental hospital? Because me and the workmen all noticed you were carrying those bricks very, very carefully. Are you taking the bricks back as mementos or are you trying to build another mental hospital?"

"Cheeky bugger."I shouted.

We went to another hospital to get some top soil for the leeks we were going to plant. We built a trench with some of the bricks from the mental hospital.

So off we go with the truck, hard hat and gloves to, this time Dryburn hospital which was being demolished. We went at night time and spoke to the night watchman. We asked if we could come on to the site and get some soil. He was very obliging and told us where to get the soil. We got loads of it and some tables and chairs for Ann Watson to put in her community hut at Finchale Abbey. We got a load of wood too for the fire. Also wood to chop up for sticks. "Owt for Nowt" is a good motto. Free fuel.

We kept the hens at this time and they were laying well. So each night we went to the hospital site to get the soil and whatever we could lay our hands on, maybe an old x-ray machine? No we weren't allowed that.

Each night we gave the night watchman half a dozen eggs for his kindness. This happened a few nights and at the end he told us to stop giving him eggs as his wife thought he was having an affair with a couple of women who kept hens. We'd rather have the top soil we told him. He said he'd rather have the eggs!

Animals

There are a lot of wild animals roam near the cottage. There are deer, rabbits, squirrels and of course rats and mice. Some come into the garden and it's lovely to see them. Not the rats or mice though.

I saw an animal grappling with a baby rabbit. The poor bunny was squealing. The nasty animal was on its back holding the little bunny with its four paws.

I went up to the animal, not knowing what it was, and I clapped my hands; making a noise to frighten it and making it drop the little bunny. I went right up to the offending animal and shouted,"Get away you nasty bugger." It dropped the bunny and the bunny ran off. But the offending animal now squared up to me and was looking at me straight in the eyes.

"Ohh my goodness."

I shouted and I began to run and the bloody animal was chasing me. I ran into the house and slammed the backdoor. I leaned against the door and said, "Bloody hell, what was that?" I rang the farmer and told him what had happened and described the animal. He said that it sounded like a weasel and I'd interrupted him, the weasel, not the farmer, catching his dinner. Well I'm pleased I did, poor little rabbit.

The farmer said that the weasel would have attacked

me!!! Aye, if he dared!!

I have a dog, a golden Labrador and she's called Martha. I have never bought a dog, dogs always seem to find me. Martha belonged to my nephew, Daniel, but Martha's a big lass and Daniel's wife felt she was too big for their house.

I looked after Martha when Daniel and his family went on holiday. Martha loved it at the cottage and so when Daniel was looking for a home for Martha I offered to look after her.

Realistically, I shouldn't have a dog because of the times I work away, but she is a good guard dog and she's such brilliant company.

Every morning I take her for a walk up the wood and she loves it. Do you know, so do I. The summer months are brilliant too. We sit with Martha in the garden sometimes until the sun goes down over the trees drinking a glass or two of wine.

During the day I weed the garden and water everything in with our special brew seaweed fertilizer. OoohAaaah. There's always plenty to do.

We go collecting sloe berries and blackberries during the autumn not to make pies but to make sloe gin and blackberry whiskey. Rosehips for schnapps and raspberries for vodka. Not that we have a problem or anything like that but the bottles of sloe gin etc make nice Christmas presents and it's a lovely tipple.

We've made carrot wine before, from carrots we grew in the garden, and it was so lethal we lost two whole days out of our lives so we packed in making wine.

While collecting the sloe and blackberries I get my hands scratched to bits but it's a 'labour of love'.

Colin the Camper

I had some work in Weston-Super-Mare and whilst driving down there loads and loads of VW campers vans passed us. They all looked brilliant and I thought to myself that I would love to own one. I called off at a motorway services and bought a VW magazine and had a bit read of it over a cup of coffee. Yes they looked wonderful.

I was staying in digs in a place called Brean and on entering the small town I looked towards some houses on my left and on the driveway was a VW campervan and it was for sale.

I went to the digs and directly made my way back to the for sale campervan. It had a number on the side, 81.

I asked what that symbolised and the man said that was the year Colin was born.

"Colin?"

"Yes his name is Colin and it's not to be changed."

I looked around Colin and he looked amazing. The price was £4,900. Anyway I went for a test drive in Colin and he felt bloody great. I asked if he would accept £4,600 and the man said he would.

I went to the bank the next day and drew the money out of my bank. I got the insurance sorted and I went back to the house and picked up 'Colin the Camper'. I was now the proud owner of a VW Campervan called Colin.

I rang both the boys and they were both chuffed to bits. Our Peter said,

"Is it a split screen?" I said,

"No, it's a T25." Upon which Peter said,

"Aw Mam you should have got a split screen." I told him that Colin was much bigger inside and he was fantastic. So there!

Colin the camper before his makeover,
myself and Martha my dog

I drove him back to Durham and I felt very proud,
although tractors and joggers were overtaking me, but I
didn't care. There was also blue smoke billowing out of the
exhaust, but that could be fixed too. I didn't care.

It was love at first sight. I booked him into a garage for
the engine to be rebuilt. Our Peter got him lowered, new
suspension and white wall tyres fitted. He looked the
business. He was a bonny lad and I loved him to bits. He
was the only man in my life.

Mind I don't know where I'd find the time to go out in him
but I'm sure I'd sort it somehow.

Our Eileen's grandchildren, Mila and Isaac came over
to see him and they loved him too.

"Oh, Auntie Brenda can we go out in Colin?"

"Of course." I said.
"Where shall we go?"
"Let's go to Whitby."
"Yesssss, yipppeeee."

So off we went to Whitby. We had fish and chips, which were brilliant. I put the table up and we ate them inside Colin.

Our Richard had got himself a nice girlfriend called Lesley. Richard rang me and asked me what time I was arriving in Whitby and I said that it would be in one hour. We got there and when we drove up to the chip shop, there was Richard and Lesley waiting to surprise us and what a lovely surprise.

We all had fish and chips then made our way up to Saltwick Bay where I always went for holidays with me Mam and Dad and where John and I holidayed with Richard and Peter.

The coastline is Jurassic and in the bay you can find fossils. So off we all went fossil hunting. Lesley wasn't having much success in finding any fossils so Mila planted some in her tracks so she could find some. Lesley would shout,"Oh I've found some fossils." Mila kept it a secret that she had planted them.

Of course, Martha was with us and she swam in the sea. She was minging but loved it. We rather ignored her while we were fossil hunting and so Martha went off on her own and joined another family who had a dog. We really forgot about her because we were enjoying ourselves so much as was Martha albeit with another family.

We all had a brilliant time and made our way back in Colin. We had to keep Mila and Isaac entertained by a quiz to stop them falling asleep. They were exhausted but very happy.

Colin has been a very useful investment because when I work away I use Colin as accommodation. He is still amazing I love driving him. He makes it a 'feel good' drive. I pip the horn when I pass golf courses and golfers even stop their game and wave. It's brilliant. Bye the way he's still the only man in my life!

Computers

I felt I must become a bit more computer literate so I enrolled on a course at a local college.

At my first lesson all the students sat in a long line in front of a computer. Our teacher introduced herself to us and then gave us a typewritten script to type out on our computers. I set away and did it in no time. The girls on either side both asked what I was doing on the course. I explained that I trained as a typist but I wasn't on the course for that but for all the other bits. I don't think they understood.

The teacher then asked us to take the mouse and drag it click on one of the pictures at the top of the screen. I chose a frog. She then proceeded to say,

"Right girls drag the mouse down from the top of the right hand corner down to the bottom right hand corner and your picture should get bigger.

I began to drag mine but the frog didn't get any bigger. All of a sudden another one appeared on the other one's back. I showed it to my fellow students sitting next to me and they started laughing. I told them to stop because it was causing me unwanted attention. Oh dear.

The teacher was wondering what was going on and she was on her way over to my desk. This I didn't want! She looked at my screen and saw the frog with the other frog on its back and immediately said,

"We don't want that. Do we?" Upon which she pressed a key on my keyboard and walked away sternly saying,

"Pick another picture Brenda."

I picked a horse but by the time I'd tried to move the mouse the lesson was thankfully over. I never went back and now I just try to learn the computer as I go along.

Cremation

My friend's friend had died and we said we'd meet everyone at the Crem. We got there; no-one was there so we thought everyone must have already gone inside. So we went into the crem and sat at the back.

The big doors shut with a bang, as they do. I said to my friend, "Have you got a hanky?" So she passed me one.

Well the service started. The hymns were lovely. We both had a bit cry. Then the vicar said, "Dear Tom." Well I looked at my friend and she looked at me at the same time.

"Tom." We said together. "Who's Tom?"

We had to sit through the whole of the service and shake the vicar's hand and view the flowers and say how wonderful they were and what a lovely service it was.

We didn't know anyone and there and I bet they wondered who we were. Anyway we got out, went round to the front of the crem and there was my friend's sister who said,

"Where've you been?"

We said together, "In the first funeral." So off we went in again this time for the right funeral. We could be professional mourners.

Dear Poppy

My Dad had a visit from the Dog Warden saying that there had been a complaint against Poppy, who was now 20 years old. A neighbour had complained that she had been running all over fouling the place where my Dad lived. (A crescent of bungalows with a large grassed area in the middle).

Well Poppy couldn't run her back legs were failing and she was blind too. Everyone still loved Poppy and she knew when anyone came into me Dad's bungalow; she would still get excited although much more restrained now that she was an old lady. All my Dad's grandchildren grew up with Poppy, my boys in particular. My Dad's great grandchildren loved Poppy and, of course, my Dad adored her. She was his soul mate, his companion, ever since my Mam died. The entire village loved Poppy. She was everyone's friend. Well so we thought.

But apparently Poppy wasn't everyone's friend. Someone had reported my Dad. So when my Dad got a visit from the Dog Warden complaining about Poppy he rang me and told me to get over quick. I got there as quick as I could. My Dad said, "She has to go."

"No Dad she doesn't have to go it's just your bloody neighbours. Not all of them, but maybe one." Yes one, who wanted to cause trouble and was jealous.

My Dad was 93 years old and Poppy 20. They had grown old together. My Dad said, "No she has to go because whoever had reported her will do it again." "She's old Brenda."

"So are you but we're not putting you down."

"Take us to the vets." Oh dear me.

I rang our Eileen and my two boys and prepared them for what was going to happen. It would have been nice for Poppy to die in her own way in her own time when she was ready, not like this. Poor Poppy she didn't deserve this.

My Dad was adamant. We got in the car, Poppy on my Dad's knee. We got to the vets and we went in and registered Poppy's name. She sat on my knee.

People came in with their pets and looked at Poppy and said, "Oh what a lovely little dog." Oh dear me this was

308

awful. I agreed with them.

"Yes she's a lovely little girl." It was very sad for me and my Dad to hear other pet lovers saying what a lovely dog Poppy was and here she was going to be put to sleep.

"Dad we don't have to do this."

"Aye she has to go; they'll only report us again."

"Don't Dad."

Poppy's name was called I gave her a kiss. My Dad took her in his arms and took her into the cubicle. He wasn't in long. He came out with her collar and lead. Poppy was gone...Oh dear. She had gone to sleep. We'll never forget her.

When my Dad got into the car he said,

"He put a needle into her leg and she went to sleep. She was alright."We drove back in silence. Then when we got back to my Dad's bungalow he said,

"Nothing lasts forever Brenda."

He hung her collar and lead up on the hook where they normally stayed. It was so sad.

I rang everyone and told them Poppy had gone to sleep. A very, very sad time but we as a family have wonderful happy memories of our Poppy, the cheeky Jack Russell crossed with a whippet. By, she couldn't half run!!!!

After that I never spoke to the neighbour who I thought had reported her. How nasty.

My Dad missed Poppy so much. When I took him to a club and when he returned home he expected to find Poppy. But of course she wasn't there.

Imagine all those years together; my Dad riding his bike, Poppy running alongside him. It was like a marriage. My Dad was lonely.

I visited my Dad every day, making sure he was alright. I came up with an idea. I know I'll get him a couple of budgies. He was too old for another dog. I could clean the cage out for him.

I discussed it over with our Eileen and it was agreed I was to get my Dad some budgies. We bought the cage and a mirror and of course the budgies. They were two male blue ones. My Dad wasn't keen but we all said it was a good idea, they'd keep him company and he could teach them to talk.

They in fact did the opposite. They got on his nerves with the chirpy chirpycheepcheep. (That's a good name for a song, do you remember it?)

My Dad loved the television especially the sport. Well the birds chirped and chirped. He ended up covering them up and putting them in the kitchen. He rang me up one day and said, "Brenda, get rid of those birds. I don't want them."

"Right," I said, "I'll be over to get them." I took the budgies to my friend's who was helping me out at the time.

"Can you have the budgies? I'll clean them out for you." At first she said no then she agreed.

Well I suffer a lot from chest infections. This comes with singing into microphones which other people, who've had a chest infection, have used. Therefore I catch their germs.

At this time I had a very bad chest infection and I went over to my friend, the one looking after the budgies. I cleaned them out for her then I went back home.

Next night I had a booking in Nottingham so I went over to pick her up. Well her breathing was dreadful. Obviously, I thought she had caught the chest infection from me. She said that she'd been to the doctors and they'd said if it doesn't get any better to come back. Well the sweat was dripping off her. She was coughing and her breathing was very laboured. She said, "Oooohhhhh IIIII'll bbbbbeeeeeeaaallllllriiiiight."

I took her to a local A & E. We sat in the waiting room and her name was called. They did a hydration test and immediately they rushed her to Intensive Care. I followed and thought, "Oh dear me, what's happening?" They put her on oxygen immediately.

"Quickly, quickly, such and such a drip." A nurse shouted. They got her to Intensive Care and placed her on a bed. A drip was up and they were injecting her with something into her tummy. I stood back but I did ask

"What's happening?" A sister said, "We'll give her 24 hours. It's touch and go."

"Eh?"

This was a lot to take in. I told them her family lived in Australia. I told them I was off to Nottingham. They said to give six hours to see if she was responding to the antibiotics. There was a full team working on her. Again this was a lot to take in. And I had to get to Nottingham.

Lyn always set the sat nav because I couldn't. I got to my car and thought, "Oh the sat nav." So I went back into Intensive Care and went up to Lyn who was all cabled and tubed up with oxygen.

"Can you tell me how to set the sat nav 'cos I've got to get to Nottingham? I said.

"Ggggggivvvvvemmmmmeeeeeeee the saaaaatnaaaavvvvandddddddl'llllllldoooooitttttttt."She said in a very breathless voice.

"OUT!" The sister shouted to me upon which I about turn and made my way to the door. I turned round to the sister and said, "It's alright I'll find my own way or could you set it?"

"OUT." was the reply.

Lyn recovered I'm pleased to say. She had caught the infection from the budgies. Some carry a tick and it attacks the respiratory system.

I took the budgies back to the pet shop explaining what had happened and that they were carrying a tick. The shop took them back and put them up for sale. I think they named them Tick and Tock.

Cyprus

My show has changed over the years and I do try to keep up to date with current events and fashions.

I carry in my suitcases two false hands, two false legs, three boobs, a blow up doll, ET, Darth Vader, Angel of the North wings. I put the duty free booze down the false legs in order that it doesn't get broken.

We disembarked from the ship when we docked in Cyprus. We were allowed off the ship first because of all the cases.

We got to the part where our cases went through the X-ray. We lifted the first case onto the rollers of the scanner. This was the case containing most of the props and the operater of the machine looked at his monitor and saw the legs, hands, boobs, a figure of a person (blow up doll), ET and he moved his face slowly closer to the screen. I knew what was happening but I didn't realise what he was thinking.

"Oh it's my husband"; I said to him jokingly "he likes to come along with me." WRONG! The man's face changed and he blew a whistle and some sort of security arrived, may have been the police. Anyway they were in uniform and wore a badge.

"Open, open, quickly, quickly." They shouted at me; they were very intent and on a mission. Well I had to find the keys. There was a queue now forming with all the passengers from the ship.

Everyone knew me. I started panicking.

"What are you doing here?" The man in uniform shouted. The queue of passengers all said in unison,

"She's the comedian." That didn't help and the passengers shouting didn't either. They thought it was all great fun.

"Come on Brenda, get your keys, and show them your

three boobs." All very rude. They meant my three boobs for once twice, three times a lady.The authorities were not happy bunnies, and making a joke of it didn't help. Oh dear here I was again in trouble. Once we got the case opened they realised they were all false body parts. They were quite interested in the three boobs. Dirty b....ers. Another case of men behaving badly. Anyway they let me go; we locked the case up and walked away quietly pushing the cases out of the port terminal.

I felt like Dick Emery pulling my case along and saying to the man in uniform, "Oh you are awful, but I do like you." I'm sure my name is flagged in Cyprus!!!! We were the talk of the bus on the way to the airport.

"Eeeh Brenda we thought you were going to be arrested there." One of the passengers said.

"So did I" was my reply.

The sketch of Swan Lake has progressed so much that now I ask the Cruise Director to join me in dancing the ballet. It's such a powerful opening of my second show. I love it so much that I have promoted myself to Dame Brenda Collins. My favourite part of the sketch is where I lift my legs behind my head. I tell everyone that the legs are my own but they can't be conned they all know they are false.

Dad

My Dad was still very active, riding his bike and of course spending a lot of time with his grandchildren and great grandchildren. Our Daniel and his wife had Mila and Isaac and they loved visiting Grandad Alfie. He was brilliant with the children. Whenever I was abroad I was always on the lookout for toys, either furry or otherwise, which made a noise, or rolled over. I bought a toy Santa Claus which played the drums. Mila and Isaac loved them and when they visited my Dad he would switch them all on. You can imagine our Eileen loved it!! Not!!

Bowburn Community Centre held an annual fete and my Dad was the oldest man in the village and he had his photograph taken with the youngest boy, a baby who had just been born. He also planted a commemorative tree in Bowburn. That was nice.

My Dad still came to venues when I was working locally. He loved it.

I went over to my Dad's and found an ambulance outside his door with a blue light flashing. Oh dear what's happened, maybe he's fallen off his bike again. I saw his neighbour and she said that she thought he was having a heart attack. The paramedics checked his heart – no, no heart attack. They gave him some paracetamol.

Days went by and he was still in extreme pain. I spoke to his GP and suggested we take him to hospital. The Doctor rang the hospital and he was admitted and tests were carried out.

They put him on morphine to help with the pain. He was very confused, so much so he thought that when he looked outside the windows he could see the sea. We were all very concerned.

A woman consultant wanted to have a word with both my Dad and I in private. I said that I would like to speak to Miss Green, his former Consultant, but they said that she wasn't available. I thought "Oh dear this is not good."

We went into a room. My Dad was shuffling along, so unlike him, as he always so spritely. The doctor was about to tell my Dad some very bad news. I knew she was and so I stopped her and said, "No, he doesn't need to know, he's a very old man."

She said that she had to tell him. I said that she didn't have to at all. Anyway she said to my Dad that the cancer was in his liver. My Dad said, "What's she saying Brenda? Is it liver for dinner?"

314

"No Dad we have to look after you now." Then I said, "Come on Dad, I'll take you back to your bed." The cancer had returned.

I rang our Eileen and told her the bad news. My Dad had only about eight weeks to live. No-one could believe it.

He was prescribed a variety of medication but they were having an adverse effect on him. I was just on my way home from a venue when the hospital rang to say I had to get there as quickly as possible as my Dad was being held down by two security guards at the hospital.

"Why?" I asked, because my Dad was 94 and I couldn't understand why two security men should be holding him down. Apparently my Dad had been asking for me and the nurses thought Brenda was his wife. The nurses then said that Brenda was no longer with us. Well I was his little girl and you can imagine how he felt. He thought I'd had an accident. My Dad had gone crazy. The staff should have got their facts right.

The nurses were very harassed probably because of the challenging patients. What a shame.

Anyway, my Dad got transferred to Bishop Auckland hospital a much better atmosphere as the staff didn't seem so harassed.

He asked if he could go back to his bungalow. We had to say, "Maybe next week Dad." He didn't understand. He always had plenty of visitors and he was pleased to see everyone. This hospital got his medication right. So that was good.

Social Services informed Eileen and I that Dad should be admitted to a Nursing Home. We found a nice one in West Rainton. He had a nice room and I got his television and his rocking chair. He said to me,

"Brenda, is this a hotel?"

"No Dad but it's a place where they will look after you."

He loved his rocking chair, because he could move his

legs while rocking. He always said, "If you don't use them you lose them." That's why he loved his bike. It kept him fit. We brought over the toy box from the bungalow and all the colouring in books and pencils so Mila and Isaac could play when they were visiting him in the Nursing Home.

I had a cruise booked for the week after. I would be away for seven days. I talked it over with our Eileen and she thought it would be okay for me to go. She would keep in touch with me daily. I spoke to the matron of the home and she said,

"Oh he'll be fine." She told me not to worry.

I told my Dad that when I got back I'd perform a show in the communal room of the home. He was over the moon at the thought. He said, "Aye, Aye I'll tell them all about you." And he would. You see whenever I took him to clubs he would say to the members of the audience he was sitting next to.

"Have you seen our Brenda?"

On the day before my cruise I called to see Dad and as I was leaving he stood waving with both arms in the air, as he always did, waving and shouting,

"Tarra, Tarra, Tarra Brenda." He was in very good spirits.

I went on the cruise and about three days in I got a phone call from the matron saying that my Dad had deteriorated and perhaps only had hours to live. They had given him morphine.

I frantically rang our Eileen and she was on her way to the nursing home. She phoned me as soon as she arrived at his bedside and said he was unconscious. I asked her to put the phone next to my Dad's ear. I said,

"Tarra Dad Tarra."

My Dad died on the 15th June 2010 about 15 minutes after I had said tarra. What a man!!!!!!!! I hope my boys take after their Granda. I know I'm turning like him and it feels good. The Hotel Manager of the ship asked if they could fly me home. I said there was no need. Our Eileen said that she would deal with everything.

I got back and we had to sort out my Dad's bungalow. Eileen took a few things, I did and my boys and our Eileen's children both wanted items to remember him by.

The funeral car set off for the crematorium from the bungalow. We were all dressed in bright colours. Our Peter had his denims on with slits across the knee. We all had button holes made out of plastic flowers and a plastic flower arrangement was placed on his coffin. Vicki, our Daniel's wife got the job of making the button holes and arranging the flowers. Me Dad always got confused over her name so he called her Sylvia.

As I mentioned earlier, my Dad's garden was full of plastic flowers because they were easy to look after and they created colour all the year round in his garden. He loved his front garden and I was always taking photos of it with him and Poppy sitting on the garden seat.

Daniel did the eulogy at the service about his Grandad. He started off by saying.

"My wife Sylvia and I... " Then the laughter started. The funeral was laughter all the way through, and of course tears but mostly tears of laughter and of memories.

His favourite song was played at his funeral – 'The Story of my Life', by Michael Holliday, and, of course, a recording of me singing 'The Working Man'. When we left the Crematorium his other favourite song Que Sera Sera was played. He called it My Mother and Me.

We all have wonderful memories of a man full of colour, a wonderful Dad, a wonderful Grandad and Great Grandad. Never to be forgotten. I still believe he is guiding me and he's there at my every show asking the passengers,

"Have you seen our Brenda?" Tarra Dad Tarra!!

Next Stage – An Audition

I was asked to go down to Bridgend in South Wales to do a showcase. The guests invited were representing different cruise lines. I'd been with Thomson's for eight years and I'd had a brilliant time, as you can tell by the stories I've told you.

I thought it was maybe time for a change for a couple of years. Mind I wasn't keen to go to this showcase because the next day at 7.00am I was flying to Majorca from Newcastle airport to meet a Thomson Ship. So I was pushing it.

I even rang the agent to say I wasn't going to turn up. He went crazy and said. "Oh you must Brenda."

"Oh alright, but I want to be on first or second, if not I'm going home." And I would. He told me I would be definitely on second.

I drove down and met up with fellow artistes who were also part of the showcase.

I did the audition then zoomed up the country back to Newcastle. Eeeh I just got to the airport in time to board the plane. Phew. That was hard work.

A few weeks later the agent who held the showcase rang me and said that the invited guests from the cruise lines were impressed with me and would like to book me. Eeeh that was good. Fred Olsen gave me ten cruises for that year, which was good news.

I gave the other two to Thomson. Peel, the agents for Thomson Cruises asked me which ships I would like to do because of all the hard work I'd done for them over the years. I chose The Majesty and The Celebration.

When I boarded The Celebration and checked in I discovered the senior staff on board had upgraded me to a suite. Thank you very much Thomson I hope I'll see you all again. It's been a fantastic eight years and I have thoroughly enjoyed working onboard all of your fleet. Thank you so much

Celebrating the Queen's Jubilee

Beautiful Songstress

I turned up at a club because an agent had said it was local, one spot, and I'd pick my money up. All these were positive reasons to accept the booking.

Sometimes some agents, would book an artiste into a club and it would be a 'no pick up'. This meant the artiste would entertain at the club but his or her money would be sent direct to the agent; he would forward it to the artiste less the commission, which could vary from 15% + VAT to 20% + VAT. Eventually we get the fee, but it all depends on whether it is the beginning or the end of the month. An agent, you see, would invoice a club at the end of a month and then the club would pay them at the end of the next month so if the booking was at the beginning of a month it takes quite some time for the fee to reach your bank. Maybe two months.

At this particular club I noticed in the window a poster advertising me and a 60s double act. I thought, "Oh that's a good line up."

I got set up and the Concert Chairman came in the dressing room and said,

"Right lads, double act, you do the middle spot and she'll open and close the night."

"Excuse me but I'm a comedy vocalist and I work on the cruise ships." Oh get me. It was a lame excuse to him because he said,

"Look lass on the poster and on the contract it says you're a 'Beautiful Songstress' so you're opening and closing the show."

The agent had sent the poster and the contract.

"But the billing is incorrect. I'm a comedy vocalist."

"Now do you want an argument?" he asked, "Because if you do you'll go before the committee and we can fight it out there. The contract says, A Beautiful Songstress, so that's final."

"Well that's libel if ever there was a description of me." I was 61 at the time.

I went on stage first and just had to do 25 minutes. It just wasn't long enough and the audience were shouting for more.

"I'm sorry I can't do more because I'm 'A Beautiful Songstress' and the Concert Chairman says I am and 25 minutes is all he wants me to do." The audience went wild and started booing the Concert Chairman. He apologised to me and I said, "Don't worry you'll be hearing from my

solicitors. I've never been a beautiful songstress."
I got banned!! Again!

I Need a Man

I was working at Thoresby Hall Hotel and during my show I say, "I need a man. I want all the men to move from side to side. If you don't you come up here with me."

All the men started to move from side to side through fear. I saw a young man on my left hand side. Umm yes. Well I normally use someone out of the show team because members of the audiences are usually unsuitable and of course, I have to consider health and safety.

"It's you." . I said to the young man. He got up on stage and I asked him what he did for a living. He said he was a rugby player.

"Perfect." I thought. He was very fit very muscular and very handsome.

He got into the dress with no problem at all and threw me up into the air with the greatest of ease. In fact I'd never been thrown so high for a long time. Even a short time. The whole sketch went really well. He even did the strip tease perfectly. I think he'd done that sort of thing before!!

The next morning I went into breakfast and everyone stood up and applauded me. The Maitre d' escorted me to my table. I was flabbergasted. Eeeeh me just coming down to breakfast and everyone standing up and applauding me!!! It was movie star treatment, usually for film stars not little Brenda Collins. They did though. I didn't know where to put my face. I said, "Thank you," and they all said in unison

"No, thank you Brenda." Well I went over to one table to talk to guests. One young girl said to me:

"It was a wonderful evening last night." I said, "Yes I really enjoyed myself especially with that young rugby player

I got up on stage."

"Oh that was funny."She replied. "Where did you go after the show?"

"Oh I slept with that young man, the rugby player." I said jokingly.

"Oh" she said "did you? He's my fiancé."

Gulp – Get out of that one if you can!

From Russia with Love

I was on a cruise from Leith, Scotland, this time with a company called Cruise Maritime. The ship was The Marco Polo.

I arrived at the port and my Cruise Director, Matthew Dallan was there to greet me. My boarding card was in the name of Brenda Collins. On all my other cruises over the many years maybe 10 years by now, my boarding card has been in the name of Brenda Woods, my married name.

We thought it strange but apparently there was a passenger on board also called Brenda Woods (another one hum)

Anyway, all was well up to the day of trying to enter St. Petersburg. We got to the passport control whereupon I handed my passport, my Seaman's Logbook and boarding card to the lady in the booth.

My name Brenda Woods was not on their crew sheet. Brenda Collins was though. So I was told to go back to the ship. I went to reception and my boarding card was changed to Brenda Woods.

Off I went again to passport control. I handed all the relevant documents over to the officer. They never smile, they just stare at you. She looked at me with distaste and said,

"No, you go back to ze ship."

By this time all the passengers had returned from their tour of St Petersburg and were back on board the ship. There was gossip on the ship about me being refused entry twice.

Passengers were saying, "Did they not let you in Brenda?"

"No," I said, "I think it's because I have ginger hair."

So I decided to adapt one of the jokes I tell in my second show to include the ladies who work in Passport Control in St. Petersburg. Their evening jobs are that of ladies of the night!!

One is called OnyabackYebitch, her colleague is Knickers Offalot. Her brother is the local lemonade factory owner, his name is DropusaBottleofPopoff and her husband who smokes 50 cigarettes a day is called Ivor Chestycoff. The joke went down extremely well with the passengers. They giggled for days.

A guest speaker on board was a lady called Jenny Hanley. I remembered her from the programme Magpie. Well she came up to me and told me she was my number one fan. Oooooooh!

She'd worked with Noel Coward and she talked with a very posh accent and her ancestors were Russian. Jenny had no problem getting into Russia passing through passport control.

I tell you "It's not what you know but who you know!!!"

Fred Olsen

I now work for Fred Olsen cruise line. The ships are lovely and the passengers are too. Just recently I was offered the World Cruise for 2014 which I am very excited about. We'll be going to some very exotic places and countries I've never been to before.

Well I'll have to behave myself on these cruises. All the

cruises I have worked on so far have been amazing. They have smashing Cruise Directors and Deputy Cruise Directors. One Cruise Director always cuts and colours my hair in my cabin

"Were you a hairdresser?" I asked him.

"No, but my Auntie was."

These cruises sail from ports in the UK so no flying, which suits me down to the ground, although when we do the world cruises we will be flying out to certain countries to greet the ship.

As part of one particular world cruise we flew from Newcastle airport to Dubai, then to Singapore where we were met by a coach which took us to our ship, the Black Watch.

The ship was to sail to India and then to Jordan. Me and my fellow artistes boarded the ship and met Cruise Director, Anthony Borradaile. We were told that we were to sail through a corridor which would put the ship under the threat of being boarded by pirates.

We never gave any thought to the seriousness of it until we docked in a port and we noticed crew were working on the outside of the ship and were attaching some sort of wire. When we boarded we found out that it was razor wire. We had a look around the deck and saw the wire. Six water cannons were also placed around deck 7. Oh dear this all looked serious.

The Captain made an announcement that everyone on board was to take part in an exercise to ensure we were familiar with the procedure and where to go in the event of the pirates boarding the ship. This was getting more serious by the minute.

The alarm was raised for the exercise and we were instructed to go to our allocated safe havens. Here we were to sit on the floor and the water-tight doors were to be closed and we were to stay there until further instruction. No one panicked we all just proceeded to our safe havens.

Some elderly people found it hard to get down on the floor but everyone managed. The Captain also announced that should the pirates try to board he would turn the ship around very quickly. When this announcement came we were all to lie down wherever we were on the ship.

Armed guards were on board. There was a machine gun at the front of the ship and a one at the back. Crew members were positioned around the ship on lookout with their binoculars.

All activities carried on as usual. Every day we played deck quoits. One morning we saw a fishing boat approaching. Someone said, "Oh I wonder if this is the pirate ship we're expecting?" We all carried on playing quoits.

You see we all had confidence in the Captain.

The lights around the ship were blacked out on a night so that we couldn't be seen. When we eventually got through the corridor everyone gave the Captain a big cheer. Well done Captain.

On that cruise I won 'I'm a Celebrity Get Me Out of Here'.

We had docked in Sweden and the ship was I think the Boudicca. We got off and we started to make our way to the town by following the arrows on signposts.

We gathered quite an entourage because passengers were saying, "Do you know the way to the town?"

"No I'm just following the arrows." I said. The arrows didn't get us to any town but to a small harbour with some lovely boats and a nice cafe.

We all sat on a wall and admired the view. I saw a young lady walking towards us and so I said to our gang,

"Here's a nice Swedish lass, I'll ask her the way to the town."

I approached her and said in my best broken English,

"Hello, can you tell me the way to the town?"

She said, "Sprechen Sie Deutsch?" I turned round and said,

"Can anyone here speak French?" The gang all laughed.

I had another go. "No we want the town." She replied, "You are Brenda, no?" Well all our mouths dropped, mine the most.

"You are the comedian Brenda?"

"Well, yes I am." Again I spoke in my very best broken English. I turned to look at the gang. They sat gobsmacked. We all looked at one another.

"Have you worked in Sweden?" one asked.

"No, no I haven't."

"Well how does she know you?"

"I haven't a clue."

In the end she burst out laughing. She couldn't keep her laugh in any longer. And said,

"You daft buggers I'm the nurse from the ship and Brenda I saw your show last night."

The sod. We were all well and truly taken in by her. She said on seeing us all sitting on the wall, she just couldn't resist it.

Cyprus in the winter

A mile with a smile

A Big Thank You

Getting older doesn't bother me. I feel exactly the same inside as I did when I was 17. I've just changed on the outside. I nip myself regularly, in fact most days.

Little Brenda Swainston has come a long way from being put down a grade in the junior school because of not being able to do the work, but by this happening I found my voice.

I feel I owe a great deal to my teacher in the junior school, Miss Crampton who saw me as a very shy young girl and found that I could sing. She encouraged me and sat with me and taught me subjects such as maths which I didn't understand. Also to Mr. Whittaker, the music teacher at Bowburn Modern School and the rest of the teachers who influenced me and pointed me in the right direction, which was to train as a shorthand typist at Spennymoor West Modern School.

I owe a lot to all the teachers, in particular Mr. Prest, the headmaster, and Mrs. Newland the music teacher who both encouraged me and guided me with my singing. I am deeply grateful to all of these wonderful teachers.

Also to my Guide Captain, Miss Mitchinson and Miss Trusswell who both moulded me into the person I am today. I have to stop and think that at this present time I travel to all corners of the world on beautiful ships full of lovely passengers and crew.

I now have a website and it's all down to a lovely lad called Graeme Paterson.

I still thoroughly enjoy entertaining. I never sit back and think, "Oh it'll be alright I'll just do my show." Oh no, I don't ever just 'do my show'. I work hard on my show and keep it up to date. I know only too well the power of timing, mannerism, facial expression and the use of a catchphrase to create a character that help me bond with an audience.

You just have to look back at some amazing comics such as Hilda Baker, Larry Grayson and of course Dick Emery.

I never forget my roots either. In my mind I'm still little Brenda Swainston.

When I first arrive on board not many passengers know me and so I'm 'wallpaper' but once I've been on stage I become part of their holiday and I like that.

I still get very nervous because when I work at a hotel, I go to the venue, perform my show which involves interacting with the audience but then at the end of the night I go home.

When I'm on a ship I'm already at the venue and when I have performed my show I, obviously remain at the venue so it's very nerve wracking. Once I've performed my first show I feel better because I then feel as though I'm that bit nearer to getting to know the passengers.

I love it.

Next Stage

Both Richard and Peter have partners and are settled nicely. When I get back from a cruise or about to go on one I take them all out for dinner. It's nice. I have a lovely family.

Richard and his partner Lesley come over to the cottage to go logging (collecting logs for our respective fires). We both have open fires. I am very thrifty if you remember, and so collecting logs is a way of not putting the gas on!!!

Anyway Lesley said, "I'll not be doing anything strenuous because I'm going to have a baby." Well you could have knocked me over with a feather.

Yes I was going to be a grandma. Grandma Brenda. Can you imagine it? You'd better not answer that. Lesley was pretty sick during the first four months but started to enjoy the pregnancy once she was over that. The bump got bigger and bigger and it was nearly time for the birth. My next chapter will be the birth and whether my grandchild is a boy or a girl! Wait for it...

The Birth of Alfred James Woods weighing in at 7lb 11ozs

Yes Lesley gave birth to a baby boy. Neither Richard nor Lesley wanted to know whether they were going to have a boy or a girl.

Anyway, a little boy was born and they named him after my Dad, Richard's Granda, Alfie and Lesley's Granda, James, which was lovely.

Richard rang me through the night and said,

"In the blue corner weighing in at 7lb 11ozs." I said to him,

"Well is baby a boy or a girl?" He said,

"Mam, blue corner." "Oh that's lovely it's a baby boy then. Are they both alright?"

"Yes they're both fine and he's beautiful."

"Oh that's good, night, night Richard I'll see you all tomorrow."

Well done Richard, well done.

What a Proud Mother

I have two wonderful boys, and I am extremely proud of both of them.

Richard is a music teacher at Durham School and Peter is a master plasterer.

I have loved watching them grow into the two fine young men and I look forward to the future as mother and grandma. It has been an amazing journey.

Messages received from passengers:

Accolade to Beautiful Brenda
Instantly likeable
Never forgettable
Bright as a button
And sassy as hell
Red-headed bombshell
You leap across the footlights
Making us all laugh
Vocally excellent
Fully eloquent
Full of nostalgia
And memories gone by
Unique little trooper
You stand out alone
Beautiful BrendaYou shine on your own
- LizHooley

Dear Brenda

Thank you for making us laugh until we cried, for your joy of life, your talent and thank you for being such a wonderful person and 'sharing' yourself with us.

You have an immense talent for such a little mini person.

Stella, Ernie, Jenni and Gabbi xxx

Happy Memories

My sister Eileen and her husband, Steve

Lyn and me

Lee Brannigan and Cruise Director Bram

Having a drink in uniform

(left-right) Lyn, Jo, Peter, Ray, Pauline, Mavis and Ray

Charlotte Baker

Christmas party

Relaxing at the cottage

Jill Bowerbank - proof reader

Jill, me, Christine, Irene

Richard, Lesley and Alfie

Best of friends - Peter and Alfie

Me Mam

Me Dad